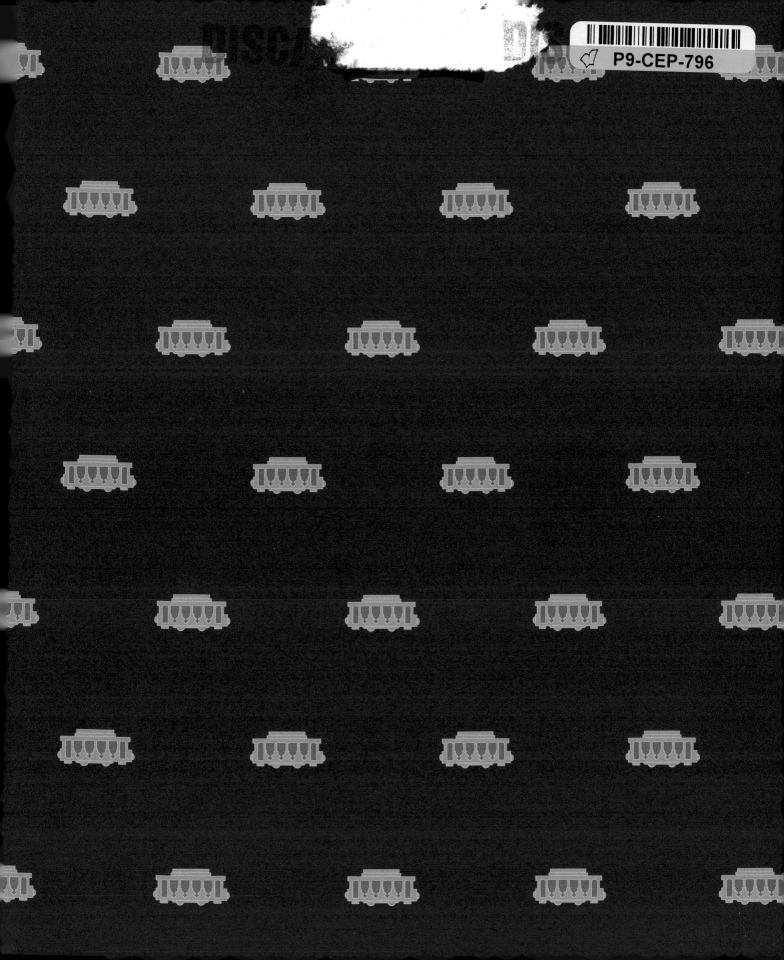

A VISUAL HISTORY

MISTER ROGERS' NEIGHBORHOOD®

A VISUAL HISTORY

Written by Melissa Wagner,
Tim Lybarger, and Jenna McGuiggan
Foreword by Tom Hanks

CLARKSON POTTER/PUBLISHERS
NEW YORK

CONTENTS

1

Our Television Neighbor: *Fred Rogers and the Beginnings of the Neighborhood*

2

Hi, Neighbor!: *Our Television Visits with Mister Rogers*

3

A Place Where Anything Can Happen: *The Neighborhood of Make-Believe*

4

**The People
Behind the
Neighborhood:**

A Tour of Studio A

5

**That's What
I Sing About:**

*The Music and
Its Messages*

6

**It's Such a
Good Feeling:**

*The Legacy of
Fred Rogers*

FOREWORD

Along with being the best neighbor a kid could want, Fred Rogers was also an ordained minister, though not one with ceremonial robes or a collar, but rather a zip-up cardigan sweater and a pair of blue sneakers. He had no church of his own, if you consider church as a place of brick and mortar, pews and stained-glass windows, pipe organs and hymnals. He did have a cozy living room and kitchen, an aquarium of hungry if nondescript fish, and he sang songs that sprung from the conversations he was having. He gave no sermons to his parishioners, instead speaking with them in simple, commonsense tones, often asking questions. Despite having a daily TV show for so many years, he was by no means a TV preacher.

Fred Rogers knew where his ministry was, in the few feet on the other side of the TV screen. His congregation was the children who made watching Mister Rogers a part of their day. Without ever mentioning God, or using the word *religion*, Fred tended to the needs and the worries of his flock with ardent passion and preparation. His television programs were studied and precise works meant to address the infinite fears and questions faced by children: Can I get sucked down the drain of my bathtub? Am I safe in an airplane? Why am I so sad sometimes? For an appreciation of just how much Fred Rogers strived to make his congregation understand the workings of its world, look at his broadcasts dealing with death, assassination, and divorce.

What many people cannot fathom in Fred Rogers is that his affection, delight, and care for children was sincere. It was. His true faith was stated in the continuous message of his ministry, that each of us are special in our own way, that what is essential in life is invisible to the naked eye, and that he really did want us to be his neighbor.

Tom Hanks

The set of TriStar Pictures' *A Beautiful Day in the Neighborhood*, starring Tom Hanks (see page 312 to learn about the making of the movie).

INTRODUCTION

No matter where you go, it's easy to meet someone who has a personal story about Mister Rogers. From those who live in southwestern Pennsylvania—home to Fred Rogers' real-life neighborhoods, where his presence is still felt—to all across the country who faithfully "visited" his television *Neighborhood*, millions of children have grown up feeling as if Mister Rogers truly was their neighbor. People who knew Fred will tell you that this is exactly how he wanted you to feel. Whether he was talking to you in person or through the television screen, he was the same soft-spoken, deep-thinking, and radically compassionate person who took a genuine interest in the world and the people around him.

Fred worked in television for fifty years, devoting his life to creating quality programming for children and families. Now for the first time ever, we can trace his legacy in visual form—from the creation of his first children's programs to his ongoing impact on the field of early childhood development to his enduring influence in popular culture. Decades in the making, this book collects hundreds of rare photographs, unique documents, and never-before-seen ephemera—including original scripts and sheet music with Fred's handwritten notes—all gleaned from the Fred Rogers Archives, various museums, and even private collections.

Delightful on-set and behind-the-scenes photographs will transport you to Mister Rogers' television house and the Neighborhood of Make-Believe. A set of hand-labeled Polaroids documents how staff helped Fred, who was color-blind, keep track of his many cardigans and ties. Through exclusive interviews, original members of the cast and crew share their stories of working with Fred and the *Neighborhood* community. Casual viewers and faithful fans alike will encounter familiar faces and perhaps some forgotten places as they read. After all, 895 episodes over thirty-three years makes for a lot of television visits!

In addition to writing scripts for those many hundreds of *Neighborhood* episodes, Fred composed more than 200 songs, authored dozens of books for children and parents, and created several television series for adults. He was, in short, prolific. Much of Fred's writing—published and unpublished—is housed at the Fred Rogers Archive in his hometown of Latrobe, Pennsylvania. The Archive contains scores of yellow legal pads covered in black ink—Fred's preferred writing tools.

Tucked away in an old file at the Archive lie several pages of undated notes written in Fred's unique, whirling cursive that sketch out his idea for an "interview program" for adults called *Two or More*. He envisioned that he and a guest would discuss a topic and pose conversation-starter questions to viewers, who would be encouraged to watch at home in groups of two of more. "This is a program [that] should encourage dialogue at home by not talking too much in the studio," he wrote. "The whole idea is to get the audience to enjoy each other." Fred imagined that in some episodes, the camera might show him making tea and bringing it to his guest. He'd look at the camera and tell viewers he wished he could pass a cup to them through the television, "but maybe they're having some of their own."

Although *Two or More* was never produced, the concept of it illuminates the values that shaped Fred's life and work: hospitality, honest conversation, and human connection. It also highlights his abiding belief that television is a medium that—when used well—can educate and edify viewers. Fred often said that he believed the space between the television and the viewer was "holy ground." He considered television to be an "exceedingly personal medium," saying that it "reflects the story back to us. Whatever we happen to be watching, we bring our own story to the screen. And so consequently, it's like a dialogue." Fred noted, "I do feel that what we see and hear on the screen is part of who we become."

Over the past five decades, *Mister Rogers' Neighborhood* has become part of everyone who has seen and heard it. Wherever you live and whenever you watched the program, *you too* are part of Fred's Neighborhood. As always, he said it best: "You know, we have pieces of the people that have cared about us all through our lives, and they're all part of us now. And so each one of us represents so many investments from others. No one of us is alone."

"I'll never forget the sense of wholeness I felt when I finally realized what in fact I really was: not just a writer or a language buff or a student of human development or a telecommunicator, but I was someone who could use every talent that had ever been given to me in the service of children and their families."

Fred Rogers

Fred Rogers with puppets King Friday XIII and Sara Saturday before the royal wedding in 1969.

Our
Television
Neighbor

1

FRED ROGERS
AND THE
BEGINNINGS
OF THE
NEIGHBORHOOD

F red Rogers created one of the most iconic and influential programs in the history of children's television—but he'd never even watched TV until his senior year of college.

That first encounter with television put Fred on the path he would follow for the rest of his life. After graduating from college with a degree in music composition, he went to work for NBC in New York City; became a charter staff member of WQED, the nation's first community-supported television station; helped to develop WQED's first children's program; and hosted his own program for the Canadian Broadcasting Corporation. Along the way, he also studied childhood development at the graduate level, completed seminary studies, and was ordained as a Presbyterian minister. But to millions of children, he was known as Mister Rogers, the soft-spoken, kind-hearted, cardigan-wearing television neighbor and host of *Mister Rogers' Neighborhood*, one of the most loved and longest running programs in the history of American children's television.

For more than thirty years, Fred Rogers invited young viewers and their families into his television house. He helped children learn that each and every one of them was special just the way they were, and that no one else in the world was exactly like them. Fred credited his grandfather, Fred Brooks McFeely, with having a profound influence on this philosophy. One day when the younger Fred was a boy, his grandfather (lovingly known to his family as Ding Dong) said to him, "You made this day a special day, just by being yourself. Always remember there's just one person in this whole world like you—and I like you just the way you are." This message of love and acceptance infused everything Fred Rogers created.

For multiple generations blessed with the opportunity to visit *Mister Rogers' Neighborhood,* this was far more than a simple television program. It was a daily practice in kindness, peace, and appreciation that was destined to meaningfully shape and influence children and families for decades to come.

OPPOSITE: Fred Rogers with puppets King Friday XIII and Lady Elaine Fairchilde in November 1971, on the set of the M Room, "inside" the castle in the Neighborhood of Make-Believe.

Fred McFeely Rogers was born in 1928 in Latrobe, Pennsylvania, a small town forty miles southeast of Pittsburgh. His family was known for its successful local manufacturing business, and for its philanthropy. As a quiet, shy child, Fred found joy in the very things that would become hallmarks of his life's work: music, imagination, and whimsy. Young Fred spent many afternoons in his attic playroom, immersed in a world of make-believe populated with puppets. He started playing piano by the age of five, and through music he discovered a way to express his feelings, something he would later share with children through *Mister Rogers' Neighborhood.*

Fred's love of music and the arts carried him through high school and into college. After a year at Dartmouth College studying Romance languages, he transferred to Rollins College in Florida to focus on music composition. Fred flourished at Rollins, where he met Joanne Byrd, a talented pianist and fellow music student, whom he would marry in 1952.

A few months before Fred graduated magna cum laude in 1951, he watched television for the first time. He recognized that this new technology and communication medium could be "a wonderful tool for education," but the children's programming he saw troubled him. More than forty-five years later, he recounted seeing "people dressed in some kind of costumes, literally throwing pies in each other's faces. I was astounded at that." This kind of silly and almost violently boisterous approach struck Fred as demeaning to children. He believed that children should be respected, and he wanted to give them something of dignity and substance to watch.

Fred had planned to attend seminary after college, but he decided to explore a career in television. He became an apprentice and then a floor manager at the National Broadcasting Company (NBC) in New York. In 1953 he and Joanne moved back to western Pennsylvania. He became program manager for WQED in Pittsburgh, which would go live in 1954 as the first community-supported television station in the country.

A PRESBYTERIAN MINISTER

While working on *The Children's Corner,* Fred enrolled in Western Theological Seminary (later known as Pittsburgh Theological Seminary). After eight years of part-time study, he received his master of divinity degree and was ordained as a Presbyterian minister. Rather than be a pastor in a church, Fred received a special ordination to serve children and families through television.

OPPOSITE, CLOCKWISE FROM TOP LEFT: Fred as a boy with a camera; Fred and his sister, Laney; Fred (*center*) at the piano with (*from left to right*) his mother, Nancy Rogers; his grandmother, Nancy McFeely; his sister, Laney Rogers; and his father, James Rogers.

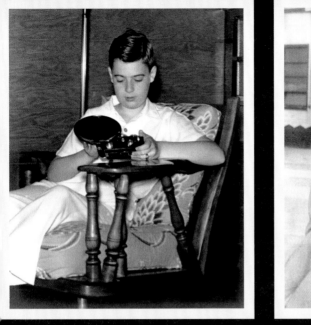

Here, exuding good cheer and champagne bubbles, we have Joanne Byrd (supporting friend) and Fred Rogers (supporting Joanne). This happy trio reaped top honors at the Lambda Chi costume ball last Saturday night.

student music guild

855044-2

WESTERN UNION

W. P. MARSHALL, PRESIDENT

(49)..

The filing time shown in the date line on telegrams and day letters is STANDARD TIME at point of origin. Time of receipt is

PA22

P·NB119 PD=FI NEWYORK NY 8 1035A=

MRS J H ROGERS=

1951 00

737 WELDON ST LATROBE PENN=

ASSIGNED TO FIRESTONE HOUR MUSICAL SHOW 830

CALL COTTAGE ABOUT 10 ALL WONDERFUL=

FRED=

TELEPHONE N
TELEPHONED
TIME
BY
ATTEMPTS
TO DELIVER

THE COMPANY WILL APPRECIATE SUGGESTIONS FROM ITS PATRONS CONCERNING

THIS PAGE, CLOCKWISE FROM TOP LEFT: Joanne Byrd and Fred dressed as Raggedy Ann and Andy for a college costume ball; the Rollins College Student Music Guild (Fred and his friend John Reardon, who was later a frequent guest on *Mister Rogers' Neighborhood*, are in the second row from the top); a telegram from Fred to his family sent during his first weeks at NBC; Fred and Joanne playing a duet.

OPPOSITE, CLOCKWISE FROM TOP: Fred's senior piano recital program at Rollins

ROLLINS COLLEGE CONSERVATORY OF MUSIC

Harvey L. Woodruff, *Director*

Presents

SENIOR RECITAL

of

ORIGINAL COMPOSITIONS

by

FRED ROGERS

Assisted by

Alphonse Carlo, *violinist*	Shirley Christensen, *soprano*
Natalie Miller, *violinist*	Jeannine Romer, *pianist*
Frederick McFalls, *violist*	Ross Rosazza, *baritone*
Katherine Courtney, *violoncellist*	John Carter, *pianist*

FRIDAY, MAY 25, 1951, at 8:30 P.M.

ANNIE RUSSELL THEATRE

Winter Park, Florida

PROGRAM

I.

FUGUE IN D MINOR (Three voices)
Mr. Carlo, Mr. McFalls, Miss Courtney

II.

TWO SONGS FROM "CHAMBER MUSIC" (James Joyce)
"He who hath glory lost"
"Rain has fallen"
Miss Christensen

III.

VARIATIONS FOR PIANO ON A THEME OF CHOPIN
Miss Romer

Intermission

IV.

THREE FOLK SONGS

"I wish I was Single Again"
"Twenty One Years"
"Tobacus and Bohunkus"
Mr. Rosazza

V.

STRING QUARTET IN ONE MOVEMENT
Allegretto
Mr. Carlo, Mr. McFalls, Miss Miller, Miss Courtney

Senior Recital — Sunday evening, May 27, 1951, at 8:15 p.m. Annie Russell Theatre. Frederick McFalls, *violinist*.

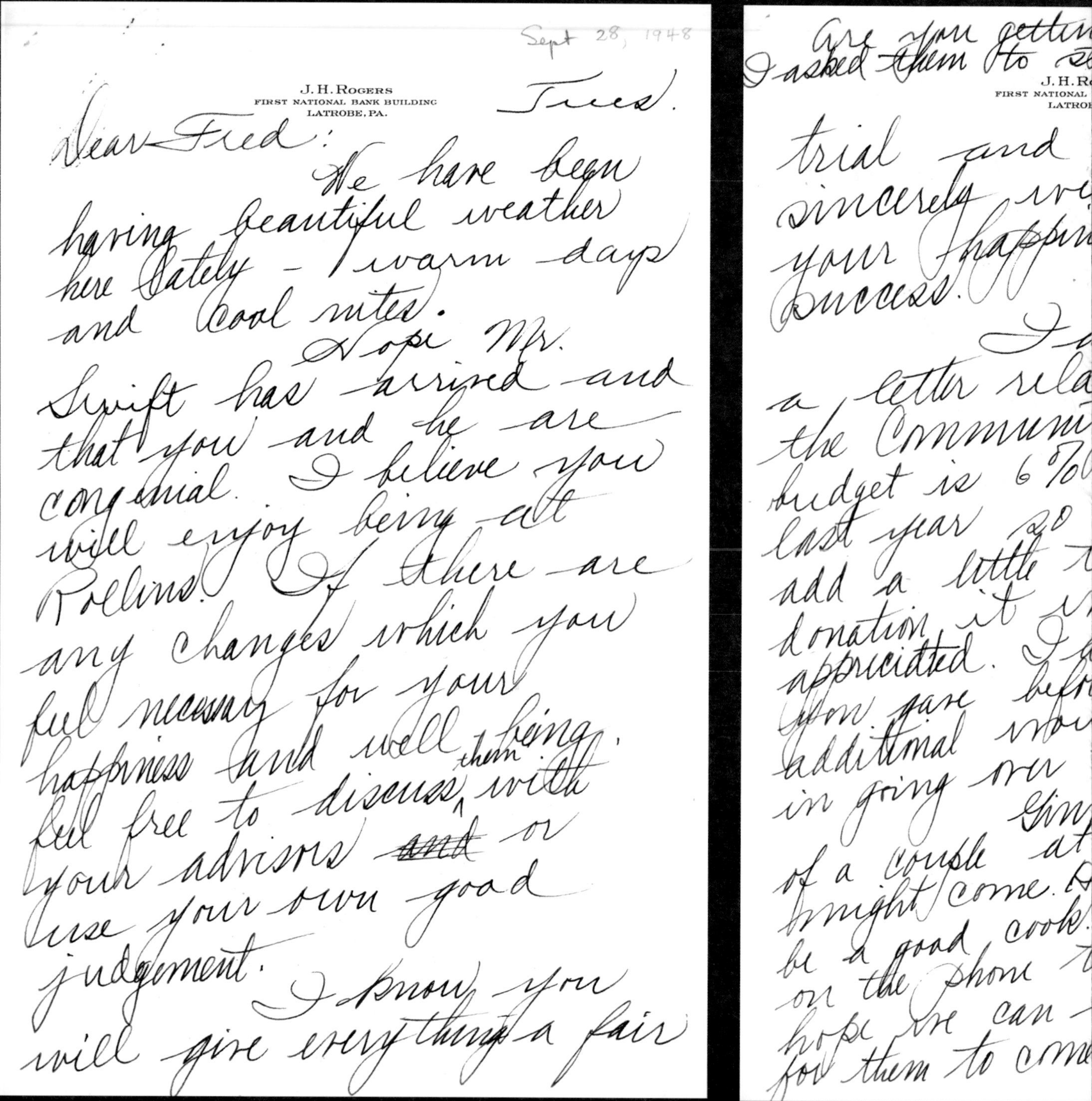

Sept 28, 1948

J. H. Rogers
First National Bank Building
Latrobe, Pa.

Tues.

Dear Fred:

We have been having beautiful weather here lately - warm days and cool nites.

Hope Mr. Swift has arrived and that you and he are congenial. I believe you will enjoy being at Rollins. If there are any changes which you feel necessary for your happiness and well being, feel free to discuss them with your advisors ~~and~~ or use your own good judgement.

I know you will give everything a fair

Are you gettin
I asked them to s

J. H. Ro
First National
Latrob

trial and
sincerely wi
your happin
success.

I a
a letter rela
the Communi
budget is 6%
last year 20
add a little t
donation it w
appriciated. I
you gave befo
additional wou
in going over
Gin
of a course at
might come.
be a good cook.
on the phone
hope we can
for them to come

A letter, dated September 28, 1948, from James Rogers to his son, Fred, at Rollins College. Fred had just transferred to Rollins from Dartmouth College in New Hampshire.

the Bulletins
t 9/23/48

ILDING

I most
for
band

n enclosing
re to
Chest. Our
higher than
you can,
last years
ld be
t recall what
but $5.00
be helpful
TP.
Scott knows
Woodstock that
is supposed to
They will call
ite and I
ake arrangements
soon as posible
over

Please return the chest card to me. Thank you for your continued interest & support of this very worth-while project.

Best wishes to you and your friends.

Sincerely
Dad

During his early days at WQED, Fred considered pitching a children's program called *It's a Small World*. Before he could do so, the station's general manager, Dorothy Daniel, asked the staff if anyone was interested in developing a children's show. Fred and another employee, secretary and aspiring actress Josephine Vicari (who later changed her name to Josie Carey), volunteered. The two hit it off creatively and began brainstorming ideas for what would become *The Children's Corner,* a live, one-hour program. The original plan was barebones: Josie would sing while Fred accompanied her on the organ; they'd feature local people doing interesting things; and they'd show whatever free films they could find, which ended up including topics such as "how to grow grass in New Hampshire."

The Children's Corner was set to debut on WQED's first day on the air, which was April Fool's Day, 1954. The night before, Dorothy Daniel threw a party for staff where she gave everyone a small present. Knowing that Fred liked puppets, she gave him a little tiger hand puppet. This, of course, was the birth of Daniel Striped Tiger, who would make his surprise TV debut the next day. On that first showing of *The Children's Corner,* Daniel popped through a cuckoo clock drawn on the set and announced, "Hi, Josie! It's 5:02, and Columbus discovered America in 1492." Daniel (named for Dorothy Daniel) would go on to become nearly synonymous with *Mister Rogers' Neighborhood* and the legacy of Fred Rogers.

THE CHILDREN'S CORNER

Most of Fred's work on *The Children's Corner* was behind the scenes: playing music and working Daniel and other puppets, including X the Owl and King Friday XIII. Over time, the puppets became an increasingly important component of the program. Fred recalled that the free footage they showed sometimes broke because the film was so brittle. Since this was live television, they had to fill the time with something. "The puppets, I think, saved us," he said many years later. Fred brought them to life and Josie talked to them as honestly and sincerely as she would to a real person.

The Children's Corner aired on WQED from 1954 to 1962 and was immensely popular in Pittsburgh. NBC even aired a weekly national version of the program for a short time. In 1955, it won a Sylvania Award for the best locally produced children's programming in the country.

ABOVE: Josie Carey and Fred with their cast of puppets for *The Children's Corner,* including (*clockwise from top right*) Daniel Striped Tiger, Henrietta Pussycat, X the Owl, Lady Elaine Fairchilde, King Friday XIII, and Grandpère.

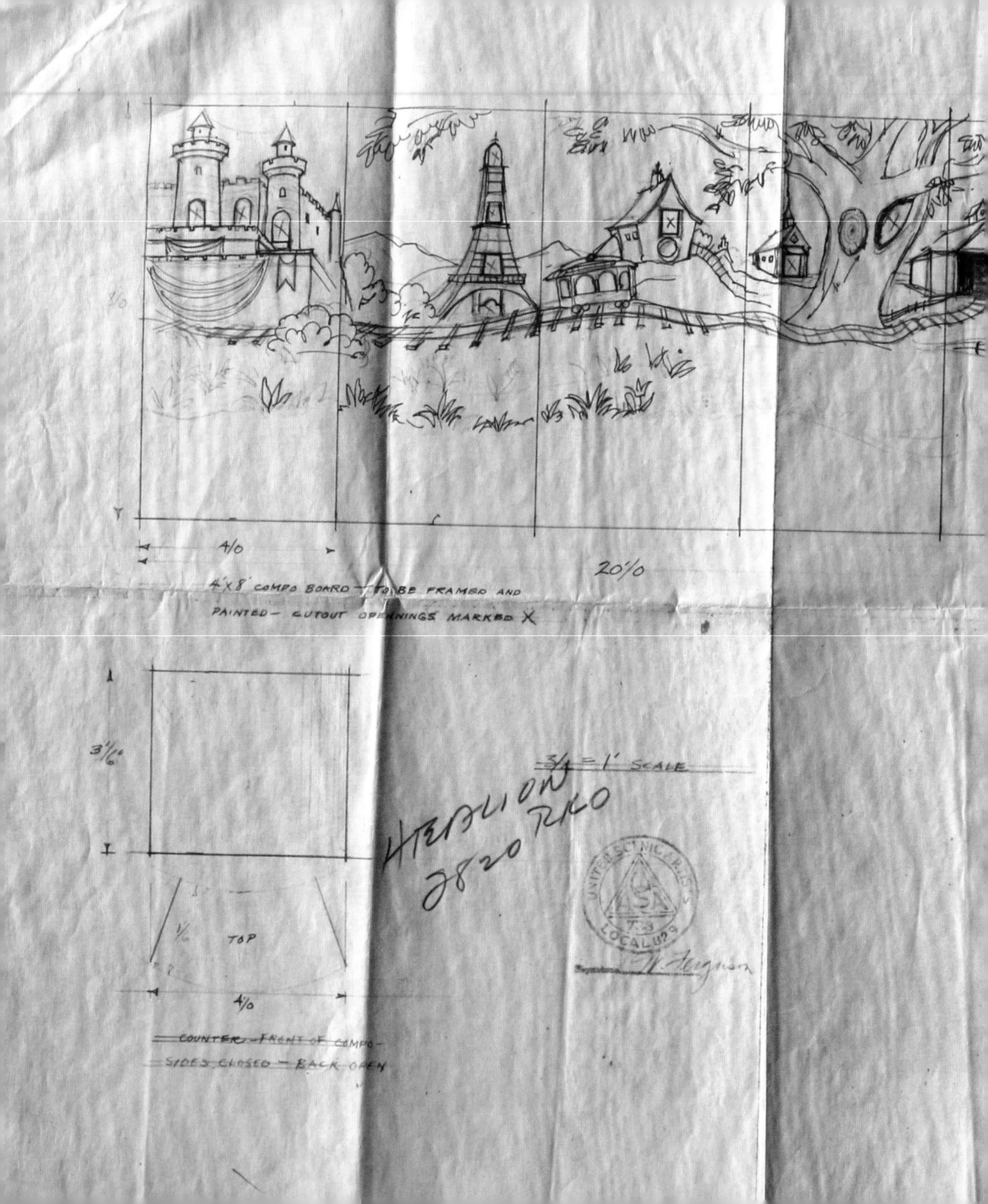

4/0

20/0

4'X 8' COMPO BOARD — TO BE FRAMED AND
PAINTED — CUTOUT OPENINGS MARKED X

3'/6"

3/4" = 1" SCALE

HEADLION
2820 RKO

TOP

4/0

COUNTER — FRONT OF COMPO —
SIDES CLOSED — BACK OPEN

UNITED SCENIC ARTISTS
LOCAL 829

EACH OPENNING TO
HAVE 6" STRIP 4" ABOVE

NBC
T.T.T.

THE CLOCK
WQED
4337 FIFTH AVE
PITTSBURGH 13, PA.

Dear Tame Tiger,
It is 11:13 A.M. AND I am writing to TELL you the GOOD news. YOU HAVE BEEN passed by our Tame Tiger Board of Directors AND you may now be called a TAME TIGER.
Welcome to the TTT
Torganizationally yours,
T.T. Daniel S. Tiger

After *The Children's Corner* went off the air Fred, Joanne, and their young sons, Jim and John, moved to Canada. Fred Rainsberry, the head of children's programming for the Canadian Broadcasting Corporation (CBC), had invited Fred to do a fifteen-minute children's show with puppets and music. But Rainsberry had witnessed how Fred talked with children in person, and he encouraged Fred to come out from behind the set and talk directly to his viewers. The program, called *Misterogers,* gave Fred experience in front of the camera, talking to both the puppets and viewers, honing what would become his signature television style.

Within a few years, the Rogers family decided to move back to western Pennsylvania. A local department store sponsored a series of *Misterogers* holiday episodes on WTAE (the local ABC affiliate). While Fred waited for WQED to secure funding for a children's program, he worked

with preschoolers at the Bellefield Presbyterian Church and at the Arsenal Family and Children's Center, where he had previously studied under the guidance of child development expert Dr. Margaret McFarland while working on *The Children's Corner*.

The neighborhood of Mister Rogers had come to Pittsburgh, but it would take a little longer for *Mister Rogers' Neighborhood* to find a permanent home on WQED.

ABOVE: Joe Negri talks on the Tele-can in the Neighborhood of Make-Believe on the set of *Misterogers* at the WTAE studios in 1964.

OPPOSITE: Mister Rogers on the set of the CBC's *Misterogers* in 1963, with the characters of Mrs. Frogg and Cornflake S. Pecially seen on the screen in the background.

Margaret McFarland

"[Fred] was a creative musician. He was a creative dramatist. And he was a creative linguist—he loved languages. These were things I wasn't. At that time, I was what he wasn't, too, because my professional career had been invested in the understanding of children and of parenthood."

Dr. Margaret McFarland

Dr. Margaret McFarland, world-renowned child psychologist and professor of child development at the University of Pittsburgh, became Fred's mentor, friend, and closest adviser. Since Fred was interested in working with children, one of his seminary professors suggested that Dr. McFarland should supervise his training. With Dr. McFarland's guidance, Fred worked with children at the Arsenal Family and Children's Center, which Dr. McFarland had cofounded with Dr. Benjamin Spock and Erik Erikson. For more than thirty years, the two met weekly, sometimes even talking daily, to discuss child development theory. Fred would incorporate the themes and concepts they discussed into his scripts and songs for *Mister Rogers' Neighborhood*.

Pretend and real.

Big and little

Alone and together

Hate the same people you love.

(Afraid of same people who are comforting)

What's inside?
(See from the inside out what
you're like.)
∧Will to find out helps learning
X representing adolesᵈⁿᵗ discretion.
(King says until you know who)
(owns it you can't open it)

You don't learn by magic

Notes on possible program themes developed in conjunction with Dr. McFarland.

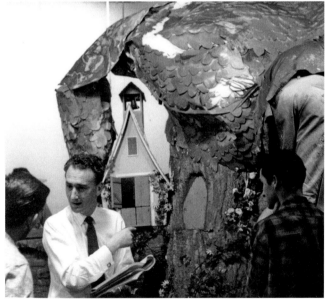

F red returned to WQED in 1966 with a half-hour program, now called *Misterogers' Neighborhood*. The black-and-white version aired locally in Pittsburgh from October 1966 through May 1967. In that first year, the budget was so small there wasn't enough money to produce new Neighborhood of Make-Believe segments. Instead, they created new content only for the portions of the program set in Mister Rogers' television house, and they included kinescopes of the puppet stories that originally aired on *Misterogers* on the CBC. The Eastern Educational Network, forerunner of National Educational Television and the Public Broadcasting Service, also showed the program in several other major U.S. cities. As a result, *Misterogers' Neighborhood* began developing a loyal following of children and families around the country. So loyal, in fact, that when funding for the program ran out and word reached mothers in Boston that it might go off the air, a group of them took up a door-to-door collection seeking contributions toward saving the program.

OPPOSITE: A portrait of King Friday XIII in front of an early version of his castle; **ABOVE:** a collage commemorating the first season of *Misterogers' Neighborhood;* **LEFT:** crew members in front of the oak tree on the Neighborhood of Make-Believe set.

FOLLOWING PAGE: Fred Rogers poses with Trolley in the Castle Garden on the Neighborhood of Make-Believe set in 1968.

"We all have only one life to live on earth. And through television, we have the choice of encouraging others to demean this life or to cherish it in creative, imaginative ways."

Fred Rogers

Classic Moment

Episode 0001
Original air date: February 19, 1968

⟩ **THE FIRST NATIONAL**
broadcast of *Misterogers'*
Neighborhood dealt with the
topic of change. Along with
changes to the program's source
of funding, the sets for both
Mister Rogers' house and the
Neighborhood of Make-Believe
had been updated from those
used during the show's more
limited distribution. In Make-
Believe, Lady Elaine Fairchilde
had rearranged all of the
buildings with her magic, and
the characters reacted in their
typical fashions. Daniel Striped
Tiger fretted about getting used
to new things—but then he
remembered that the *people*
in Make-Believe were still the
same, which comforted him.
Henrietta Pussycat declared
that she's too shy for change.

X the Owl, on the other hand,
seemed to enjoy things being
"topsy-turvy" because, he said,
"it's a little like a treasure hunt,"
except you know what you're
looking for. King Friday, who
always opposed change, was
up in arms and commanded
Handyman Negri to find Lady

Elaine, who had gone into hiding
after her mischief. Back at his
house, Mister Rogers discussed
the idea that change can be good
and can give people new ideas.
He knew that while change can
be difficult for children, talking
about it could make it easier
to manage.

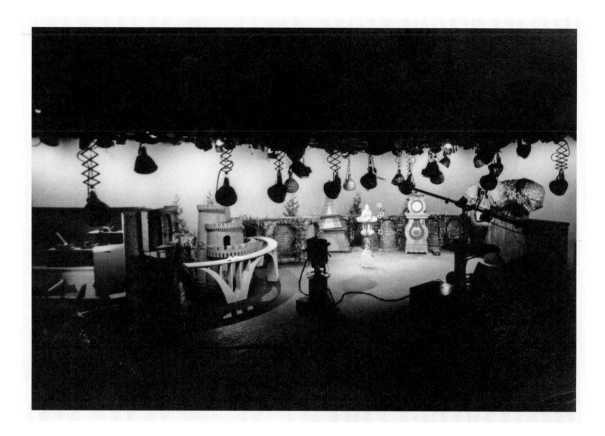

A National Audience

On February 19, 1968, *Misterogers' Neighborhood* (the spelling didn't change to *Mister Rogers' Neighborhood* until the fourth season, in 1971) went national with funding from the Sears-Roebuck Foundation. Even though the program would evolve throughout the next thirty-three years, many of its core elements were present at the start. The opening sequence and song, for example, remained largely unchanged for the life of the series. The slow pace of the program and many of the characters were also consistent throughout the years.

In some ways, the early episodes were more fantastical than in later years. The line between reality and make-believe was less defined in the beginning. Although Mister Rogers never appeared in the Neighborhood of Make-Believe, characters from that fantasy world, such as Handyman Negri, would occasionally visit Mister Rogers' house. Over time, Fred became more focused on the importance of helping children understand the difference between reality and make-believe, and the two neighborhoods became more distinct.

OPPOSITE, ABOVE: Behind-the-scenes look at the Canadian set of the Neighborhood of Make-Believe. Note the placement of the Eiffel Tower and the oak tree, which would both change locations with the program's first national broadcast in the United States.

OPPOSITE, BELOW: Fred Rogers peeks out of X's door in the oak tree and poses with Henrietta Pussycat. Mister Rogers never appeared on camera in the Neighborhood of Make-Believe.

RIGHT: Early sketch for King Friday's throne room.

BELOW: (*from left*) Sam Silberman, Eliot Daley, Fred Rogers, Johnny Costa, Michael Taylor, and Betty Aberlin watch playback of a scene in 1971.

MR STICKS HIS HEAD IN THE DOOR.

MR (sings) "Won't You Be My Neighbor?"

MR INVITES FRIENDS TO PORCH WHERE

HE'S UP ON A LADDER SECURING THE

(Play up away)

BOLTS (OR WHATEVER) ON THE SWING.

To have things stay in just the same way

Like to keep bed in same place. Then when you awaken you get a brand new idea 'cause you see world in a new way. I liked my studio

MR GOES INSIDE

HE TAKES OFF JACKET-IF HE HASN'T ALREADY.

Sometimes though it would be more comfortable just the way it was.
(i.e. New houses w/ many new

MR MOVES KITCHEN TABLE AND CHAIRS

INTO PLACE.

features. Still remember the old.)

MR: Did you notice any of the changes inside?

Some of my neighbors came in this past weekend

and helped me rearrange this studio of mine.

Soon as I finish this we'll go in.

I've been thinking about you all weekend--

wondering how you would like it.

You know what a Studio is
(A studio is a place where people can create-

we can create plays, songs, cookies, block build

ings.)

MR (Showing map of his Neighborhood): Did you

come down this way and then around here, watch

when you cross this street, and then come up thi

side? That's the ~~best~~ *easiest* way to come.

SONG: "I Like You As You Are".

Did you see the traffic light? (You can move it

all around.) Let's call King Friday XIII and see

what's going on in Make-Believe today.

(WITH CAN ON TRAFFIC LIGHT) Hello? Edgar? How

are you?

A KNOCK AT THE DOOR INTERRUPTS

MR (TO EDGAR) *Could I call you back?* ~~Can you hold on a minute?~~ *There's*

Someone at the door.

MR GOES TO DOOR, OPENS IT.

THE SPEEDY DELIVERY MAN IS THERE
(He even runs when he's standing
waiting--always in a hurry!)

HE HANDS MR A NOTE
(He has his bike beside him)

Mr. McC.: Speedy Delivery Message for Misterogers.

MR: Thank you.

HANDS MR PAD AND PENCIL.

Mr. McC.: Please sign here.

MR (Signing): You're certainly always in a hurry
aren't you, Mr. McCurdy?

Mr. McC.: Speedy Delivery never lets you down.
Fastest delivery service in any city or town!

MR (Reading note): It's from Mrs. Russellite.
You know the lady who ~~wears the~~ Collects old lamp shades.

HE READS NOTE SILENTLY.

Do you read? It's a mighty handy thing. I learned
how. You'll learn. Mrs. Russellite says she had She
hoped to come over and see what we had done inside
here but she doesn't feel like coming today. She's
~~got something bright for us though.~~ She wishes we'd
come over to her house. insteed

MR Mr. McCurdy Could you tell Mrs. Russellite we'll
come over to her place later on today.

Mr. McC.: Speedy Delivery Man at your service!

MR: How much is delivery today?

New episodes of *Mister Rogers' Neighborhood* were produced until early 1975. The production then took a hiatus that would last for several years. At first, it wasn't clear whether it *was* merely a hiatus. No one, including Fred himself, knew if they'd make more episodes. After eight years and hundreds of episodes, he felt he'd created a well-rounded catalog of programs that addressed the needs of children, and he intended for these to continue to play in rerun for years to come. He organized some of the existing episodes into a three-year cycle to be shown on the more than 230 public television stations that carried the program. In this way, he ensured that the episodes would have continuity rather than being aired in the haphazard way of some television reruns.

Even as Fred was taping the final 1975 episode, he left the door open to returning, telling a reporter that the program had "been a good vehicle, and I don't say we won't use it again."

A few years into the hiatus, Fred became increasingly concerned with the way media often blurred the lines between reality and fantasy, which he knew could be confusing or dangerous for children. And so, in August 1979, *Mister Rogers' Neighborhood* returned to produce new episodes. One significant change in these post-hiatus shows was the introduction of weekly themes, such as Superheroes, Day and Night Care, Alike and Different, Fathers and Music, and Imaginary Friends. A theme would weave through every element of that week's episodes, from events in Mister Rogers' real Neighborhood into the dreamlike realm of the Neighborhood of Make-Believe, and back again.

Elizabeth "Betsy" Nadas Seamans, who wrote for the program and also played Mrs. McFeely, described how weekly themes would play out in Make-Believe. Each one, she said, "was like a little soap opera that you started on Monday, and something was going on. By Wednesday you had a crisis, and by Thursday you began to resolve it. By Friday everything was okay. It was a little drama that had five days' arc to it." Fred would continue to produce new episodes until August 2001.

OPPOSITE: The Royal Family, Neighbor Aber, and Lady Aberlin gather for the grand opening of the new Caring Center, a day care at Corney's Factory. The episode first aired in 1989, addressing the theme of "When Parents Go to Work."

BELOW: When the *Neighborhood* resumed production in 1979, the first week of new programming was themed "Mister Rogers Goes to School." In Make-Believe, François Clemmons and Lady Aberlin visit the new students in Miss Harriet Elizabeth Cow's classroom.

Classic Moment

THE FIRST EPISODE IN COLOR

Episode 1001
Original air date: February 10, 1969

> **AFTER 130 EPISODES IN BLACK AND WHITE,** the *Neighborhood* came to life in vibrant color for the first time with the start of the second season. Though Mister Rogers never mentioned the change during the program, viewers discovered that King Friday's castle and X the Owl's feathers were blue, the Neighborhood Trolley was a brilliant red, and the iconic cardigan sweaters Mister Rogers donned at the beginning of each day's visit came in a variety of colors.

OPPOSITE: Fred Rogers at the kitchen table in his "television house," 1970.

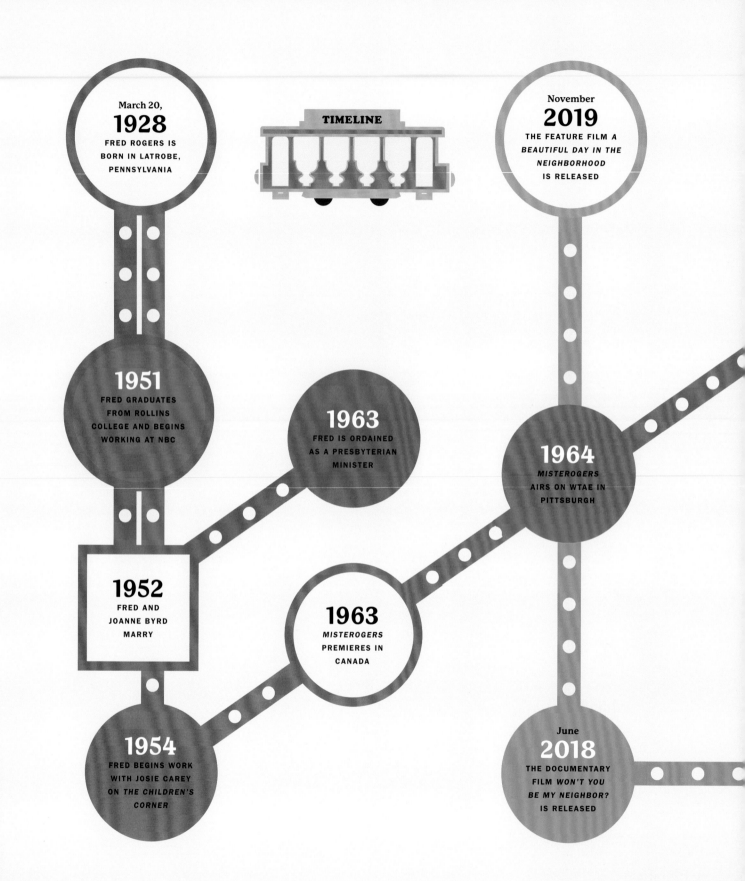

TIMELINE

March 20,
1928
FRED ROGERS IS
BORN IN LATROBE,
PENNSYLVANIA

1951
FRED GRADUATES
FROM ROLLINS
COLLEGE AND BEGINS
WORKING AT NBC

1952
FRED AND
JOANNE BYRD
MARRY

1954
FRED BEGINS WORK
WITH JOSIE CAREY
ON *THE CHILDREN'S
CORNER*

1963
FRED IS ORDAINED
AS A PRESBYTERIAN
MINISTER

1963
MISTEROGERS
PREMIERES IN
CANADA

1964
MISTEROGERS
AIRS ON WTAE IN
PITTSBURGH

November
2019
THE FEATURE FILM *A
BEAUTIFUL DAY IN THE
NEIGHBORHOOD*
IS RELEASED

June
2018
THE DOCUMENTARY
FILM *WON'T YOU
BE MY NEIGHBOR?*
IS RELEASED

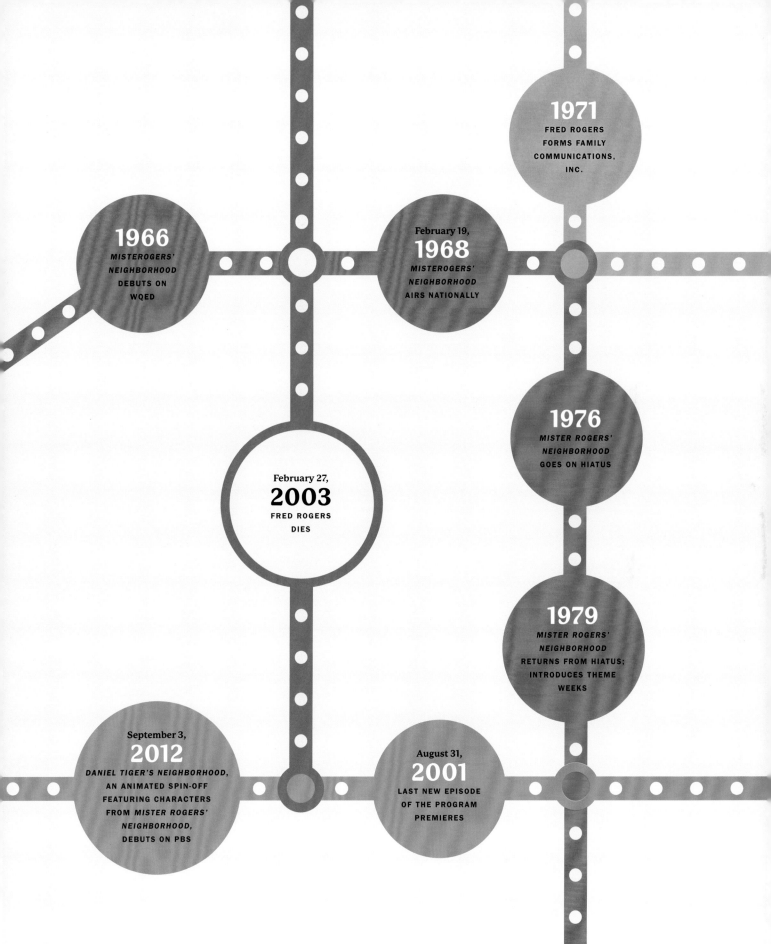

A Neighborly Chat *with*

HEDDA SHARAPAN

Assistant Director, Associate
Producer, and Director of
Early Childhood Initiatives

HEDDA SHARAPAN has worked with Fred Rogers Productions (formerly Family Communications, Inc.) for more than fifty years, starting as an assistant director in October 1966. She has filled many roles over the years, including assistant producer, associate producer, and director of Early Childhood Initiatives. Hedda continues to serve as a child development consultant for the company, working on special projects and speaking about Fred Rogers' messages to audiences around the country.

TIM LYBARGER: How did you start working with Fred Rogers?

HEDDA SHARAPAN: I went to college at Carnegie Tech, which is now Carnegie Mellon, and graduated with a degree in psychology. That was the summer of 1965. And I thought, "Well, I'll just check around Pittsburgh. If I don't get into grad school, what else might there be here?" Just kind of on a lark, I went over to WQED. And I said, "Is there anything here for children on television?" At the time, Fred was working with children, learning through Dr. McFarland, Dr. Nancy Curry, Linda Philbrick, and the others in the preschools that were connected to the Arsenal [Family and Children's Center]. He was kind enough to meet with me. And he said, "If this is really what you want, why don't you think about a master's degree in child development?"

I was fortunate enough to get a fellowship [at the University of Pittsburgh]. The second year that I was in graduate school, Fred remembered my interest, and he asked if I would help. That was October of 1966. They were taping at night because of [musical director] Johnny Costa's schedule. We were taping three nights a week, I think, from six to eleven. So I was in graduate school in the daytime, and then I'd come into the studio at night. And I would watch Fred play out all the things I had learned about—ritual; transition; helping children with aggression, fears, and separation; the difference between reality and fantasy. I was in this incredible position of really understanding what he was doing.

TL: What was the program like in the beginning, and what was your role in those early years?

HS: I was the assistant director. In that first year, there was no pay the first couple months. There was no pay and no staff. We didn't have money for the Neighborhood of Make-Believe segments. We used those from the kinescopes, from the CBC, when Fred was in Canada. Those were all timed. We knew it was like eight minutes and thirty-five seconds. We did *Mister Rogers' Neighborhood* that first year almost like a live show.

He would do the introduction. We would then roll in the Neighborhood of Make-Believe. And while that was playing, I had to sit with pencil and paper—there were no back-timers or calculators. I had to sit and figure out how much time until the end of the show. And I also had to fill out a log of any problems that made us go over budget.

TL: From the '60s all the way through, a lot of the things on the *Neighborhood* stayed the same, but what kinds of things did you see change over the years?

HS: Well, there are a number of things. But one that I was very much involved in—in the early years, Mister Rogers used to say things like, "Stand up and let me see how tall you are. Oh my, you really have grown." Or also with the death of the fish, it was the projector, Picture-Picture, that showed the words *"Dead fish."* And Fred asked Picture-Picture, "Where?" And on Picture-Picture we saw the word *"Here."* Fred rethought a lot of that and felt that he didn't want children to think that he really could see them through the television when he would say, "Stand up and let me see how tall you've grown." And he also didn't want them to think that Picture-Picture had a mind of its own and could tell him things. So while Fred kept the basics the same, he allowed some things to evolve and change, things that he felt would be more meaningful to children.

There was also a time when he would say, "Let me see if it's time for the Trolley." And he would take out the telescope, look through it, and we would see the Trolley coming through the tunnel into Make-Believe. And he would say, "There's the Trolley." In later years, he felt that it was more important to show that he was bringing out the Trolley with a switch by the Trolley tracks in his television house. He would then say to children, "Let's pretend that . . ." And we could see that he was in charge of the pretending, as children pretend in their play.

TL: It seems like over time he became more intentional about making a clear line between reality and make-believe. Was there a particular reason for that?

HS: I really don't know what made Fred rethink that. I do know that children have a hard time distinguishing between what is real and what is just pretend. I just think that the advantage of doing something that was solid over time allowed him to keep looking at it. And Fred was that kind of person that any writing he did, he looked at it again, and again, and again. And I think he just became more comfortable being this person who was the honest adult in the life of a child.

TL: It's been said, from multiple sources, that Fred was very particular about every last detail of the program. Everything was very calculated and very intentional. Did that present any kind of challenge for the rest of the staff?

HS: Well, we were a small group. We were maybe twelve of us in the office, maybe fourteen at the most. And my feeling is that we all bought into the sense that we were doing something really meaningful through this television experience, and that Fred had incredibly high standards and we could help him.

"He was able to see deeper, higher, stronger, simpler, more meaningful. And that's what I learned from him."

I will tell you that when people ask me, "What was it like working for him?" it was two things. One is, it was incredibly challenging. I always felt stretched, like anything I was presenting to him had to be the very best, thought-out, carefully worded.

Part of that feeling comes from the incredibly complex work that Fred did with *Mister Rogers' Neighborhood*. Yes, it looked simple, but it truly was complex, with many layers and many themes. I was often called upon to do workshops or speeches about some approach of his, on topics like helping children deal with death, helping them with angry feelings, strengthening the bonds with families, tragic events in the news, communication, literacy, STEAM [Science, Technology, Engineering, Arts, Math], and helping families with children in the NICU or in need of painful medical treatments. And I worked hard on researching—talking with Fred and Dr. McFarland and others in the field—in order to learn all I could to be able to understand enough about Fred's approach to articulate it. Then came the effort of figuring out how to communicate it in such a way that others would want to learn it, understand it, and hopefully apply it to their own work with children and families, as well as their own lives. That's hard work!

But on the other hand, I also felt incredibly rewarded. Fred was very appreciative. There was no "favorite son." He appreciated what each of us brought, and he told us, often in notes or comments. When I would write anything—an article that I was writing on his behalf, or another bit of work—I would put a Post-It Note on it and say, "For your revision." And then I got smarter, because I saw what was coming back to me. I started to write, "For your *elevation*." Because he always elevated. I miss him terribly, because he did that. He was able to see deeper, higher, stronger, simpler, more meaningful. And that's what I learned from him.

He used to refer to himself as my elevator operator. He'd sometimes sign a note with, "Your E.O." Your elevator operator. That's the advantage of working in a small staff with someone who is dedicated to a mission. And we were all committed to that mission—and still are.

TL: Are there any particular episodes that stand out to you as being especially memorable?

HS: In the early years, there was a wonderful moment at the beginning of a program. Fred went to the closet. He got a sweater out and he started buttoning it as he was singing the song. He got to the end of the song, looked down, and said, "Oh, did you ever do anything like that?" when he realized he buttoned it wrong. And he re-buttoned it, saying, "I thought I was doing that just right." It was just such a human moment, and he didn't retape it. He left it in.

The death of the goldfish was one that really helped a lot of people through their understanding of "How do we talk to children about this?"

The treasured visits with Yo-Yo Ma, with André Watts, with Eric Carle. There are so many moments. I almost hate to say names—everyone was so incredible in their own way. And I remember Fred saying he wanted to offer a kind of smorgasbord of so many ways that people could be who they are and express who

they are to the world and find meaning in life.

TL: Did you ever think that Mister Rogers would have come into the forefront of pop culture as he has today?

HS: I knew what he was doing was so right-on. And I knew how helpful it was. I'll tell you, there was a time, somewhere in the late '90s, where we were concerned that people had forgotten about him and that he was considered old-fashioned.

In 2003, when he died, there was such an outpouring of gratitude for what he had given to children and families over the years. Then it quieted around 2005, or until we started with *Daniel [Tiger's Neighborhood]* and even past. But what I'm hearing now, especially since so many people have seen the documentary, *Won't You Be My Neighbor?*, is an outpouring of affection and respect. And you can't get any better than those two words.

Over the years, Fred Rogers' work forms such a solid gift to the world. There are just so many moments . . . It's the humanness of it all. And the beauty is that people are still appreciating it and want more.

📺

"Childhood isn't just something we 'get through.' It's a big journey, and it's one we've all taken. Most likely, though, we've forgotten how much we had to learn along the way about ourselves and others."

Fred Rogers

Twelve-year-old Jermaine Vaughn teaches Mister Rogers some breakdancing moves before performing a routine in Episode 1543, which originally aired in 1985.

Hi, Neighbor!

**OUR TELEVISION
VISITS WITH
MISTER ROGERS**

For more than thirty years, Mister Rogers would zip up a warm cardigan, slip on his comfy sneakers, and settle in for time with his television neighbors. Visits may have been just twenty-eight minutes long, but that was plenty of time for talking, singing, learning, playing, and pretending.

At the start of each episode, Mister Rogers would arrive singing his signature song about what a beautiful day it was. As he swapped his coat for a cardigan and sat down to change his shoes, he'd invite viewers to be his neighbor. It was a lovely reminder that everyone belonged here. Then it was time to share what he'd brought with him on this visit. It might be a musical instrument, a toy to play with, or even a puppy!

Next, he might show a film on Picture-Picture about how people make crayons or bake pretzels, before going to the kitchen for a craft project, experiment, or snack. More often than not, Mr. McFeely would swing by with a Speedy Delivery. And, of course, every visit included space for dreaming and pretending in the Neighborhood of Make-Believe.

In Mister Rogers' real Neighborhood, he often caught up with his neighbors at Negri's Music Shop, Brockett's Bakery, and Betty's Little Theater. Sometimes he'd tour the kinds of places his young viewers might recognize from their own neighborhoods: a factory, school, museum, or library. Through these special visits, children could broaden their perspectives and learn to feel more comfortable in new situations.

Special guests might drop by Mister Rogers' television house or join him out in the neighborhood. These excursions were always interesting and exciting. Where else could you attend ballet class with Pittsburgh Steeler Lynn Swann or visit the home of renowned musician Yo-Yo Ma?

While there was tremendous variety in the program's daily topics, the framework of these television visits remained consistent, providing children a sense of ease and security as they experienced new ideas and things. Mister Rogers was a calming presence among the flashy and fast-paced programs saturating the airwaves in the 1970s, '80s, and '90s. No matter the topic or the agenda, each "visit" to *Mister Rogers' Neighborhood* offered viewers a placid sense of personal connection unlike any other found in children's television at the time.

Every episode ended the same way, with Mister Rogers changing back into his loafers and jacket as he sang goodbye. The song reassured young viewers that he'd be back when the day (or the week) was new, and they'd all have more things to talk about. And out the door he went— but everyone knew he'd be back again, just as he'd promised.

WON'T YOU BE MY NEIGHBOR?

"It's a beautiful day in the neighborhood . . ."

As the program's opening music swelled, Mister Rogers walked through the door singing his welcome. His first order of business was always to change out of his "work" clothes and into his "play" clothes. First he'd stop by the closet to swap out his jacket for one of his colorful zip-up cardigans. Next, he'd sit down on the bench in the living room to exchange his loafers for a pair of blue canvas sneakers. On the surface, it was a simple one-two wardrobe change, but like so much in *Mister Rogers' Neighborhood,* the purpose of this routine went much deeper.

Fred Rogers knew that young children often find it difficult to move from one task or experience to another. He helped viewers to feel calm, safe, and focused by including purposeful transitions in every segment of the program. The simple ritual at the opening of every episode helped children to settle in for the television visit and feel ready to learn from whatever he was going to talk about or show. It assured them that Mister Rogers was ready to spend mindful time together.

OPPOSITE, ABOVE: Since Fred was color-blind, he and crew members worked out a system to tell him which sweater to wear that day: the one placed to the left of the empty hanger.

THE ICONIC SNEAKERS

Mister Rogers' iconic blue canvas sneakers signaled to viewers that it was time for a relaxing visit together. He started wearing them while filming *The Children's Corner* because their soft soles allowed him to run quietly behind the scenes between the organ and the puppets during live television.

A young viewer once wrote to Mister Rogers to ask why he tossed his shoe in the air when he took it off. Mister Rogers replied, "One day I was in an especially playful mood when our visit began, and I tossed my shoe. It was fun, and it's become a kind of game between Mr. Costa, our musical director and pianist, and me. He tries to play certain notes on the piano just as I catch my shoe. Sometimes we do it together just right, and sometimes we don't, but it's fun for us to try each time because it's like a game."

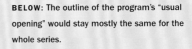

BELOW: The outline of the program's "usual opening" would stay mostly the same for the whole series.

LEFT: An overhead shot of Mister Rogers walking through the front door on the set of his television house.

THIS IS CONSIDERED "USUAL OPENING"

CUE MUSIC

FADE UP ON WIDE SHOT OF MODEL OF MR's NEIGHBORHOOD (constructed to correspond with drawing of his neighborhood which is in his kitchen)

SUPER "MISTEROGERS NEIGHBORHOOD" SLIDE

ZOOM IN SLOWLY TO TOP OF HILL,
FOLLOW HILL DOWNTOWN AND FOLLOW THE STREETS WHICH WOULD LEAD TO MR's HOUSE
ON MODEL.

ZOOM EXTREMELY TIGHT ON HIS HOUSE AND
DISOLVE TO INTERIOR AND PAN.

PICTURE-PICTURE GIVES A GREETING.

CONTINUE TO PAN TO DOOR.

DOOR OPENS

A RAINBOW OF SWEATERS AND TIES

For years Fred's mother, Nancy, knitted the sweaters he wore on the program. After she passed away in 1981, the original sweaters began to lose their shape due to age, and the crew found alternate sources for the sweaters, including a style worn by Canadian postal workers. The cotton sweaters were off-white, so the art director dyed them bright colors before Fred wore them on the program. Over the course of his career, Mister Rogers wore more than twenty-four different cardigans.

BELOW: Mister Rogers changes out of his jacket in an episode produced in 1994.

ABOVE: The tag in a sweater knit by Fred's mother, Nancy Flagg, who had remarried after Fred's father passed away.

RIGHT: Producer Margy Whitmer labeled Polaroid photos of Mister Rogers' sweaters and ties to help Fred (who was color-blind) keep track of matching wardrobe items.

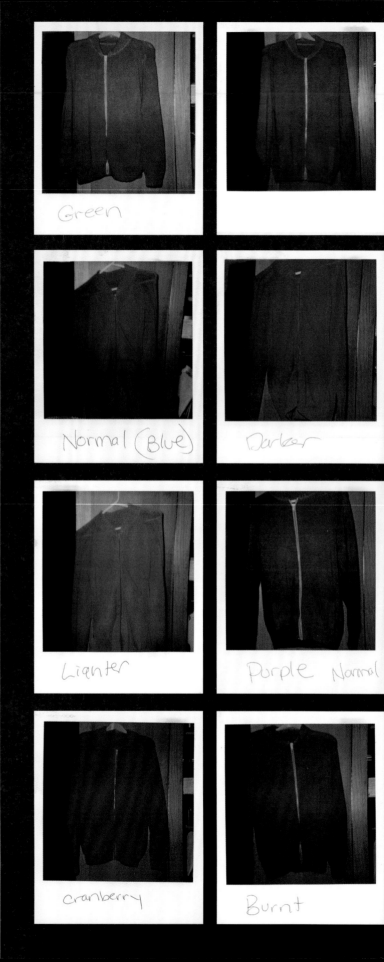

Green

Normal (Blue)

Darker

Lighter

Purple Normal

Cranberry

Burnt

Brown Silk with White and Red Daisies

Liberty of London — (Dark Green w/ small circles)

Macfarlane Tie

Brown w/ Red Trolley Trolley Tie

Blue w/ red trolleys

Garfinckel's 1

Garfinckel's 2 (Purple)

Bloodhound and Stirrup

Clergy Tie

Murray Tie

Red with gold trolleys

Red Silk with Blue, Green and Brown Diagonals

Nantucket

Skeleton Keys

Black with Bubbles

Boomerang Tie
Giorgio Armani Black with Half Circles (Beige, Aqua + Mustard)

COME ON IN!

A TOUR OF THE TELEVISION HOUSE

Mister Rogers' television house may have been an oasis of calm and quiet, but one design element stood out as relatively loud and busy: the curtains! Fashioned from kettle cloth, a type of fabric popular in the late sixties and seventies, they featured illustrations depicting former political campaign ephemera, including the slogans "Keep cool with Coolidge" and "Votes for Women."

The inside of the house changed very little throughout its three decades. The furniture, décor, and kitchen appliances stayed mostly the same, no matter the year. This gave the space a kind of old-fashioned familiarity, similar to that childhood feeling of stepping back in time when visiting the house of a dear grandparent or great-aunt. The relative consistency—and simplicity—of the set was another way Mister Rogers tailored every detail to his young viewers' need to know what to expect. Fred knew that plain, calm surroundings help children feel safe, offer their full attention, and be more open to learning without making them feel overwhelmed or distracted.

The Neighborhood Trolley was controlled electrically through a panel located under the window seat, where its tracks passed through Mister Rogers' house. Mister Rogers showed viewers the controls in several episodes, explaining that machines like Trolley do not operate on their own without the help of people.

Hidden from the cameras at the end of the couch was the "knock-knock box," a wooden box with a microphone clipped above it. When Mister Rogers had a visitor, floor manager Nick Tallo tapped on the box to make a sound like someone knocking at the door.

Front Porch and Yard

On his small front porch, Mister Rogers might welcome visitors or sit in the swing for a chat or song with his viewers, or "television neighbors," as he called them. The front yard was no bigger than the porch itself, but there was plenty of space to connect with friends.

The Living Room

The living room was the heart of Mister Rogers' house. This was where many of the scenes took place, from Mister Rogers' arrival and departure rituals, to playing films on Picture-Picture, to summoning Trolley to take viewers to the Neighborhood of Make-Believe. Sometimes Mister Rogers (or a guest) would sit at a small upright piano to play a song or two. When he needed to answer the phone or make a call, he sat on the orange-and-brown plaid couch.

The Neighborhood of Make-Believe models, most of which were made by Bob Trow, were sometimes used in lieu of the Neighborhood Trolley to make the transition into Make-Believe.

On either side of the refrigerator, a framed image can be found—one detailing Mister Rogers' Neighborhood and the other the Neighborhood of Make-Believe. These pictures changed slightly throughout the series, but they always maintained their representation of the two separate neighborhoods.

Mister Rogers cared for his pet fish by ensuring they were regularly fed. Often he would stop at the fish tank to sing a song, talk with viewers, or simply to feed the fish.

The Kitchen

The kitchen was a treasure trove of fan-favorite items, including hand-colored illustrations of the two neighborhoods (the "real" and the "make-believe") hanging on either side of the refrigerator, and the corner shelves that held models of the buildings and characters from the Neighborhood of Make-Believe. After feeding the fish, Mister Rogers might sit at the kitchen table to drink a glass of fruit juice or to build a tower with paper cups. Sometimes he might make a snack, giving him an opportunity to talk about healthy eating. These simple, quiet moments allowed him to demonstrate common, everyday activities or to engage in open-ended, imaginative play.

Backyard

The sandbox, housed inside a tall wooden workbench, gave Mister Rogers a place to play and pretend in his backyard. In Episode 1425, which featured the opera *The Key to Otherland*, the camera zoomed in for a close-up of the sand in the sandbox and then pulled back to reveal the opera's opening scene on a beach.

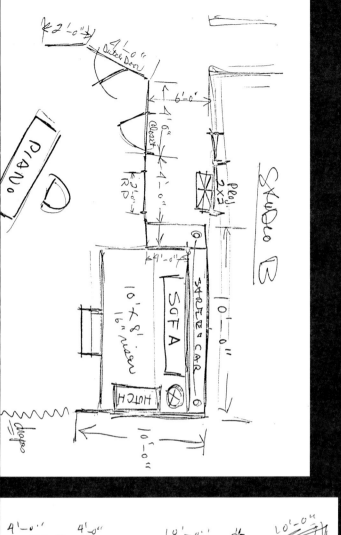

Seldom-Seen Spaces

Garage

The garage appeared in just five episodes during 1976, never to be seen again. Inside, Mister Rogers stored a wide array of items, including a massive collection of tapes of recorded *Neighborhood* visits. Since production was going on hiatus and stations were set to re-air episodes from years earlier, Mister Rogers wanted to help children understand that the programs were recorded and could be shown again from the beginning. When Mr. McFeely mentioned that he would like to remember more about the older Neighborhood of Make-Believe storylines, Mister Rogers alluded to the fact that the older episodes would be airing as the program took a break from production: "Next week we'll start to show all of these visits so everybody can see them the whole way through."

ABOVE: In an episode that first aired in 1976, Mister Rogers shows viewers shelves in his garage that hold tapes of recorded television visits.

LEFT: Early drafts for the interior of Mister Rogers' television house and King Friday's throne room. When the set was constructed for the nationally televised episodes in 1968, the house was one continuous set, with the kitchen connected to the living room rather than existing as a separate mini set.

Bathroom

In 1986, Fred received a letter from the father of a young viewer who was absolutely certain that Mister Rogers didn't poop—because there was no bathroom in his house! In fact, several early episodes (in 1968 and 1974) did show a bathroom in his house, but the room hadn't been seen in more than a decade. Some time after receiving that letter, a "new" bathroom—complete with mint-green toilet, sink, and tub—was added to the set. This gave Mister Rogers a place to talk with children about issues that are prominent in many young minds.

Computer Room

In 1999, viewers got their only glimpse of Mister Rogers' computer room, which he described as a "little room over by the bathroom where I do my writing." At the computer, he showed viewers the new "online Neighborhood" website, which included digital versions of his television house and the Neighborhood of Make-Believe. In true Mister Rogers fashion, he took the opportunity to remind children that their "own imagination is far more wonderful than any computer could ever be," because "human beings are far more wonderful than machines."

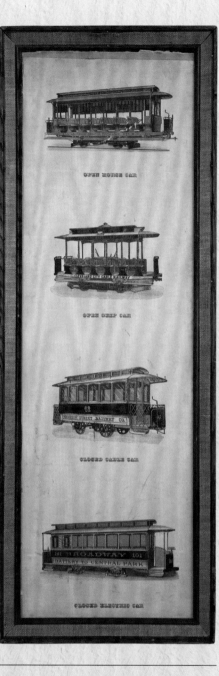

ABOVE, LEFT: The painting *October Gleaning* by Eric Sloane hung on the set of the television house.

BOTTOM, LEFT: The painting *Connecticut Grain Barn*, another by Eric Sloane, hung on the wall between the front door and closet.

ABOVE, RIGHT: *Color Prints of Early American Trolley Cars*, a series produced in the early 1950s by the New York company Autoprints, hung between the closet and window seat.

Mister Rogers rarely arrived at his television house empty-handed. In nearly every episode, he revealed something special to his television friends. What he shared could be almost anything: a book, a toy, a plant, a puppy, a photo, a song, or even just his thoughts. This was one of the ways he showed children that the world is filled with wonderful and interesting everyday things. Mister Rogers was always willing to follow his curiosity and stay open to new ideas and experiences. He demonstrated that there is always something new to wonder and learn about. When you wonder, you're learning; and when you're learning, you're growing!

Mister Rogers encouraged children to look and listen carefully, to ask questions, and to try new things. Here's a sampling of the curious and wonderful things he brought to his television house over the years:

- GROCER'S SCALE
- YELLOW PAINT FOR THE SWING
- CAN OF CAT FOOD
- ONE DOZEN EGGS
- OPERATOR'S HEADSET
- JAR OF PAPER CLIPS
- BOX OF FALSE MUSTACHES
- BOX OF RUBBER BANDS
- ALBUM OF RECORDED LAUGHTER
- MACHINE USED TO MAKE RECORDS
- SANTA CLAUS COSTUME
- BUCKET AND STOOL FOR MILKING COWS
- LEG BRACES
- TROPHY HE RECEIVED FOR WINNING A FOUR-MILE SWIMMING RACE
- ANTIQUE CAR
- BASKET OF ELEPHANT MODELS AND SCULPTURES
- SEA CAPTAIN'S DESK
- WALKING STILTS
- BRAILLE WRITING MACHINE
- INVISIBLE INK PEN AND MARKER
- LEI MADE OF PEANUTS
- DOLL OF HIMSELF
- BALL FLOAT TO REPAIR HIS TOILET
- BOX OF FORTUNE COOKIES
- COMPUTER MOUSE

OPPOSITE, ABOVE: Mister Rogers shows viewers a guinea pig in 1971.

OPPOSITE, BELOW: Mister Rogers sets down a large box before changing his shoes and sweater.

"You know me: I'm interested in all sorts of things! And I spend a lot of time trying to learn about things. I'm curious. . . . I wonder how many stop-and-go lights there are in the world. And I wonder if fish laugh or cry. . . . We learn so much by wondering."

Mister Rogers, Episode 1654

Added to the set after the program's first year, the fish tank gave Mister Rogers an opportunity to help children learn about taking care of other living creatures. Feeding the fish ("just a little bit" each day) became such a routine part of each television visit that he sometimes did so without commenting on it. That changed when the father of a blind five-year-old wrote to Mister Rogers with a message from his daughter: "Please say when you are feeding your fish, because I worry about them," she said. Ever mindful of all children's needs, Mister Rogers was happy to oblige.

"HELLO?"

So Many Wrong Numbers!

Mister Rogers was just as gracious on the telephone as he was with in-person visitors. Even though the phone was just a prop, oftentimes he'd answer it to discover it was a wrong number. Occasionally he even dialed the wrong number himself. Either way, he used these simple moments to show children how to use the phone, how to be polite, and how to handle mistakes—their own or other people's. It was just one more way that the program mirrored the everyday issues of real life and showed young viewers how to deal with them.

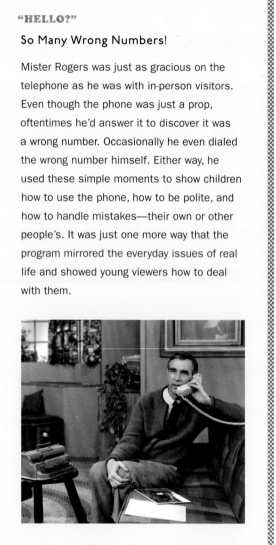

OPPOSITE: Mr. McFeely and Mister Rogers share a laugh in the television house living room.

Who might it be? More often than not, it was Mr. McFeely, stopping by with a Speedy Delivery. But plenty of other friends came around as well. Some, including Maggie Stewart, Officer Clemmons, and Marilyn Barnett, were Neighborhood regulars. Others visited just once, but left a deep and lasting impression on both Mister Rogers and his viewers.

Mister Rogers took genuine delight in welcoming visitors to his house. He made sure to look out the window to see who it was before he opened the door, and he let children know who was there before inviting them in. Unlike other television programs, in which the host and guest talked one-on-one while viewers tuned in, Mister Rogers invited his guests and viewers into the

> ## "Hospitality is one of the main things that people are looking for in this life."
>
> ---
>
> **Fred Rogers**

same conversation, so they could all spend time together as friends. This kind of inclusivity helped children feel as though he were truly talking to—and with—them. In this way, Mister Rogers helped children understand relationships with others—how to greet people, how to make them feel welcome, how to say goodbye—and showed them that everyone deserves kindness and respect.

A Neighborly Chat *with*

MARGY WHITMER

Producer

MARGY WHITMER was a longtime producer on *Mister Rogers' Neighborhood,* having joined the staff in 1981. She also oversaw a number of other projects and initiatives for Family Communications, Inc., including two series of picture books and professional development videos. Later, she produced the live-action interstitials for *Daniel Tiger's Neighborhood* and is now a scripting consultant for the series.

TIM LYBARGER: How did you get involved with the *Neighborhood* program?

MARGY WHITMER: I was working at WQED and the offices [of Family Communications, Inc.] were in the same building. I was down at the other end of the hall doing local programming. That was in 1974 or '75, so that was when they were winding down production. Over the course of the next few years, when Fred was on hiatus, I was working with a local producer, and she wanted to do this half-hour documentary about Fred, so I worked with her on that. I got a little bit of insight into him. Then I did some freelance work for his company. I remember, after both of those experiences, just one of the fleeting thoughts that

you have like, "Boy, if I could ever have a chance to work on that, I would. He's a really cool guy." Fast-forward a few years and a colleague, Sam Newbury, who had worked at WQED, got a job with Family Communications. He called me up and he said, "I need an associate producer." I called Sam back and I said, "Sam, can I interview for the job?" And he said, "Yes, but this is for the associate producer, and it's not full-time, and you're a producer now." I said, "I do studio shows. I want to do something more." So, long story short, I got the job as the associate producer and did that on a freelance basis for two or three years. Sam went on to do other things, and he said, "Which do you want to do? *Mister Rogers' Neighborhood* or some other nonbroadcast video projects?"

And I said *Mister Rogers*. I didn't even give it a second thought. That's how it happened.

TL: **So when you say he was a cool guy, what was it that drew you to him? What piqued your interest?**

MW: I always thought I'd be a third-grade teacher, because I've always been interested in kids. When I got the hang of the philosophy behind the program and saw some of the things that I had learned about in the child development courses I took in college, I started to connect the dots. I just thought, "Wow, this is so cool." I started in 1981, so I was just on the cusp when the program was becoming very popular. I still didn't think it was going to be a big deal. I didn't get it for a long time. Well, I did, but I didn't, because I was wrapped up in the day-to-day process of producing.

TL: **What was the climate of the studio as things were being filmed?**

MW: We tried to make it a well-oiled machine, and for the most part it was. I think that had a lot to do with Fred, because Fred worked really hard. He expected the rest of us to work hard—not in a dictatorial

Margy and Fred between takes in 1989.

way, but just to do our best. He was kind to everyone, and so I think everybody was much kinder on that set than they would have been on a feature or another program. There was no yelling. There were angry times and conflicts, but those were rare. Fred never reprimanded anyone in front of the crew. Off set he would say, "Let's talk about this." He would talk out his anger. Usually he got angry because something like a prop or some equipment broke or something wasn't ready and he was frustrated. Sometimes in the summer, the air-conditioning would go out, making it difficult to work because of the heat of the lights. It was no one's fault in particular. So his anger was more frustration at not being able to get the work done.

TL: **So did that present any kind of challenges?**

MW: In the studio, we were very careful about planning and organizing so that things would go smoothly. We had weekly production meetings with the art crew to go over props and review them. Often Fred would visualize something in a certain whimsical way, but he really needed someone to fabricate it first to help them know what he didn't want. We might say, "The actor needs to be able to manipulate that prop in an easier way." Fred's hardest challenge was to tell someone a particular prop didn't work or wasn't what he had in mind. He didn't want to hurt their feelings or reject their hard work—that usually ended up being my job! After the meeting, we asked for

several new samples for the next meeting, and eventually we'd work it out.

Another challenge for the studio days was to help Fred feel comfortable. When Fred looked into the camera and spoke to his audience, he appeared to be natural, as if he really were having a conversation with them. But because he cared so much about being real and trustworthy, he put a lot of pressure on himself to get it right. Everything in those moments was scripted and on a teleprompter; that allowed him

TL: How much input and influence did the production team and cast members have on the topics and the scripts?

MW: Once Fred wrote the scripts it was hard to get him to change anything. He really had something in mind. So not a lot of rewrites.

I think in the beginning, before my time, people did have much more input because they were just trying to turn out scripts quickly.

you really don't like to if you don't have to.

the next season. We would come up with five or six themes that we thought were pertinent to children's lives. We'd give him this list and say, "Pick three. Or tell us if you have something else you'd rather do."

We would also pitch ideas for specific segments that might tie into the themes. For example, people used to send me all kinds of ideas. I had this old ratty cardboard box under my desk that in my mind was my treasure chest. I would save some of those ideas from people and pitch them to Fred. We did a wonderful piece for the week on the environment with an artist who made sculptures out of recycled metal and buttons and all kinds of stuff.

TL: What was it like being with Fred in public?

MW: The first location piece I ever did was at the National Zoo when the pandas were first given to the United States from China. We were taking a lunch break, and this school group just flooded Fred. I remember I saw them coming and I panicked. I heard them all say, "Mister Rogers!" I mean, it was like me seeing Mick Jagger as a teenager. In a demanding way, I said, "Stop. You've gotta let Mister Rogers eat his lunch." Thankfully I've learned to be more diplomatic.

> ## "Because he cared so much about being real and trustworthy, he put a lot of pressure on himself to get it right . . . This was his focus, his reason to be. His mission."

to say exactly what he meant in a conversational, honest way. This was his focus, his reason to be. His mission.

We were very careful about planning and organizing. We had a leisurely schedule in terms of production. But sometimes you do everything you think is right and then it doesn't work and you have to change gears. We got pretty good at it, but you know,

They were producing sixty-five episodes a year, which is a lot. He would take suggestions from staff. Someone would say, "Hey, I know somebody who plays music on a saw," and soon they'd have a guy on the program to play "Amazing Grace" on a saw.

When I was there we did theme weeks that were added to the library of programs. We would have a staff meeting in the late spring to come up with ideas for

TL: There's been this big resurgence of the *Neighborhood* over the past year or so especially. What are your thoughts on how it's come back into the forefront of pop culture?

MW: Well, I'm just over the moon. I think it's great because even when we were in production, it was hard for us to market Fred Rogers in a lot of ways. Once we even put out a pamphlet called "The Magic Behind *Mister Rogers' Neighborhood*" to help adults understand that the program is not just another "kiddie show." Fred put a lot of thought into it. Everything was based on solid child development theory.

What's so enlightening and hopeful about this resurgence is that those kids who loved Mister Rogers and had no understanding why, now understand. I give credit to the documentary *Won't You Be My Neighbor?* because it shows parts of Fred Rogers' personality that many people never even thought about, and it makes him human. It illustrates the complexity of his personality and the depth of his commitment to everything he did. So that they now understand why they like him and why their kids like him and why some of their grandkids even now like him.

TL: So many people grew up on the show or are aware of the show, but they just saw it on a surface level. I thought the documentary did a great job of showing the depth—that it was, like you said, so much more than just another kiddie show.

MW: Fred always had this fantasy that parents would watch it with their kids. I think a lot of times when it first started, they did, because mothers were home. But as time went on, it became the babysitter. That's good and that's bad. That's good that parents felt comfortable letting their children just watch it without supervision. But on the other hand, much of what he's saying is for the parents as well as for the children. The program is good for any age person.

TL: Looking back at the cast that you worked with and guests who came on the show, does anybody stand out as especially fun to work with?

MW: This is not in any order, as I really liked everyone, but when Bob Trow was in the scripts we knew it would be a fun day in the studio. He made a lot of funny jokes, very clever. He had this great sense of humor and turn of phrase.

Of course, Johnny Costa and the guys in the band and Joe Negri were fun, too, and I loved them. We had a handful of famous visitors—Yo-Yo Ma, Wynton Marsalis, Eric Carle, Tommy Tune, and Itzhak Perlman—and all were great to work with. But we had many not-so-famous visitors equally as talented and interesting, like Sylvia Earle, a marine biologist with whom Fred went snorkeling; artist Bill Strickland, who taught Fred how to throw pots; and Mary Alice Sherred, who helped him make music with spoons! I wish I could list everyone.

TL: Any final thoughts, looking back over the years?

MW: I'm lucky. Very, very lucky that I was part of this classic children's program. But more importantly that I got to work with and know Fred Rogers. I had the perfect job. As I was doing it, intellectually I'm thinking, "He is so cool. You're gonna wish that you were paying more attention to being in the moment instead of worrying about what's happening in the next scene." But that was my job. So I have to appreciate it all now—and I do!

EXPLORING THE NEIGHBORHOOD

Human connections and relationships were at the heart of *Mister Rogers' Neighborhood*. After all, this was a neighborhood—a whole community! Mister Rogers often invited viewers to "come along" on field trips to other locations. These outings helped to broaden children's worlds, exposing them to many different people, places, and things that might exist outside their own homes.

Before leaving his house, Mister Rogers let viewers know where he was headed. The camera showed him walking out the door, and then the scene shifted to the Neighborhood model, beginning at Mister Rogers' familiar yellow house and moving down the street or around the block to his destination, as if it were following Mister Rogers on his journey. All the while, Johnny Costa played jazzy renditions of familiar Neighborhood tunes. Unlike a quick cut to a new location, this slow transition gave children time to prepare for the new scene ahead.

In the earlier days of the program, the Neighborhood excursions took viewers to other studio sets, such as Negri's Music Shop, Brockett's Bakery, or Betty's Little Theater. As technology advanced and cameras became smaller and more portable, Mister Rogers was able to add on-location visits to real places found in a larger community, including a zoo, museum, and fire station.

Illustration of Mister Rogers' Neighborhood that hung on the set's kitchen wall next to the refrigerator.

HI, NEIGHBOR!

THE MODEL NEIGHBORHOOD

During the opening and closing credits of each episode, and when Mister Rogers left his house, viewers saw an overhead shot of a model of the Neighborhood, complete with cars, people, and a moving trolley. The model changed over the years; in the first season of the program, the Neighborhood looked very different from the one that became so iconic. The instantly recognizable version, introduced in 1974, measured approximately forty-eight inches from side to side, and was made in HO scale, the most popular scale among model railroad enthusiasts.

The core of the Neighborhood—Mister Rogers' house, Negri's Music Shop, Brockett's Bakery, Betty's Little Theater, and a few other buildings—remained consistent week to week, but the outskirts of town were apt to change as needed, to represent the destinations for Mister Rogers' far-afield excursions.

One of the most recognizable structures in the Neighborhood was the large red building that was the first and last location to be seen on each episode. The slope of its roof was at the same angle as the original logo of National Educational Television, which appeared on the building during the early years of the program; though it was eventually removed, the shape of the roof remained.

Another significant change to the model was the addition of a moving trolley in the early 1980s. At director Paul Lally's request, Pittsburgh model railroader Tom Vitolo modified a Bachmann trolley to create an HO-scale Neighborhood Trolley for the model. Crew members used simple fishing line to make the Trolley (Trolley II, as it became known among the crew) move across the model Neighborhood.

WOULD YOU BE MINE?

MEET THE NEIGHBORS

The residents of *Mister Rogers' Neighborhood* comprised a community of talented and playful friends, and a walk around the Neighborhood was sure to include something new and entertaining. In any given episode, Mister Rogers might have visited Betty's Little Theater, François Clemmons' Studio, Brockett's Bakery, Bob Trow's Workshop, or Negri's Music Shop. These visits often included a demonstration or performance, such as trying a new recipe at the bakery, or meeting a musician at the music shop.

The performers who portrayed Mister Rogers' neighbors were accomplished, professional artists. Fred encouraged them to use their real names and to correlate their personal interests with those of their television personas. Most of the cast members played multiple roles on the program, appearing in both the real Neighborhood and the Neighborhood of Make-Believe. Some, like Chef Brockett, had the same character name in both. Other neighbors played slightly different characters in Make-Believe: Joe Negri became Handyman Negri; Betty Aberlin became Lady Aberlin; and Bob Trow transformed into both Bob Dog and Robert Troll.

Cast members rarely auditioned for the program. Fred had a knack for bumping into people who would be a good fit for the *Neighborhood*. And the right people seemed to have a knack for turning up at the right time. "All of these people came along at just the moment that they were needed," Fred once said.

Officer Clemmons and Mister Rogers cool their feet on a hot day in Episode 1663 in 1993.

"Neighbors are people who live close to each other. Neighbors look at each other; they talk to each other; they listen to each other. That's how they get to know each other."

Mister Rogers

PLAYED BY: Joe Negri (see interview, page 146)

IN THE NEIGHBORHOOD: As owner of Negri's Music Shop, Joe Negri offered music lessons to the residents of the Neighborhood and often hosted visiting musicians. A gifted jazz guitarist himself, Joe often played along with these musical guests. He was one of the original cast members of the *Neighborhood*, appearing on the very first episode in the Neighborhood of Make-Believe.

OFF THE SET: Joe Negri is a renowned jazz guitarist, known in Pittsburgh and around the country. By the time Joe was four years old, he was performing on stage and radio. He picked up guitar at age eight, and by sixteen he was touring professionally. A native of Pittsburgh, Joe studied music arrangement and composition at Carnegie Mellon University (then Carnegie Tech). Throughout a lifetime in music, Joe headed up his own trio on KDKA-TV, served for twenty years as a performer and musical director for WTAE-TV (Pittsburgh's ABC affiliate), and worked as a composer, recording artist, and teacher.

BETTY ABERLIN, *Proprietor, Betty's Little Theater*

PLAYED BY: Betty Aberlin

IN THE NEIGHBORHOOD: Betty Aberlin was a longtime resident of the real Neighborhood who operated Betty's Little Theater, where she hosted various musicians and performers. In addition to her work with performing artists, Betty sometimes helped out at Brockett's Bakery, where she assisted Bob Trow in constructing the soda fountain and worked as a server once it opened. She also provided cave tours of the Neighborhood cavern.

Although she appeared in the real Neighborhood dozens of times as Betty Aberlin, she is best known for her role as Lady Aberlin in the Neighborhood of Make-Believe (see page 129), where she starred in hundreds of episodes during the series, beginning with the second episode and continuing through to the end of the program.

OFF THE SET: Betty Aberlin was born Betty Kay Ageloff in New York City. She studied art, modern dance, and literature at Bennington College and appeared in numerous theatrical productions around the country, including the 1964 Broadway production of *Café Crown.* After the final season of the *Neighborhood,* Aberlin went on to further work as an actress, with roles in a number of movies. She continues to write poetry and short stories.

CHEF BROCKETT, *Proprietor, Brockett's Bakery*

PLAYED BY: Don Brockett

BAKERY EMPLOYEES

Brockett's Bakery employed several people: **Gladys Schenk** (pictured) worked at the bakery counter in the 1970s. When she went on maternity leave, **José Cisneros** took over her position and ran the soda shop in the bakery. He appeared on the program from 1973 to 1986. **Sergio Pinto** worked the bakery counter in a handful of episodes from the 1980s and '90s. All three characters were fluent in Spanish and would occasionally teach Mister Rogers a new word when he visited the bakery.

IN THE NEIGHBORHOOD: Chef Brockett owned Brockett's Bakery. Early on, he did not speak while cooking and insisted on having a quiet kitchen; however, this characteristic became less emphasized over time.

Chef Brockett walked with a limp. He and Mister Rogers often discussed coping with a physical disability and his progress with exercise, modeling acceptance for young children who were also testing and discovering their own physical limitations. Throughout the series, Chef Brockett appeared as the same character in both the "real" world and the Neighborhood of Make-Believe, where he was often seen delivering a cake or a snack or participating in one of the many Neighborhood operas. He was one of the original characters on the program, first appearing in the third episode and continuing until the actor Don Brockett's death in 1995.

OFF THE SET: Actor Don Brockett, born Richard Donald Brockett, was known around Pittsburgh for producing and starring in musicals and stage revues. He appeared as a character actor in more than thirty-four films, including *The Silence of the Lambs* and *Flashdance*.

BOB TROW, *Proprietor, Trow's Workshop*

PLAYED BY: Robert Trow

"Bob Trow walked in one day, and he looked at the whole place set up with the Eiffel Tower and the castle and the factory and the tree and Lady Elaine's Museum-Go-Round and Daniel's clock and all these fanciful places, and he said to everybody, 'You know, I remember when this was all farmland!'"

Fred Rogers

IN THE NEIGHBORHOOD: At his workshop, Bob Trow made and fixed a variety of items for his neighbors. He created the models of the castle, Museum-Go-Round, and other familiar structures in the Neighborhood of Make-Believe that Mister Rogers often used at his kitchen table. Bob was also a talented artist who painted portraits. He appeared on the program regularly from 1970 until 1996. In the Neighborhood of Make-Believe, actor Bob Trow played Robert Troll and Bob Dog (see page 158) and was the voice of puppet Harriett Elizabeth Cow.

OFF THE SET: Actor Robert E. Trow was a well-known face—and voice—in his hometown of Pittsburgh. He worked for many years as a comedy writer and voice artist for a popular local radio program. He also worked as a freelance radio and television commercial writer. Besides his performance work, Bob was a gifted artist and craftsman who really did make the Neighborhood of Make-Believe models in Mister Rogers' kitchen.

PLAYED BY: François Clemmons (see interview, page 281)

IN THE NEIGHBORHOOD: In the real Neighborhood, actor François Clemmons played both a police officer and the owner of a dance and music studio. Officer Clemmons was a caring guardian of those in the Neighborhood. When he was off-duty, he worked in his studio near Mister Rogers' house and pursued his goal of becoming a professional opera singer, which reflected the actor's real-life talents. When Mr. Clemmons received a scholarship to study opera, he left his position with the Neighborhood police department and moved to another city. He later returned to the Neighborhood to visit. This character arc showed children that adults can continue to grow and learn new things. Officer Clemmons first appeared on the program in 1968 and continued as a character in the Neighborhood of Make-Believe until 1993.

OFF THE SET: François Clemmons joined the cast after Fred Rogers heard him sing at church. François had received his Bachelor of Music degree from Oberlin College and his MFA from Carnegie Mellon University. In the late 1960s, in tandem with his *Neighborhood* character persona, he won a position with the Metropolitan Opera Studio in New York, where he performed for seven seasons. Among his many accolades, François won a Grammy award for Best Opera Recording in 1976.

AUDREY ROTH, *Proprietor, Audrey Cleans Everything (A.C.E.)*

PLAYED BY: Audrey Roth (see interview, page 156)

IN THE NEIGHBORHOOD: Audrey Roth was the kindly neighbor with an assertive demeanor who owned Audrey Cleans Everything (A.C.E.), the local Neighborhood cleaning service. She ran the business out of her home; thanks to some clever set design, she could transform her living room into her office with a few quick flicks and turns of the furniture. Audrey also occasionally worked as a waitress at a Neighborhood restaurant and filled in at the soda shop inside Brockett's Bakery. Her character came to the *Neighborhood* in 1970 and brought "an element of dignity to cleaning chores." In the Neighborhood of Make-Believe, actor Audrey Roth played the character of Miss Audrey Paulificate, the telephone operator (see page 155).

OFF THE SET: Audrey Roth studied drama at Carnegie Mellon University and appeared in plays and musicals in Pittsburgh and on Broadway. She also worked as a fashion model and taught charm courses to teens and adults.

PLAYED BY: Elizabeth "Betsy" Nadas Seamans (see interview, page 192)

IN THE NEIGHBORHOOD: Mrs. Betsy McFeely had many interests, including playing the recorder, tap dancing, and driving a bookmobile. She also helped to run the Speedy Delivery Service. Mister Rogers frequently visited the McFeely home to see an animal the couple was caring for. The McFeelys' grandchildren sometimes stopped by for a visit as well. She once arrived at Mister Rogers' house on a motorcycle. When he suggested that it was strange to see a lady like Mrs. McFeely with a motorcycle, she responded that "women can do just about anything that they want to!"

OFF THE SET: Although fans know her best as Mrs. McFeely, Elizabeth "Betsy" Nadas Seamans joined the *Neighborhood* in 1972 to work behind the scenes as an assistant producer and scriptwriter. Betsy was in her early twenties when she began playing the grandmotherly role of Mrs. McFeely. She also made short films for the program and created documentary films for Fred's prime-time PBS series *Old Friends . . . New Friends* and *Fred Rogers' Heroes*. Betsy graduated with honors from Harvard University and received a Master of Fine Arts in writing from Lesley University. In 1977 she received a grant from the National Endowment for the Arts for her film work. She continues to work as a writer and documentary filmmaker.

Mister Rogers' Neighborhood A VISUAL HISTORY

MAGGIE STEWART, *Singer and Signer*

PLAYED BY: Maggie Stewart

IN THE NEIGHBORHOOD: Maggie Stewart regularly dropped by to visit Mister Rogers, usually to sing a song. She would often sign along in American Sign Language, and sometimes she even taught Mister Rogers a sign or two. When the need arose, Maggie Stewart helped out with Mr. McFeely's Speedy Delivery Service. She stayed physically active by swimming and taking Hula-Hoop lessons. In the Neighborhood of Make-Believe, the actress Maggie Stewart played the part of Mayor Maggie (see page 162).

OFF THE SET: Maggie Stewart was a college student at Carnegie Mellon University when she auditioned for the role of Mayor Maggie. She spent a year on Broadway in *The King and I* and toured with the company for five years. She is a professional American Sign Language interpreter and has served on the board of directors of the Center for Hearing and Deaf Services in Southwestern Pennsylvania.

PLAYED BY: Chuck Aber (see interview, page 164)

BREAKING THE FOURTH WALL

In all of the theme-week episodes of *Mister Rogers' Neighborhood*, Chuck Aber was the only supporting character in the real Neighborhood who ever directly addressed the television viewers (aside from the many individuals who said "hello" as they were introduced by Mister Rogers). In Episode 1578, when Mister Rogers mistakenly forgot he had an appointment and needed to leave the house for a meeting, he asked Chuck Aber to stay with the viewers for just a bit while he was gone.

IN THE NEIGHBORHOOD: Chuck Aber was an active member of the real Neighborhood and a jack-of-many-trades. He first appeared in the Neighborhood as a guard delivering samples of gold to Mister Rogers' house. He was also the manager of the Neighborhood miniature golf course, a deliveryman for Mr. McFeely's Speedy Delivery Service, and the owner of a local dance studio. Like Maggie Stewart, Chuck Aber was fluent in sign language. In the Neighborhood of Make-Believe, actor Chuck Aber played the part of Neighbor Charles R. Aber, Westwood's associate mayor (see page 163). He was also the voice for puppets H. J. Elephant III and Mr. Skunk (see page 167).

OFF THE SET: First appearing on *Mister Rogers' Neighborhood* in the mid-1970s as a puppeteer, Chuck Aber became a more regular member of the live cast in the 1980s. Aber appeared on stage in *The Music Man* and *My Fair Lady* as well as in feature films such as *The Silence of the Lambs* and *Creepshow*.

ELSIE NEAL, *Proprietor, Elsie Neal's Craft Shop*

PLAYED BY: Elsie Neal

IN THE NEIGHBORHOOD: At her craft shop, Elsie Neal demonstrated simple craft projects for Mister Rogers and hosted other talented craftspeople. Elsie's shop also provided a variety of costumes for use throughout the Neighborhood. She appeared on the program from 1972 to 1975.

BOB AND JUDY BROWN, *Proprietors, Brown's Marionette Theater*

PLAYED BY: Bob and Judy Brown

IN THE NEIGHBORHOOD: Bob and Judy Brown owned and operated Brown's Marionette Theater. The theater, which was located directly next door to Mister Rogers' house, appeared on the program occasionally between 1971 and 1975 and staged a few marionette plays, including *The Three Little Pigs*, *Little Red Riding Hood*, and *The Elves and the Shoemaker*. In addition to his role as a marionette maker and puppeteer, Mr. Brown was a talented sign maker. His character also appeared a few times in Make-Believe.

MARILYN BARNETT, *Physical Education Teacher and School Principal*

PLAYED BY: Marilyn Barnett

IN THE NEIGHBORHOOD: Marilyn Barnett was a physical education teacher at the Neighborhood school, where she later became principal. She regularly visited Mister Rogers and taught him simple exercises and stretches that children could follow along with at home. Children from her school sometimes came with her to demonstrate their talents, such as jumping rope or yo-yoing. She appeared on the program from 1972 to 1999.

TONY CHIROLDES, *Proprietor, Toy Shop*

PLAYED BY: Tony Chiroldes

IN THE NEIGHBORHOOD: Tony Chiroldes lived in the Neighborhood in 2000 and 2001. He owned a shop named Tony's, which specialized in toys, books, and costumes. He often spoke Spanish and taught Mister Rogers new Spanish words. In the Neighborhood of Make-Believe, actor Tony Chiroldes played the part of the Royal Hula Mouse (see page 137).

BARBARA RUSSELL, *A.C.E. Receptionist and Mrs. Russellite*

PLAYED BY: Barbara Russell

IN THE NEIGHBORHOOD: Barbara Russell appeared on the very first episode of the program as the character Mrs. Russellite, a neighbor who liked to create hats out of lampshades. In later episodes she portrayed Barbara Russell, who worked as the receptionist for Audrey Cleans Everything. She also appeared in the Neighborhood of Make-Believe as a friend of Lady Elaine Fairchilde, as Posy the elephant in the opera *Josephine the Short-Neck Giraffe,* and as the voice of puppet Hilda Dingleboarder (see page 151). Her final appearance on the program was in 1990.

CHRISSY THOMPSON, *McFeelys' Granddaughter*

PLAYED BY: Chrissy Thompson

IN THE NEIGHBORHOOD: Chrissy Thompson was the granddaughter of Mr. and Mrs. McFeely. She and her sisters, Becky and Terri, occasionally visited their grandparents or stopped by Mister Rogers' house. Chrissy wore braces on her legs as a result of spina bifida, and she talked openly about her condition.

JUDY RUBIN, *Craftsperson*

PLAYED BY: Judy Rubin

IN THE NEIGHBORHOOD: During the 1968 season, art therapist Judy Rubin regularly visited Mister Rogers to show him arts and crafts created by her young friends around the Neighborhood. She and Mister Rogers would then create similar projects of their own.

MRS. SAUNDERS, *Nursery School Teacher*

PLAYED BY: Carol Saunders

IN THE NEIGHBORHOOD: Mrs. Carol Saunders played a nursery school teacher in the early days of the program. She occasionally visited Mister Rogers' house, and he visited her classroom.

Mister Rogers visited so many interesting places over the years, giving young viewers a glimpse of the kinds of places they might discover in their own neighborhoods— or even around the world.

In the late 1980s, tensions between the United States and the U.S.S.R. were high as the two countries and their respective allies endured the continuing Cold War. In a simple effort to show "we are more alike than we are different," Mister Rogers traveled to Russia where he visited the set of *Good Night, Little Ones!,* a children's television program hosted by Tatiana Vedeneeva. Later in the same week of episodes, originally broadcast in March 1988, Ms. Vedeneeva made a reciprocal effort by visiting *Mister Rogers' Neighborhood.*

ABOVE: Mister Rogers poses with Tatiana Vedeneeva and one of her puppets, the brave rabbit Stepashka, during her visit to the *Neighborhood.*

LEFT: Fred poses with Daniel during his trip to Moscow.

OPPOSITE: Tatiana Vedeneeva, Mr. McFeely, and Masha Nordbye (Tatiana's translator) pose on Mister Rogers' porch.

"One night in 1988 I was watching *Nightline*. Ted Koppel was saying, 'Here's Russian television. Let's take a look at it. The sports. The news shows. The documentaries.' They showed a children's show, *Good Night, Little Ones!* Ted said, in a voiceover, 'This is like *Mister Rogers' Neighborhood*.' Immediately, a lightbulb went off in my head. I said, 'Here's a chance to do our own foreign exchange. Fred visits Russia. She visits us.' Our countries may not be able to get along, but let's show that people can potentially get along with each other. Fred wrote the script and made the trip to Russia. [Ms. Vedeneeva] came to our studio. It was like our own little Glasnost."

David Newell

Some other locations Mister Rogers visited:

CITY BUS (1971)

CONSTRUCTION SITE (1980)

AIRPORT (1981)

MUSHROOM FARM (1981)

ART MUSEUM (1981)

DANCE STUDIO (1981)

SHOE STORE (1982)

ZOO (1982)

RESTAURANT (1982)

GROCERY STORE (1984)

PENGUIN EXHIBIT (1985)

MINI GOLF COURSE (1986)

BOWLING ALLEY (1989)

LIBRARY (1991)

Mister Rogers and Mr. McFeely visit a recycling operation. (1990)

ABOVE: Mister Rogers learns about milking cows at Turner's Dairy Farm. (1984)

LEFT: Mister Rogers learns about the responsibilities that come with being a firefighter. Captain Hayward Arnold shows him around Engine Company #15 of the Pittsburgh Bureau of Fire. (1999)

OPPOSITE: Dr. Joan Embry gives Mister Rogers an up-close look at the giraffes at the Neighborhood Wild Animal Park (which is really the San Diego Zoo). (1989)

"IT'S PEOPLE WHO MAKE THINGS": THE FACTORY VISITS

Mr. McFeely often stopped by Mister Rogers' house with a film or videotape to show on Picture-Picture, the framed screen that hung on the living room wall. These short films showed behind-the-scenes visits to factories, giving viewers a glimpse into the world of how people make things. Mister Rogers emphasized that while machines can do a lot of things, it's *people* who make the machines and who make them work. So instead of saying "how balls are made," he'd say, "how people make balls." During the narration of the films, he often asked questions that children might wonder about, or helped them make connections to the things they already knew.

NIGHT OF THE LIVING . . . NEIGHBORHOOD?

Before he made his zombie cult classics, director George A. Romero (who attended Carnegie Mellon University) created several short films for Mister Rogers, including one about how people make lightbulbs and another about a time when Mister Rogers went to the hospital for a tonsillectomy.

OPPOSITE, CLOCKWISE FROM TOP: Mister Rogers visits the Philadelphia bakery for Nabisco Brands in 1983 to see how people make graham crackers; a tour of the Carousel Works, Inc., in 1998 shows children how people make carousel horses; Mister Rogers watches as an employee at the H. J. Heinz Company factory adds corn to the ingredients for vegetable soup.

Learn how people make . . .

BAGELS (1998)

BALLS (1998)

CONSTRUCTION PAPER (1992)

CRAYONS (1981)

FORTUNE COOKIES (1998)

GRAHAM CRACKERS (1983)

GUITARS (1995)

MACARONI (1997)

MERRY-GO-ROUND HORSE (1998)

PRETZELS (1981)

SNEAKERS (1991)

SUITCASES (1988)

TOFU (1984)

TOILETS (1998)

TOWELS (1983)

TOY CARS (1991)

TRICYCLES (1985)

TRUMPETS (1986)

VEGETABLE SOUP (1984)

WAGONS (1996)

"I want children to know that people make things, they just don't make themselves."

Fred Rogers

Classic Moment

Episode 1481
Original air date: June 1, 1981

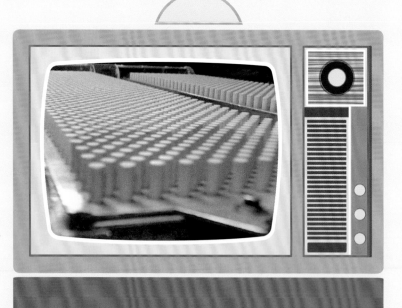

› **OF ALL THE FACTORY FILMS,** the one about how people make crayons stands out as a fan favorite. The film began with a railroad tank car carrying hot wax. Next viewers saw the wax being mixed with yellow pigment and poured into molds. The newly minted yellow crayons were then individually wrapped with labels from a machine that Mister Rogers compared to a Ferris wheel. Workers fed handfuls of sixteen different colors of crayons into a collating machine, which then filled little boxes. Little boxes filled a bigger box, and there was the finished product: packs of sixty-four crayons ready to be shipped out to stores. What a fun and colorful factory visit it was!

PICTURE-PICTURE

In the early days of the program, Picture-Picture functioned a bit like a magical screen that could play films on its own and display messages, such as *"Hi"* at the start of the episode. Over time, Fred became more concerned with drawing a distinction between reality and make-believe. He wanted children to understand that Picture-Picture was a machine that showed films, not something with a mind of its own.

In later programs, Picture-Picture showed images of famous paintings, such as *The Starry Night* by Vincent Van Gogh and *The Peppermint Bottle* by Paul Cézanne. Mister Rogers rarely talked about the artwork itself. "He was very subtle," said Hedda Sharapan, who worked with him for more than fifty years. She remembers asking Fred if he'd like to talk about the artwork so children knew what they were looking at. He told her he preferred to let them absorb the images on their own: "I just want them to be exposed to it, so that maybe someday in their life they may come across it and say, 'Oh, I kind of remember that.'"

Scattered among the many films Mister Rogers shared through Picture-Picture were some known as Funny Fast Films. Each "FFF" featured someone from the Neighborhood completing a task—Betty Aberlin making a bed, Mr. McFeely mowing the lawn, Chef Brockett in his kitchen—with the film played back at a humorously fast speed. Other FFFs included the McFeelys building a snowman; the A.C.E. crew cleaning a stadium; Mister Rogers changing into his sweater and sneakers; Mr. McFeely raking leaves; and Audrey cleaning an airplane.

A SMORGASBORD
OF SPECIAL GUESTS

During an interview late in his life, Fred explained why he chose to have so many different guests on his program. He said he wanted to "present a whole smorgasbord of ways for the children to choose. Some child might choose painting, some child might choose playing the cello. There are so many ways of saying who we are, and how we feel—ways that don't hurt anybody. And it seems to me that this is a great gift."

Over the years, Mister Rogers welcomed dozens of special guests to the program, each of them an interesting and engaging expert in their field. These visits—with artists, musicians, scientists, and others—opened up new worlds of ideas and possibilities to his viewers.

Mister Rogers liked to ask guests if they'd been interested in their subject as a child. The answer was nearly always yes. Mister Rogers wanted children to experience the beauty and value in creativity, as well as the discipline and hard work required to master any skill. "With our guests' help, I have been able to show a wide diversity of self-expression, the extraordinary range of human potential," he said. "I want children and their families to know that there are many constructive ways to express who they are and how they feel."

Susan Linn

Ventriloquist Susan Linn brought her puppets Audrey Duck and Catalion to talk with Mister Rogers. On several occasions, Linn and her puppets also appeared in the Neighborhood of Make-Believe.

Ella Jenkins

Folk singer Ella Jenkins, known as "The First Lady of Children's Music," visited Mister Rogers several times between 1974 and 1992.

Julia Child (1974)

The effervescent chef and author visited Brockett's Bakery to whip up a batch of "Spaghetti Marco Polo" to share with Mister Rogers.

Margaret Hamilton (1975)

Actress Margaret Hamilton, best known for her role as the Wicked Witch of the West in *The Wizard of Oz*, visited Mister Rogers to help children know that dressing up as the witch was a form of pretend. Mister Rogers told viewers, "When you feel as if you'd like to play something a little bit scary, a witch is a fine thing to play."

Arthur Mitchell and the Dance Theatre of Harlem (1987)

Mister Rogers visited the Dance Theatre of Harlem, where founder and choreographer Arthur Mitchell gave him a tour of the school and introduced him to young ballet dancers who were working on a piece. Mister Rogers even tried a few basic ballet positions and impressed everyone by getting his sneaker-clad feet into fifth position and doing a passé.

> "It's fun for me to tell people how much I like them, and how much I like their work."
>
> ———
>
> Mister Rogers

Sylvia Earle (1990)

Mister Rogers met marine biologist Sylvia Earle in Florida, giving viewers a beautiful glimpse of an underwater "neighborhood" filled with plants and fish. Earle later visited Mister Rogers' house and brought an underwater microphone to listen to the fish in an aquarium.

Koko the Gorilla (1998)

As he did with humans of all ages, Mister Rogers seemed to make an instant connection with Koko the gorilla. During the visit, he learned the gorilla greeting of softly blowing out air and played a game of peek-a-boo as she hid her head underneath a towel. He brought her several gifts, including a small stuffed Daniel Striped Tiger. Koko was quite interested in Mister Rogers' signature sweater, unzipping it and even removing the cardigan he was wearing.

Eric Carle (1998)

Author and illustrator Eric Carle, known for picture books such as *The Very Hungry Caterpillar,* showed Mister Rogers how he uses carpet samples to paint abstract designs onto tissue paper that he'll then use to create his collaged illustrations. As Carle brushed yellow paint onto a sheet of tissue paper, Mister Rogers talked about how everyone can create something, and that it's good to try new things.

OPPOSITE: **Captain Kangaroo** (1970) (Bob Keeshan) stopped by and talked about how he got his name: a result of his many pocketfuls of interesting items.

Other Special Guests

LOU FERRIGNO (1980) helped Mister Rogers show children that the big and scary Incredible Hulk was just a pretend character.

LYNN SWANN (1981) of the Pittsburgh Steelers showed Mister Rogers his football uniform before performing a short ballet dance. He explained that ballet helped him jump and move on the football field.

AL WORDEN (1972) talked with Mister Rogers about being an astronaut on the Apollo 15 mission.

PEGGY FLEMING (1982), an Olympic gold medalist in ice-skating, shared how she'd worked many years to learn and master her skills.

Potter and educator **BILL STRICKLAND (1991)** demonstrated how to make a clay pot using a potter's wheel.

Restaurateur **B. SMITH (1996)** gave Mister Rogers a tour of her restaurant kitchen and made a custard dessert with her head chef.

EZRA JACK KEATS (1971-1974), author and illustrator, visited Mister Rogers several times to talk about his books and how actions can make an idea become a reality.

Artist **SAIHOU NJIE (1998)** sewed a vest for Mister Rogers and showed him how he makes batik designs on fabric.

Architect **MAYA LIN (1998)** shared the small models she makes before she starts a big project.

YING LI (2000), a principal dancer with the Pittsburgh Ballet Theatre, demonstrated some ballet moves with her husband, a fellow dancer, as Mister Rogers watched.

ABOVE: **Bill Nye the Science Guy (1997)** demonstrated a science experiment by inflating a balloon using a bottle, vinegar, and baking soda.

OPPOSITE, TOP: **David Copperfield (1997)** taught Mister Rogers to do a magic trick using a piece of rope.

OPPOSITE, MIDDLE: **LeVar Burton (1998),** actor and host of *Reading Rainbow,* read *The Daddy Book,* about fathers and children around the world.

OPPOSITE, BOTTOM: **Suzie McConnell (1989),** who won a gold medal as part of the U.S. women's basketball team in the 1988 Summer Olympics, talked about the times she felt left out when playing.

"We all have different gifts, so we all have different ways of saying to the world who we are."

Fred Rogers

If there's anything you want,
If there's anything you need,
McFeely's Delivery brings it to you
here with speed.
Yes, our Speedy Delivery is a speedy
delivery,
Speedy Delivery to you!

IN THE NEIGHBORHOOD: Besides Mister Rogers himself, no one appeared on the program more than Mr. David Alex McFeely, the Neighborhood's chipper—and speedy!—Speedy Delivery man. Played by David Newell, Mr. McFeely ran the Speedy Delivery Messenger Service and often stopped by Mister Rogers' house to deliver an item from one of his neighbors. Over the years, he brought all sorts of wonderful things, including a suit of armor, an antique car, an armadillo, walkie-talkies, and a vacuum cleaner.

While Mister Rogers usually invited him in for a visit, Mr. McFeely rarely had time to stay, especially in the early days of the series. Having a *Neighborhood* character who was always in a hurry evoked the sense of exasperation that children can feel when adults hurry them and don't allow them to pursue their own interests.

In later years of the series, as Mr. McFeely became more patient and had more time to spend with Mister Rogers, he became a more complex and fully rounded character. He was a husband, father, and grandfather who enjoyed model-making and old films in his spare time. He often brought a factory film of how people make things to play on Picture-Picture; he'd even stay to narrate it while he and Mister Rogers watched it together.

Although he typically completed his deliveries on foot, Mr. McFeely sometimes used a tricycle, a small battery-operated car, or even a kayak. Throughout the series, Mr. McFeely appeared in both the real Neighborhood and the Neighborhood of Make-Believe, one of the only characters to consistently appear in both places as himself.

Mr. and Mrs. McFeely were the only *Neighborhood* characters that differed significantly from the actors who played them. Although the McFeelys were grandparents on the program, the actors who portrayed them were in their twenties in the early days of the program. In Episode 1476 (first aired in 1981), viewers got to see a "flashback" of the couple's wedding. Fans often thought the two were married to each other in real life, but they were not.

OFF THE SET: David Newell graduated from the University of Pittsburgh and began his acting

> **"It's been more than a career. It's a way of life."**
>
> ———
>
> **David Newell**

career with the Pittsburgh Playhouse. He joined the *Neighborhood* in 1967 as a production assistant. He quickly added the role of Mr. McFeely to his duties and appeared in nearly every television visit, including the first and final episodes. Newell also worked behind the scenes as director of public relations at Family Communications, Inc. In 2008, the documentary film *Speedy Delivery* featured Newell and his commitment to delivering the *Neighborhood*'s message of love and kindness. As Mr. McFeely, Newell visited all fifty states and almost every PBS station in the country at least once.

A Neighborly Chat *with*

DAVID NEWELL

Mr. McFeely

> "I think the *Neighborhood* has soul that a lot of programs don't have. It's got a depth that people don't realize at first."

Although **DAVID NEWELL** filled many off-camera production and administrative roles within Fred's production company, including prop development and director of public relations, he is best known for his many years making Speedy Deliveries as Mr. McFeely, the Neighborhood deliveryman.

TIM LYBARGER: How did you get your start on the program?

DAVID NEWELL: During the summer of 1967, I got a telegram from a mutual friend of Fred's and mine that said, "Fred Rogers has gotten funding to take the regional program of *Mister Rogers* national. He's expanding his staff. I've given him your name to be interviewed." Fred had been interviewing people, I guess, for the past month or so for the job of production assistant. But we talked for about an hour and he hired me. That first meeting, he showed me the breakdown of the scripts. There was a week of scripts that he had written. My assignment was to read them, then go out to hunt for the props and make sure we had everything ready for taping the next week.

I was in charge of all the props and costumes. I helped Fred behind the scenes. I would get the puppets ready. I did everything. If I had to play McFeely that day, I would get all that done, go to the dressing room, get ready, then come back and be McFeely.

He explained to me how the opening and the house—he called it his "TV house"—was the place where he would meet children on their level. The sweater and the sneakers were play clothes, then he would put his street clothes back on before leaving to go to his own home.

The Trolley would be a transition object that would take us to the Neighborhood of Make-Believe. The story would be worked out further there.

Fred being a musician, I always thought the way he structured the program was almost like a symphony. If you think about it, the opening of the *Neighborhood,* where Fred is putting his sneakers on and talking to the camera, is almost like a symphony setting

"Fred being a musician, I always thought the way he structured the program was almost like a symphony."

its tone. The major melody. Then the Neighborhood of Make-Believe adds variations on the theme—just as when you go to a symphony, you can hear strands of something you may have heard in the opening passage later in the composition. Coming back to Fred at the end of the program pulled all those themes together and tied it all up.

TL: I think that's a great analogy.

DN: Fred was so musical, as you know. The music throughout the program was one of the variations, I would think.

I also thought that all of us, all of the different characters, were elements of that symphony, too. The McFeely character and Fred were almost musical because Fred was very, very deliberate; he spoke slowly to the camera, took his time. McFeely, another variation coming in, was always in a hurry. "I'm on my way!" Out the door I'd go.

There's an expression in music: "contrapuntal"—one fast melody going at the same time as a slow melody. I always thought that's what the McFeely

and Fred characters represented, that strain of a symphony or music.

It was interesting. McFeely evolved over the years from somebody who made very fast Speedy Deliveries to McFeely slowing down. You probably remember the episode where Fred invites McFeely in to sit down on the bench. I think Fred sat beside me. We were doing our sitting-still exercises. That, too, in a way, is musical, I think.

TL: Who were some of the guests that stand out in your mind?

DN: One that I most remember talking to Fred about was Margaret Hamilton, the Wicked Witch of the West. Before she was even on, the subject of *The Wizard of Oz* would come up. "That movie still scares me." This would be an adult. "When I was a kid, those flying monkeys and the witch . . . I still have nightmares." I told Fred all this. "Do you think we could address the situation, since so many people seem to be bothered by it or scared by it?" They were showing it on television as a big spectacular for

years and years and years. They still do. Kids were seeing it.

Fred said to me, "If you can find her, I'll write a script." That was his way of saying okay.

So we had Margaret on the program. She came in her civilian clothes. She talked about how she's an actress, that it was one of her jobs. In the Neighborhood of Make-Believe, she appeared in the costume, similar to the one she wore in the movie.

As a result, she became a very good friend. A lovely, lovely woman. She would call my wife and me every Sunday evening. She called herself "Aunt Maggie." We'd meet her for lunch in New York with our daughter. A lovely person. Not just an actress—more of a teacher.

TL: Any other visitors to the Neighborhood that you particularly remember?

DN: Fred and I were riding in a taxi to the local public station in Hawaii. On the way there, I remember reading a newspaper article saying that a child was injured because he thought he could fly off of the garage roof by tying a towel around his neck like Superman. There was almost an epidemic of that when Superman was very popular. I said, "Fred, do you think we could deal with this superhero fascination?"

He started to put the scripts together. We couldn't get Superman because of copyrights and all of that. I said, "Our daughter was terrified of *The Incredible Hulk*. It's scary."

We contacted Bill Bixby, whom we knew. He got us into Universal. He was directing *The Incredible Hulk* episode we were going to. We watched Lou Ferrigno get into his makeup, and back out of it. That was all something that Fred wanted children to see. It's all part of the pretend.

Fred added the part about talking about angry feelings.

production meetings, and maybe through conversations that we had individually with him, and incorporate it into the program—write a script around a certain topic. I was very proud that he would take something that one of us thought about. We all contributed in some way. Those years were wonderful years.

He would also take my interests, as David Newell, and incorporate them into the McFeely character. For instance, I would go out, just for fun, to flea markets. Just dumpster dive, in a way. One time, I went out with a friend. He had a pickup truck.

McFeelys were going to tap-dance. We did. I faked it a lot. I did take tap-dance lessons. Fred wrote that in because I had mentioned, "Wouldn't it be fun if the McFeelys could do a tap-dance?"

There's this corny saying: "When you choose a career, make sure it's something you love because you'll never work a day in your life." I feel that exactly. I've never felt that I've worked a day in my life.

But thinking back on it, producing television, even a children's show, is not easy work. There were a lot of frustrating days that people were tired and cranky. Every day wasn't nirvana by any means.

I felt my years there were very productive. I'm still helping spread the message. In a way, we have sort of created a *Wizard of Oz*. The *Neighborhood* is almost timeless.

"We all contributed in some way. Those years were wonderful years."

Lou becomes this big Hulk when he got mad and burst out of his clothes and grew and all of that. It gave Fred a chance to talk about angry feelings. It's what you *do* with your anger. All of that worked into this theme very well.

TL: It seems like Fred would take different topics from conversation with other people and write scripts around these various topics.

DN: We would have production meetings every week. Fred would take ideas from our

Between the two of us, we got together stuff we'd never miss if it was all stolen from our garages and put it in the truck and sold it.

Fred wrote a little Picture-Picture film script about McFeely going out and selling at a flea market. I played Mr. McFeely at the same flea market I'd sold at as myself.

One time, we had a little variety show. I said, "I've always wanted to learn how to tap-dance." That's easier said than done. We had a variety show at Betty's Little Theater. The

TL: I think it absolutely is timeless.

DN: The *Neighborhood* is, I think, to many people an acquired taste. I think the documentary [*Won't You Be My Neighbor?*] really helped that immeasurably. It explained Fred's rationale in a way that people did not realize before.

I think we all realized it, people working on the program.

"There's this corny saying: 'When you choose a career, make sure it's something you love because you'll never work a day in your life.' . . . I've never felt that I've worked a day in my life."

That's what was frustrating at times, to take some of that child development theory and try to put it into a press release. You really need five pages to explain it correctly, but that's not what a press release is.

I think the *Neighborhood* has soul that a lot of programs don't have. It's got a depth that people don't realize at first. That's what I've been trying to do all these years with everything I've done. Little by little, you inch away at it. Every little interview you do, you can talk more about it. You're not going to cover the world.

It all built over the years. We're still building the program and still building what Fred was all about. I think we will continue doing that.

David Newell writes cue cards with the lyrics to the new song "I Like to Take My Time" in 1970.

"The sky's the limit when creativity's involved."

Fred Rogers

Lady Aberlin checks on Grandpère and Daniel Striped Tiger at the Eiffel Tower, which has been turned upside down by Lady Elaine Fairchilde during the "What Do You Do with the Mad That You Feel" theme week in 1995.

A Place Where Anything Can Happen

3

THE
NEIGHBORHOOD
OF MAKE-BELIEVE

No television visit with Mister Rogers would have been complete without a jaunt to the whimsical Neighborhood of Make-Believe. The colorful, polka-dotted path that wound through Make-Believe played host to more than thirty years of events that could only be imagined.

In Make-Believe, visitors could talk with a tame tiger who lived in a clock, watch cereal rain down from the sky, or attend a bass violin festival.

Life was never dull in Make-Believe. One day the neighbors might receive a visit from the extraterrestrial Purple Panda from Planet Purple, and the next they might find that Lady Elaine had established her own television station to broadcast throughout Make-Believe. They might deal with the aftermath of a fire at Cornflake S. Pecially's Rock-It factory or enjoy a performance at the castle with snacks to follow in the S Room. It was a place where anything could happen!

It was also a place where anything could be discussed. Feelings and ideas were just as important in Make-Believe as they were in the real world of Mister Rogers' neighborhood. Characters often expressed their feelings and asked deep questions. They turned to their friends for help and to make sense of confusing things.

Even though Make-Believe was a whimsical and welcoming neighborhood, life there was not perfect. The neighbors often had to figure out how to deal with common fears, difficult situations, and even hurt feelings between friends. In Make-Believe, people and puppets talked openly, treated one another with kindness, and found ways to work together.

OPPOSITE: Fred Rogers with King Friday XIII and Queen Sara Saturday.

Make-Believe was a dreamlike realm filled with both the familiar and the fantastical. People and things that appeared in Mister Rogers' real Neighborhood often showed up in Make-Believe, much the way a day's events might appear in our dreams at night. Fred once explained the flow of a typical episode this way:

In the opening reality of the program, we deal with the stuff that dreams are made of. Then in the Neighborhood of Make-Believe we deal with it as if it were a dream. Then when it comes back to me, we deal with the simple interpretation of the dream. That sounds very analytical, and it probably doesn't show at all, and that's fine. I hope it doesn't. But . . . when I'm writing the script that's what I think about.

Hedda Sharapan, who worked with Fred for decades, expanded on this idea: "What he wanted to do, I think, was to encourage imagination and the sense that play is a way to master situations, experiences, and feelings." Equally important was the end of the show, when viewers came back to Mister Rogers' house and he talked about the events in Make-Believe. "You talk about it beforehand, you then experience it, then you come back and you talk about it afterward. You integrate it," said Hedda. "So he took you by the hand through these experiences and let you experience them. And then he helped you reflect on it."

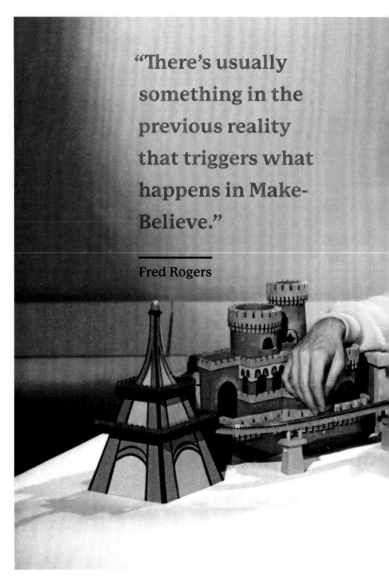

> "There's usually something in the previous reality that triggers what happens in Make-Believe."
>
> ── Fred Rogers

Fred poses with the Neighborhood of Make-Believe models that normally sat on the shelves in his kitchen. This photograph was the cover image for the album *A Place of Our Own*, originally released in 1970.

Why Make-Believe?

Fred knew that children use imaginative play to express feelings and to gain a sense of competence over things they find difficult or frightening. So while Make-Believe was fun and fanciful, it also supported children's healthy development.

The puppets were particularly important in this way. "Puppets can say and do things that children might feel but may not have the language to express," explained Susan Linn, a ventriloquist and child psychologist who occasionally appeared on the program. "Fred was so good at that. The puppets could say things that Fred understood might be frightening to a child, or to some children. It was just an incredibly safe way of being able to express those feelings. When you are playing, and especially when you're using puppets, you can say and do things that you wouldn't do otherwise."

Even though a few human characters appeared in both Make-Believe and the real Neighborhood, Mister Rogers himself never appeared in Make-Believe. He was careful to distinguish between the two worlds, especially as the program developed over the years.

To help young viewers make the transition from reality to pretend, Mister Rogers would say, "Let's have some make-believe." Then he'd use an object to help facilitate that shift. "Transitions give children some time to leave behind where they've been and to get ready for what's ahead," Fred explained. In the earliest days of the program, he would look through a telescope to "see" into Make-Believe. Sometimes he would use the little model buildings of Make-Believe that he kept in his kitchen. But usually, he'd call on Trolley to shuttle viewers' imaginations from the real world of his television house to the world of Make-Believe. "The boundaries of make-believe are really, really important, because it's those boundaries that make make-believe safe," noted Susan Linn.

LET'S HAVE
SOME MAKE-BELIEVE!

HOP ON THE
TROLLEY AND TAKE
A RIDE INTO THE
NEIGHBORHOOD OF
MAKE-BELIEVE!
DING! DING!

Illustration of the Neighborhood of Make-Believe
that hung on the wall beside the refrigerator in
Mister Rogers' kitchen.

MEET THE PUPPETS (AND PEOPLE) OF MAKE-BELIEVE

People and puppets both played important roles in Make-Believe, and the relationships among them were complex. In many ways, the puppets of Make-Believe expressed different aspects of Fred Rogers' personality. "Every one of them has a facet of me," he said. But they were also archetypes that represented the kinds of feelings and thoughts that *everyone* experiences. While Daniel was shy and sensitive, King Friday boldly declared his thoughts to one and all. Good-natured X the Owl represented the adolescent who displayed a deep curiosity about the world, and Lady Elaine was, in Fred's words, "the fun-maker, the mischief-maker." And yet, these were not static, single-dimensional characters. Everyone in Make-Believe—people and puppets alike—had a multifaceted personality and intricate relationships, just as people do in real life.

> "This is a history of a make-believe universe. The ties are intricate!"
>
> **Fred Rogers**

ABOVE: The studio set of the Neighborhood of Make-Believe.

OPPOSITE: Trolley and the puppets of Make-Believe at King Friday's castle.

Trolley

NEIGHBORHOOD HOME: Car Barn

PERSONALITY: steadfast, dependable

TALENTS: transporting us from reality to fantasy and back again

FAVORITE FOOD: pretend peanut-butter-and-jelly sandwiches

PERFORMED BY: Johnny Costa (whistles, music), production crew (movement)

FIRST APPEARANCE: Episode 0001 (1968)

AS SOON AS TROLLEY APPEARED on the tracks behind the window seat in Mister Rogers' television house, viewers knew where they were headed. In almost every episode of the show, the little red and orange trolley car trundled along its track, accompanied by that rolling, vamping piano music—and voilà! We arrived in the Neighborhood of Make-Believe.

As a prop and a mode of transportation, Trolley helped viewers make the transition between the worlds of reality and pretend. But Trolley was more than that; it was a character in and of itself. In his real world, Mister Rogers often addressed Trolley by name, and Trolley responded through bells, whistles, and music. Though it's clear that these "conversations" with Mister Rogers were meant fancifully, once Trolley arrived in the Neighborhood of Make-Believe, the other characters responded to Trolley as though it were speaking a full, understandable language.

In Make-Believe, Trolley even seemed to have feelings at times, such as when it was sad that its neighbors might like the visiting Express de Grandparents (a flying trolley) better than they liked it.

Trolley adapted well to the given weather and time of day, and in some episodes it was equipped with a snowplow, a flashlight, and even an umbrella.

ORIGIN STORY: A trolley first appeared on *The Children's Corner* to provide an element of movement on the set. Fred knew that "anything on wheels can be a special delight for a young child just gaining confidence walking and running." When Fred moved to Canada to develop the CBC program *Misterogers,* a Canadian craftsman made the now-familiar Trolley for that program, with a placard that read *"Neighbourhood"* (spelled the Canadian way) on its roof.

"[Trolley] was a very low-tech, Fred Flintstone kind of thing. It had a little electric motor, and it ran on electrified tracks. It ran through a transformer with a toggle switch, like forward, reverse, and off. I would sit behind the castle with a black-and-white monitor in front of me so I could see what the camera was seeing. The trolley would come out, and one of the actors in the scene would talk to it. The trolley would respond by bumping back and forth. That took a little bit of skill. The trolley had to jog back and forth at the right time—you wouldn't want to do it too soon, because that wouldn't make sense. But if somebody asked the trolley something and two seconds would go by before it would jog back and forth, you'd have to do it over. Over the many years we did those shows, there were a handful of other trolley operators that did it as well. I just happened to be the one in the latter years."

Joe Abeln, production crew and Trolley operator

PITTSBURGH

Fred had fond memories of Pittsburgh's trolleys from when he was young. "One of my favorite vehicles from my childhood in Latrobe was the 'Toonerville Trolley' that took us from Latrobe to Ligonier into Idlewild Park for our school picnics," he wrote. "I also remember crossing those train tracks every day on my way to and from school. And of course I loved riding on a real trolley when our family came to visit in Pittsburgh." Here, Mister Rogers visits the Pennsylvania Trolley Museum for episodes that first aired in 1984.

Daniel Striped Tiger

HOME: Clock

PERSONALITY: sweet, gentle, sensitive

FAVORITE THINGS: clocks, toy dump truck

SPECIAL FRIENDS: Lady Aberlin, Prince Tuesday, Ana Platypus

TALENTS: kindness, feeling his feelings, being honest

PERFORMED BY: Fred Rogers

FIRST APPEARANCE: Episode 0001 (1968)

DANIEL STRIPED TIGER LIVED ON THE far west side of the Neighborhood of Make-Believe, but he was the tenderhearted center of this imaginary world. Soft-spoken and tame, Daniel lived in a big grandfather clock with no hands. Fortunately, he had his handy wristwatch to help him tell time!

For Daniel, the time was always right to share his feelings. He was easily frightened and tended to be quite the worrywart, but he found comfort in talking with his best friend, Lady Aberlin. She often helped Daniel cope with difficult situations or sad feelings. Daniel and Lady Aberlin showed their affection for each other by rubbing noses and saying "Ugga-mugga," which was their way of saying "I love you."

Daniel was a friend to everyone in Make-Believe, including his schoolmates at Some Place Else: Prince Tuesday and Ana Platypus. Daniel was also a tiger of many talents. He was a founding member of Make-Believe's Reindeer–Tiger sports team, was known to attend the occasional clock-lovers' meeting, and was even able to communicate with Yo Yo LaBelle (the visitor from the stars) when no one else could.

Daniel showed children that they can be scared and, with the help of a friend, be brave. Whether he was nervously meeting Santa Claus, spending his first night away from home, or dealing with the sadness of being forgotten by a friend, Daniel approached the world and people with openness, courage, and trust.

ORIGIN STORY: Daniel Striped Tiger was born in 1954, the night before the premiere of *The Children's Corner*. Station manager Dorothy Daniel gave Fred the little hand puppet as a gift. He recalled how "the art department had painted this fanciful set and there happened to be a clock on it. So I just put a little slit in the clock and poked Daniel [through]." He'd intended to use Daniel just once on the program, but viewers liked him so much that he became a regular character.

DANIEL'S WHISKERS

Paul Lally, who directed the *Neighborhood* from 1982 to 1989, recalled a moment on the set with Daniel:

One day, we were setting up for a scene with Lady Aberlin and Daniel Striped Tiger at his clock. Fred had Daniel up and in position, Betty was going over her lines, and I was checking camera angles when I noticed that Dan was missing some whiskers.

I leaned over and peered down into the shelf of the clock. Sure enough, the studio lights gleamed off of two stray strands. I called for the hot glue gun, one of the most important tools on a television set.

Seconds later, it's in my hand, glue oozing from the tip.

"Hold still, Daniel," I said.

The little tiger froze and asked, "Is something wrong?"

"Not at all. Just a little repair work."

He reared back. "On what?"

"Your nose. Some whiskers fell out and I have to stick them back on with the glue gun. Only take a second."

"A second's a long time when you're using hot glue."

"Good point—but it won't hurt a bit."

"Why not?"

I rubbed the little tiger's furry head. "Because you're a puppet, Daniel, remember?"

A long pause. He rubbed his cheek with his paw, contemplating my comment. "You're right. I forgot."

"Me, too," I said.

Daniel let out a deep sigh. "I'm ready, Mr. Lally."

I reached out, and he moved back slightly. "You're sure I'm a puppet?" he asked.

"Yes, Daniel. Absolutely positive."

"Okay, then."

Ten seconds later, whiskers back in place, we started rolling.

Daniel dressed as a wolf in Episode 1623 (1990).

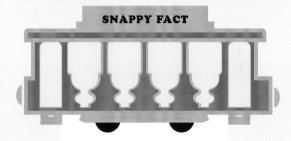

SNAPPY FACT

Daniel received his wristwatch as a gift from a young viewer of *The Children's Corner* who was concerned that Daniel's clock had no hands. When another child wrote to Mister Rogers to ask why the clock didn't have hands, Mister Rogers replied, "We decided we would pretend there was no time in Make-Believe, like the timelessness of love."

"Fred once told me, 'It's not the puppet that's real, it's Betty's absolute belief that it's a shy little tiger that makes the magic work.'"

Paul Lally

TOP: Daniel shows Lady Aberlin his 143 sign and explains that the numbers are a code for "I love you."

BOTTOM: In one of the series' most touching scenes, Daniel confides in Lady Aberlin, singing "Sometimes I Wonder if I'm a Mistake." He's concerned because he's not like anyone else. She reassures him, singing: "I think you are just fine as you are." The moment is part of Episode 1578, which first aired in 1987 during the theme week about "Making Mistakes."

LEFT: A 1971 promotional photo featuring Betty Aberlin, Daniel Tiger, and Fred Rogers. The "Magician Show" tickets were for a performance by Mr. Appel in Episode 1216, which originally aired in 1972.

"Betty is a brilliant performer, and her ability to relate to the puppets and her sparkle—she really brings life to the Neighborhood of Make-Believe. She's the animating spirit of the Neighborhood that all the puppets can relate to. Her tenderness with them, and her playfulness with them, and her very adorable relationship with King Friday—that she can be kind of obedient and kind of tease him and needle him a little bit, very obediently. She could do a layered thing, where she was saying one thing and communicating much more."

Betsy Nadas Seamans, writer, actor (Mrs. McFeely)

Lady Aberlin

HOME: the castle

PERSONALITY: kind, sweet, strong

SPECIAL FRIEND: Daniel Striped Tiger

TALENTS: singing, dancing, caring for others

PERFORMED BY: Betty Aberlin

FIRST APPEARANCE: Episode 0002 (1968)

OPPOSITE: Lady Aberlin talks with her uncle Friday and aunt Sara at the castle.

THE CHARACTER OF LADY ABERLIN, played by actress Betty Aberlin (see page 79), was the niece of King Friday XIII. She was a kind and caring presence in the Neighborhood of Make-Believe, and she played a big-sister role to many of her neighbors, celebrating with them and helping them in times of struggle. She was particularly close with Daniel Striped Tiger. Their intimate conversations and playful interactions created some of the program's most touching and memorable moments.

Lady Aberlin often expressed herself through song and dance, and she appeared in all of the Neighborhood operas. Even though she was usually positive and compassionate, she was not afraid to express her own difficult emotions like anger, frustration, and disappointment, such as when she felt King Friday was making unreasonable demands of his subjects. By showing a full range of emotions, Lady Aberlin helped children know that life naturally has its highs and lows, whether you're a puppet, a child, or a grown-up, and that talking about whatever you're going through can help.

ORIGIN STORY: Actress Betty Aberlin responded to a general talent call held before *Mister Rogers' Neighborhood* went national in 1968. Fred Rogers described their introduction: "She knocked on our door and said, 'I sure would like to help.' Well, she was a great addition."

KING FRIDAY XIII RULED OVER the Neighborhood of Make-Believe, where he lived in the castle with his wife, Queen Sara Saturday, and their son, Prince Tuesday. King Friday's arrivals were typically announced with fanfare. He addressed visitors to the castle by name (for example, "Handyman Negri, I presume") and required a respectful response ("Correct as usual, King Friday"). He was a proud monarch who sometimes created outrageous rules within his kingdom, and he expected his subjects to obey his every command. But when he felt the love of his family and his subjects, he revealed his kind and understanding nature. Fred described King Friday as "a kind king" who also "worries that people won't love him unless he's very important—and one way he feels important is by thinking he's always right."

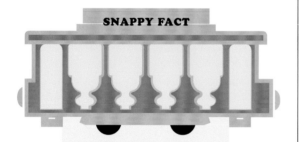

SNAPPY FACT

Fred Rogers chose the name "Friday XIII" for the King because he wanted to make Friday the thirteenth a fun day instead of one attached to ominous superstition.

King Friday XIII

HOME: castle

PERSONALITY: proud, authoritarian, demanding but loving

FAVORITE THINGS: hearing himself talk, bass violin, pet birds Mimus Polyglottos and Troglodytes Aedon

FAMILY MEMBERS: Queen Sara Saturday, Prince Tuesday

TALENTS: whistling, playing bass violin, making grandiloquent speeches

PERFORMED BY: Fred Rogers

FIRST APPEARANCE: Episode 0001 (1968)

OPPOSITE, ABOVE: King Friday with his pet bird on a stick, Troglodytes Aedon.

OPPOSITE, BELOW: King Friday (on bass violin) and Handyman Negri (on guitar) play a duet in the castle garden.

In addition to making numerous decrees, King Friday played the bass violin and loved to perform for his subjects. He enjoyed showing off his royal vocabulary in long-winded speeches and creating kingly versions of common songs and poems.

ORIGIN STORY: King Friday XIII originally appeared on *The Children's Corner,* where he was the king of Calendarland who celebrated his birthday every Friday the thirteenth (regardless of the month). In the Canadian program, *Misterogers*, he evolved into the king of the whole universe. Eventually, on *Mister Rogers' Neighborhood*, his kingdom was limited to the Neighborhood of Make-Believe.

A NURSERY RHYME FIT FOR A KING

King Friday loved to elevate common things to royal status. Here is his
kingly version of "Row, Row, Row Your Boat," alongside the original.

Propel, propel, propel your craft	*Row, row, row your boat*
Gently down liquid solution.	*Gently down the stream.*
Ecstatically, ecstatically, ecstatically, ecstatically,	*Merrily, merrily, merrily, merrily,*
Existence is but an illusion.	*Life is but a dream.*

Classic Moment

THE ROYAL WEDDING

Episode 1015
Original air date: February 28, 1969

› **WHILE VISITING THE NEIGHBORHOOD** of Make-Believe from nearby Westwood, Sara Saturday caught the royal eye of King Friday XIII. Following a brief courtship, Sara Saturday was crowned Queen as she and King Friday married at a gathering of their closest neighbors. The royal wedding was officiated by Mr. Anybody (Don Francks), who was provided authority to do so by the arch-clergy of Make-Believe. This marriage set the stage for many years of Make-Believe monarchy overseen by King Friday XIII and Queen Sara Saturday.

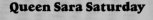

Queen Sara Saturday

HOME: castle

PERSONALITY: kind, diplomatic, loving

FAMILY MEMBERS: King Friday, Prince Tuesday

INTERESTS: being a mother, helping others

PERFORMED BY: Fred Rogers

FIRST APPEARANCE: Episode 0038 (1968)

ORIGINALLY FROM WESTWOOD, Sara Saturday wed King Friday in a royal ceremony in 1969. When deciding what name to use after the wedding, Sara gave a nod to the feminist movement of the 1960s by opting to keep her last name; her official name was "Queen Sara Saturday Friday," and "Queen Sara" for short.

OPPOSITE: A royal family portrait.

SNAPPY FACT

Queen Sara is named for Fred's wife, Joanne, who was born Sara Joanne Byrd.

The queen was a kind and benevolent ruler. She helped to temper King Friday's sometimes outrageous demands and acted as a mediator between him and his subjects. Queen Sara was quick to see the best in people and worked for good causes such as Food for the World.

Queen Sara helped her son, Prince Tuesday, navigate the normal highs and lows of a child's life. In this way, she showed viewers how they might celebrate their accomplishments and deal with their fears and mistakes. When she and King Friday argued, she reassured Prince Tuesday that people can be angry with each other and still love one another. She modeled how to stand your ground while also being respectful.

ORIGIN STORY: Sara Saturday met the King while working in the castle kitchen. She made him one of his favorite treats: cup custard. He tried to impress her by wearing his finest crown, but she was more interested in his "beautiful eyes."

PRINCE TUESDAY WAS THE SON OF King Friday XIII and Queen Sara Saturday. He was born on—you guessed it—a Tuesday (April 14, 1970, to be exact), and he made his first appearance to his neighbors one week later. His character showed viewers what it's like to be a child in a loving family. Tuesday was one of only two characters in the Neighborhood of Make-Believe who aged over the course of the series. Like Ana Platypus, viewers saw him grow from a newborn baby to a school-age child.

While Tuesday respected his parents, he also helped them to see things in a new perspective. When King Friday made rules that were too strict, such as banning all play (because Bob Dog got hurt when he was playing), his son spoke up and explained why people need to play. Tuesday demonstrated how children can respectfully express their thoughts, opinions, and needs to the adults in their life.

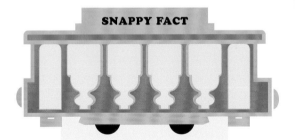

SNAPPY FACT

Prince Tuesday's voice changed many times over the years. He was performed by no fewer than five actors.

Prince Tuesday

HOME: castle

PERSONALITY: respectfully outspoken

SPECIAL FRIENDS: Daniel Striped Tiger, Ana Platypus

TALENTS: Reciting the alphabet quickly, yo-yoing

PERFORMED BY: Adair Roth, Fred Michael, Charles Altman, Carole Muller, Lenny Meledandri

FIRST APPEARANCE: Episode 1122 (1970)

Castle Helpers

EDGAR COOKE (1968) sang every word he uttered in an operatic tone to fulfill his role as King Friday XIII's "singing cook." He sang in a minor key when sad and a major key when happy. Early in the television series, Edgar was the first line of communication between Mister Rogers and Make-Believe, but this role was phased out as the difference between fantasy and reality became more distinct. Edgar, who was performed by Fred, was too timid to rebel against even unreasonable authority.

THE ROYAL HULA MOUSE (1999) was one of King Friday's many royal helpers. He spoke Spanish and had a magic Hula-Hoop that transported him anywhere he wanted to go. Hula Mouse once traveled to the planet A.O.P. (Altogether Other Planet) to rescue the lost Prince Tuesday and Little Panda. The role of Hula Mouse was played by Tony Chiroldes (see page 88).

ROYAL COACH WILLIE SAUNDERS (1968), performed by actor Willie Saunders, was Make-Believe's fitness guru. Although he traveled throughout the Neighborhood, he was most often found exercising inside the castle with the king.

Lady Elaine Fairchilde

HOME: Museum-Go-Round

PERSONALITY: mischievous, fun, self-confident

FAVORITE THINGS: her magic boomerang

SPECIAL FRIEND: Betty Okonak Templeton Jones

TALENTS: whistling; playing piano, oboe, and accordion; flying in her spacecraft

PERFORMED BY: Fred Rogers

FIRST APPEARANCE: Episode 0005 (1968)

When not on camera, Lady Elaine could serve as an outlet for Fred's mischievous side. "Lady Elaine was the troublemaker," said floor manager Nick Tallo. "In thirty-one years, I never heard Fred swear, but I heard Lady Elaine swear."

LADY ELAINE FAIRCHILDE WAS the neighborhood rogue. She regularly addressed others as "toots." Having learned magic from the Wizard of Lupovich, she often used her magic boomerang to make mischief, but she had many other interests and talents. She discovered Planet Purple while flying in her spaceship and was the founder and manager of Make-Believe's television station, MGR-TV, where she interviewed guests and produced a soap opera called *As the Museum Turns*.

Lady Elaine's brazen honesty inspired honesty in others. She often stood up to King Friday when his rules and declarations went too far. She knew that she was ornery, and sometimes she worried that people didn't like her. Even though she could be brash, her neighbors often reassured her that they liked her just the way she was.

SNAPPY FACT

People often wondered if Lady Elaine was named for Fred's sister Elaine, but he never confirmed that, saying only, "We tease her because she thinks that I must have named Lady Elaine Fairchilde for her."

Fred wrote that Lady Elaine gave the program "a way to help children think about how important everyone can be in a neighborhood. She often adds adventure, mischief, pleasure, and fun in a way that others do not." Whenever Lady Elaine hurt someone's feelings or caused a problem, she apologized or found a way to make things right. In this way, she helped children understand personal responsibility and social boundaries.

> "Lady Elaine is the mischief maker in the Neighborhood of Make-Believe—she keeps everybody honest because she's so honest herself."

Fred Rogers

ORIGIN STORY: Lady Elaine first appeared on *The Children's Corner* as proprietor of the Rapid Walking Beauty Counseling and Professional Bridesmaid School. On *Mister Rogers' Neighborhood,* she hid during most of the program's first few national episodes in 1968, but she was on everyone's minds nonetheless: She'd used her magic boomerang to rearrange the location of the buildings in the neighborhood, causing King Friday to ramp up security measures to fight against "the changers." Throughout the first season, Lady Elaine lived in Some Place Else; it wasn't until Episode 1003, in 1969, that she found a permanent home in the Neighborhood of Make-Believe as the curator of the Museum-Go-Round.

BOOMERANG-TOOMERANG-SOOMERANG!

Lady Elaine often turned Make-Believe upside down by using her magic boomerang and the words "Boomerang-Toomerang-Soomerang!"

But where did this magic boomerang come from? In 1968, Lady Elaine revealed her boomerang for the first time, comparing its shape with "the wings of a swallow." The next year, Lady Elaine's magician friend, the Wizard of Lupovich, visited Make-Believe and revealed that he'd given Lady Elaine her boomerang and taught her how to unleash its magical powers.

Henrietta Pussycat

NICKNAME: Hen

HOME: house in the oak tree, next door to X the Owl

PERSONALITY: sweet, shy, needed encouragement to feel confident

FAVORITE THINGS: fancy dresses and hats

SPECIAL FRIENDS: X the Owl, Lady Aberlin

TALENT: fashion

PERFORMED BY: Fred Rogers

FIRST APPEARANCE: Episode 0001 (1968)

HENRIETTA PUSSYCAT LIVED IN A COZY little schoolhouse perched in Make-Believe's big oak tree, next door to her best friend, X the Owl. When friends came to call, they pulled a rope with a golden tassel to ring her doorbell. Henrietta loved fancy things, including pretty dresses and hats. She enjoyed taking care of others, but she was also a shy kitty who sometimes struggled with feelings of insecurity and jealousy, especially when someone (or something) else received special attention. With the love and support of her friends, she was able to be braver and to feel more secure in who she was—reflecting children's own experiences growing up.

ORIGIN STORY: Henrietta originally appeared on *The Children's Corner* as the governess of nine nice mice, but those duties faded away over the years. Henrietta's English-language vocabulary was limited in the early years; she could say only three words besides "meow": "beautiful," "telephone," and "Mister Rogers." Though her vocabulary expanded significantly over time, "meow" remained her predominant word.

OPPOSITE: Mr. McFeely and Henrietta at the oak tree in an episode from 1994.

X THE OWL WAS a blue-feathered owl who lived in the oak tree in the center of the Neighborhood of Make-Believe. X was happy and inquisitive, and also a bit naive. He was sometimes frustrated when things did not go his way.

X was an eager learner and frequently immersed himself in lessons delivered by the Owl Correspondence School (OCS). He idolized his hero, Benjamin Franklin, and emulated him by keeping a printing press in his tree. He also found great joy in teaching others the things he'd learned. He reflected the pride one can have in oneself after learning something new or accomplishing a task.

With a helpful and caring spirit, X often comforted his neighbor Henrietta, though like most friends, they sometimes disagreed. His friendship with her represented the pleasure children often feel when they have someone to protect and instruct.

ORIGIN STORY: X the Owl's name was based on the word "escape," as detailed in the 1954 *Children's Corner* book, *Our Small World:* "My friend and true tame tiger pal, Daniel S. Tiger, let me out of my cage at the county fair. . . . Daniel said to me, 'X SCAPE,' and I said, 'WELL, HOW ABOUT THAT.' I flew out, and I've been his pet ever since, and now I live in a tree right next to Daniel's Clock."

The Owl Family

COUSIN MARY OWL (1970), performed by actress Mary Rawson, lived in Shadyville and worked as an instructor at the Owl Correspondence School. She often assisted X with his studies.

X the Owl

HOME: hole in the oak tree, next door to Henrietta Pussycat

PERSONALITY: inquisitive, happy, easygoing

FAVORITE THINGS: learning, oranges, Benjamin Franklin

SPECIAL FRIENDS: Henrietta Pussycat, Lady Aberlin

TALENTS: conducting experiments, printmaking, teaching

PERFORMED BY: Fred Rogers

FIRST APPEARANCE: Episode 0001 (1968)

COUSIN STEPHEN OWL (1994), played by actor Stephen Lee, enjoyed roller-skating and occasionally assisted X the Owl with his Owl Correspondence School studies.

Cousin Mary Owl

Cousin Stephen Owl

TOPICS STUDIED AT OCS

In order to satisfy his desire to learn about new topics, X frequently enrolled in educational courses through the Owl Correspondence School (OCS). Often, he was not aware of the new topics he would study until the course materials were delivered. Here is a selection of the many OCS courses he took:

Count to Ten by Twos (1328)
Early American Owl History (1231)
Hide and Find (1349)
Native Americans (1518)
OCS Cookbook (1508)
Owl History (1199)
Owl Music History (1223)
People Watching (1595)
Printmaking/Lettering (1373)

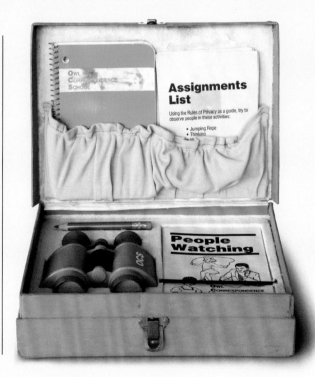

HANDYMAN NEGRI, played by actor Joe Negri (see page 78), was the royal fix-it man in the Neighborhood of Make-Believe. Skilled at fixing, cleaning, and building things, Handyman Negri was often called upon for his help in keeping Make-Believe in order. When a new school was being considered for the Neighborhood of Make-Believe children, Handyman Negri went to work and built a school at Some Place Else.

In addition to his handiwork, Handyman Negri also served in other roles at King Friday's request, such as a border guard and member of the volunteer fire department. Because he was so busy with so many things, Handyman Negri didn't always have time to chat with his friends and neighbors right away. But if they were patient and waited, "Handy" was always happy to come back to spend time with them or help with special projects. Through these interactions, children might see that even if adults don't have time for them immediately, they still care about them.

Handyman Negri, like the real-life Joe Negri, was also a talented musician. He often performed for and with his neighbors. He sang with Lady Elaine Fairchilde, played guitar to accompany King Friday on the bass violin, and gave music lessons to Prince Tuesday. He also took an active role in several of the Neighborhood operas, including playing W. I. Norton Donovan, the villain in *Windstorm in Bubbleland*.

ORIGIN STORY: In early episodes, before taking on "handyman" status, Handyman Negri was referred to as "Mr. Negri." On a few occasions, Handyman Negri appeared in the real Neighborhood, but he was usually seen there as Mr. Negri, the owner and operator of Negri's Music Shop.

Handyman Negri

NICKNAME: Handy

PERSONALITY: outgoing, busy, helpful

FAVORITE THINGS: guitar, baseball cap

TALENTS: fixing and building things; playing guitar and singing

PERFORMED BY: Joe Negri

FIRST APPEARANCE: Episode 0001 (1968)

OPPOSITE: Handyman Negri chats with Henrietta and X the Owl outside their homes in the oak tree in 1972.

A Neighborly Chat *with*

JOE NEGRI

Handyman Negri, Mr. Negri

JOE NEGRI was a cast member on *Mister Rogers' Neighborhood* for the duration of the series. He shared his guitar talents in the Neighborhood of Make-Believe as Handyman Negri, as well as in the real Neighborhood, where he owned the music shop.

TIM LYBARGER: How did you start out on the *Neighborhood*?

JOE NEGRI: I worked with Fred at a commercial station where I was the musical director. It was WTAE, an ABC channel here in Pittsburgh. They brought him over to do a fifteen-minute show that was a prototype of what became the *Neighborhood*. He actually opened up in his little apartment at the piano and then, a few minutes later, he would take the trolley and go to the Neighborhood of Make-Believe. That was the format of the show.

My job at the time was to help him any way I could with music or whatever he might need. We were already a little bit acquainted because in those days there weren't many people in television, so we knew each other. After a week or so, he started asking me if I would go

into the Neighborhood and just walk around and chat with the puppets. So I would talk to King Friday a bit, I'd talk to X the Owl, I'd talk to Henrietta, this and that.

The show didn't last because Fred and the sales department were not amiable—they just didn't get along. Fred didn't want to do commercials, so he didn't. He wasn't cut out for commercial television. [Later] I got an unexpected phone call from him saying, "Hey Joe, how would you like to be the handyman in the Neighborhood?" And that became our little standard joke. I said, "You're kidding, because I'm not very handy. I'm not very good at anything. I can't even put in a nail straight." So he said, "Don't worry about it. It'll be all pretend." And it was all pretend. I believe I was on the very first episode of that new series of the *Neighborhood*.

TL: You and Betty Aberlin were the humans most frequently in Make-Believe. What are some of your thoughts on the characters that you commonly interacted with?

JN: You know, Fred had such a knack. Every one of the characters had a distinct personality. The King thought he was king. Fred once said to me, "One of the best forms of life is to have a king who is a good king," and in a way I think King Friday was a good king. He was fair, he was equal with everybody, and he liked to run the show. And a character like Daniel Tiger, who's afraid of this and that—you have to calm him down periodically—his was a totally different personality. X was a little outgoing, boisterous—a little bit comedic. Henrietta was on the timid side.

> ## "Johnny and I took Fred's basic songs and we enriched them in a very jazz-like manner, which gave them the language that the people hear. I am very proud of that."

One of my favorite characters, believe it or not, was Lady Elaine, who didn't take anything from anybody, including King Friday.

She was kind of tough. She stood her ground about everything. And Corney was a typical businessman, ran a factory, and that kind of stuff. It was amazing how each of them were individuals.

TL: Were there any particular story lines from Make-Believe that stand out to you? Any that were especially impactful that you felt were a little larger than the typical story?

JN: I remember one that had to do with divorce. I had a friend at the time, she was a young singer here in Pittsburgh, and she came on the show. She was the one going through the divorce.

The operas were very special, all of them. The one opera I remember is *Windstorm in Bubbleland*. I played the wind, which was an amazing experience for me because, well, I'm not an actor. I'm basically a musician and a little bit of a performer. I played the wind, and I actually got up

there on the same contraption that they used on Broadway and flew across the studio. The other thing about it was that I had to be a little bit on the rough side. [The wind] wasn't such a nice guy. I was looking to hurt some people, and that was quite a role for me, to be able to do that. I remember that well.

TL: There were a lot of different people that came in and out of Make-Believe and Negri's Music Shop. Do any specific guests stand out to you?

JN: The first one that comes to mind is always Yo-Yo Ma. I've always been a jazz musician and Yo-Yo Ma, I had such respect for him. He's a beautiful classical musician. He comes to the music shop and then Fred has me with a guitar, and I'm going, "Uh-oh, what am I going to play with this guy? He's a real classical artist, and I don't know if I'm up to this or not." We decided to do Fred's simple song called "Tree Tree Tree." Yo-Yo Ma played it beautifully, with a gorgeous tone. So that solved that problem.

Another special guest, of course, was Wynton Marsalis. We all got along with him. He was an interesting guy. His family had been on prior to him. His father was a very good stride piano player, which is the old-style piano with the left hand where they hit the bass and the chords. They were from New Orleans, and he was a Dixie player. The family came on and we did a show with all of them, but not with Wynton. I'll never forget the father [Ellis Marsalis] saying to me, "Oh, could you get me a little rhythm like Freddie Green?" Now, Freddie Green is a name only known to guitarists. He was the very famous rhythm player with the Count Basie Orchestra who made the Count Basie Orchestra unique. And I said, "Yeah. I can do that." And he went, "Boy, is it wonderful to say 'Freddie Green' to somebody and they know what you're talking about." That was really cute.

TL: Any overall thoughts on your experience over the years on the *Neighborhood*?

JN: Honestly, it was something that I never dreamed would ever happen. When we began, we began on a very small scale, and little by little, Fred would add things. I'll never forget when he decided to go into the reality segment, and he made me the music shop, he made Betty Aberlin the theater, Bob Trow the art studio, Don Brockett the kitchen—that was a big addition. The operas were very, very special. I think I must have done maybe all of them but one or two. I was really happy to be able to be a part of all of that stuff because, as I told you, I was not an actor. I remember Spencer Tracy saying, "I'm not an actor. I usually just play myself." That's what I did, I was just myself. But it worked, and it was fine. I loved being with all the people. We all got along beautifully. There were never any personality clashes.

One big moment for me was when one day Fred came in and said, "The show's going to be playing in the Pacific Islands." I went, "What?" He said, "Yeah, and it's also going to be playing in Europe [on the U.S. Armed Forces Network]." I said, "You're kidding?" I never dreamed the show would get out of Pittsburgh.

TL: You never expected it to get out of Pittsburgh, and look how widespread it became.

JN: Yeah. Well, the revival has really astounded me. It's been so popular. I remember being disappointed that the educational channels were not playing the old Mister Rogers show anymore, and we had stopped receiving our residuals. And I thought, well gee, does that mean the show is going under? But the show has a longevity about it, and Fred's messages are still vital today.

TL: It's a universal message that's timeless.

JN: "You are my friend, you are special."

TL: That's something that will never lose its importance.

JN: And "I like you as you are." Every one of us has a unique personality, and we're all valuable and we're all important. I was so glad that I was able to use my jazz talents and be a part of that show. Johnny and I took Fred's basic songs and we enriched them in a very jazz-like manner, which gave them the language that the people hear. I am very proud of that.

CORNFLAKE S. PECIALLY, known to his neighbors as Corney, was Make-Believe's lovable, tuxedo-wearing, snaggle-toothed entrepreneur. He lived and worked in the salmon-colored Rock-it Factory located next to the castle. Though the factory sometimes produced items such as baseball bats or King Friday dolls, Corney's specialty was the "Rock-it," a rocking chair that you sit in and, naturally, "rock it."

Corney enjoyed his work and took pride in what he produced. He was more interested in his work than in his appearance. Despite his fancy clothes, he almost always forgot to comb his hair. He was a handy and innovative business owner, but sometimes he became overwhelmed and needed help understanding his own limits. He was also prone to an occasional accident. Because he wasn't perfect, children often felt close to him.

Cornflake S. Pecially	
NICKNAME:	Corney
PERSONALITY:	good-natured, hardworking
FAVORITE THINGS:	Rock-its
TALENT:	manufacturing
PERFORMED BY:	Fred Rogers
FIRST APPEARANCE:	Episode 0003 (1968)

ORIGIN STORY: In early episodes, Corney was occasionally referred to as "Cornelius." This name was eventually dropped, and Corney's full name became Cornflake S. Pecially, named for the cereal "corn flakes," which one of Fred's sons liked "especially."

Corney's theme song was "I'm a Man Who Manufactures."

ROCK-IT VARIATIONS

Cornflake S. Pecially created many items within the walls of his unique factory, but he was best known for his "Rock-its"—rocking chairs made in various shapes and sizes, including:

Auto Rock-it

Block Rock-it

Covered Rock-it

Dance Rock-it

Floating Rock-it

Hair Chair

Instant Assembly Rock-it

Kite Rock-it

Piano Rock-it

Pretzel Rock-it

Rain or Shine Rock-it

RC81351 Rock-it

Rocking Throne

Rock-it to the Moon Carnival Ride

Scroll-back Rock-it

Stroller Rock-it

Umbrella Rock-it

Underwater Rock-it

Factory Employees

HILDA DINGLEBOARDER (1989), performed by Barbara Russell (see page 88), was an employee at Corney's factory. She had a young daughter named Daphne ("D.D."), who was cared for by Lady Aberlin, Princess Zelda, and Henrietta Pussycat while Ms. Dingleboarder was at work. When the Neighborhood of Make-Believe faced a garbage crisis, Hilda invented a recycling machine to help reduce waste.

JOEY HOLLINGSWORTH (1968) played a character of the same name who appeared in twenty-five episodes between 1968 and 1974. He was part of the regular cast of *Misterogers* in Canada, and Fred invited him to be on the *Neighborhood* version of the program. He was a skilled tap dancer and traveled the world as a representative of Cornflake S. Pecially's Rock-it Factory.

OPPOSITE: Corney's Rock-it Factory featured a showroom of various Rock-it models.

The Platypus Family

HOME: Platypus Mound

PERFORMED BY: Dr. Bill and Elsie Jean: Bill Barker; Ana: Carole Muller Switala

FIRST APPEARANCES: Dr Bill: Episode 1016 (1969); Elsie Jean: 1017 (1969); Ana: 1111 (1970)

RIGHT: Elsie Jean and Dr. Bill with baby Ana.

BELOW: Elsie Jean, Dr. Bill, and Ana (who is now school-age) enjoy the garden on the side of their Platypus Mound.

DR. BILL AND ELSIE JEAN PLATYPUS arrived in Make-Believe after the Frogg family moved to Westwood, making their first appearances in Episodes 1016 and 1017. The married couple lived in the Platypus Mound next to the Museum-Go-Round. Their daughter Ana joined the family in Episode 1111. The Platypus family served as another example of family life in addition to the royal family. Fred's friend Reverend Bill Barker voiced both Dr. Bill and Elsie Jean, who were named

DR. WILLIAM DUCKBILL BAGPIPE PLATYPUS IV spoke with a thick Scottish brogue. He often substituted the phrase *very, very* with *bill, bill*, as in "It's a bill, bill good day today." Dr. Bill served as both pediatrician and veterinarian in Make-Believe, and he had an office inside the Eiffel Tower. He was also a talented bagpiper.

Dr. Bill was married to **ELSIE JEAN PLATYPUS**. She loved to tend to her garden on the Platypus Mound, and she was a dedicated mother to Ana. Her magic pie recipe inspired Lady Elaine to open a pie restaurant, where Elsie Jean also worked.

ANA PLATYPUS was the daughter of Dr. Bill and Elsie Jean. Her official name was Ornithorhynchus Anatinus Platypus, which derived from the scientific name for the platypus and reflected Fred's love of playing with language. (Her name was also a nod to psychoanalyst Anna Freud, whose practice Fred observed one summer at the Hampstead Clinic.) Ana attended school at Some Place Else along with Prince Tuesday and Daniel Striped Tiger. She was a kind young platypus who thought deeply about things and loved animals.

Grandpère

HOME: Eiffel Tower

PERSONALITY: patient

FAMILY MEMBER: Collette Tiger

TALENTS: making *pommes frites*, writing

PERFORMED BY: Fred Rogers

FIRST APPEARANCE: Episode 0004 (1968)

near King Friday's castle. His full name, seen on the cover of his book *Pommes Frites*, was Henri Frederique de Tigre. With his jaunty green beret, handlebar mustache, and tiny goatee, he was the quintessential *tigre français*. He spoke French and often taught his neighbors French words and phrases. (Fred was fluent in French and thought Grandpère could help children learn a few French words.) He was known around the Neighborhood for his excellent *pommes frites,* or French fries, made with Donkey Hodie's best potatoes. A proud and loving grandfather to Collette, who occasionally visited him from France, he also served as a grandfatherly figure to his Make-Believe neighbors.

COLLETTE (1971) was the beautiful, French-speaking granddaughter of Grandpère who occasionally visited him in the Neighborhood of Make-Believe. On one such visit, she arrived via a flying trolley called the Express de Grandparents. Performed by Fred Rogers, Collette appeared in just a handful of episodes.

MISS AUDREY PAULIFICATE served as the telephone operator in the Neighborhood of Make-Believe. During the earliest years of the *Neighborhood,* Miss Paulificate was just the unseen "voice" of a tinkling bell on the other side of a telephone at the castle switchboard. Audrey Roth (see page 83) joined the cast in 1971, and Miss Paulificate came out from behind the castle wall. She was an assertive but nurturing woman who took great pride in her work, and King Friday often ordered her to complete various tasks in addition to her duties as telephone operator. When she was not hard at work, Miss Paulificate enjoyed dancing around the Neighborhood, visiting with the neighbors, and often comforting them when they were feeling low. Her straightforward personality served as a contrast to some of the more low-key characters in Make-Believe.

Miss Paulificate was named after the three children of Fred Rainsberry, head of children's programming at the CBC: Paul, Iffy (a nickname for Elizabeth), and Cate. She shares her first name with Audrey Roth, the actress who played her.

Miss Audrey Paulificate

HOME: castle

PERSONALITY: assertive, nurturing

TALENTS: dancing, singing, telephone operation

PERFORMED BY: Audrey Roth

FIRST APPEARANCE: Episode 1139 (1971)

TELE-CAN

When a call was required in Make-Believe, the Tele-can—a large contraption suspended near the oak tree—would lower over the head and body of the caller, who would use a can on a string to place a call. The calls were typically received by Miss Paulificate, Make-Believe's switchboard operator, who sounded like a tinkling bell on the other end of the line. As the 1970s progressed, the Tele-can was used less frequently; instead, Miss Paulificate typically used an antique phone. However, the Tele-can does appear in a few episodes produced in the mid-1980s.

A Neighborly Chat *with*

AUDREY ROTH

**Audrey Cleans Everything,
Miss Paulificate**

"Lady Elaine was always my favorite. Probably because I envied her ability to just say whatever she wanted to say."

Actress **AUDREY ROTH** played the owner of the Audrey Cleans Everything cleaning service (A.C.E.) and the character of Miss Paulificate, the telephone operator in the Neighborhood of Make-Believe. Audrey passed away in 2016. In 2012, she recorded this interview with Tim Lybarger for *The Neighborhood Archive Podcast*.

TIM LYBARGER: How did you get to be involved with the program itself, and how did you meet Fred Rogers in the first place?

AUDREY ROTH: With Chef Brockett and his wife—Don and Leslie Brockett. My daughter [Adair] and I—the whole family— we've been very good friends for years. And Don and Leslie always went to Nantucket for a few weeks in the summer, and they invited Adair and me to share their cottage. It was across the street from where Fred had his summer home—called the Crooked House on Nantucket. That's how I met him first.

The following fall after I met Fred, I was doing the part of Mama Rose in *Gypsy* at the Pittsburgh Playhouse, and Fred came to see it. And the following summer we were with them again, and that fall he called and he said, "I have two new characters on my show." And I said, "Really?" And he said, "Mm-hmm." He said, "They're both named Audrey." And I said, "Oh, did you name puppets for me? How nice!" And he said, "No. I have scripts written. And they're both real people, and they're you." So I was very pleased. And he said, "Would you be interested?" and of course I was interested.

The parts were Audrey Cleans Everything, A.C.E. is what they called it, and that's in the real Neighborhood. And in the Neighborhood of Make-Believe, there was Miss Paulificate. In a lot of those shows, Audrey Cleans Everything didn't appear after a time, which was kind of a shame, but there were some criticisms from women, if you can believe it. And somehow the part sort of was just phased out.

We had some wonderful shows—funny, fast cleaning. I cleaned a stadium. I cleaned a huge plane at the airport . . . I dusted off a plane. I had no idea planes were so tall until I had to clean them! At any rate, that part phased out and then Miss Paulificate just went on.

I was thinking about the parts I played in the operas. Don and I were swans, potato bugs, I was a mama cat and a mama elephant for the *Josephine the Short-Neck Giraffe* opera. The operas were so much fun. Then I was the bubble seller in [*Windstorm in Bubbleland*]. And a fish . . . I think there was hardly an animal that I didn't play.

TL: Do you have a personal favorite opera that stands out?

AR: Yes. *Bubbleland*. I love that one. I think Joe was wonderful in *Bubbleland*. John Reardon was so perfect as the newsperson. Betty was wonderful. She's good in all of them. And *Potato Bugs* was fun. They were all fun to do.

TL: They were so detailed and so creative, I think it would be the kind of thing that would be hard not to have fun doing.

AR: I think Fred was kind of a genius in picking people, because everybody got along well. Everybody admired everybody else and respected their talents. Most of the people had multiple talents. It was an absolute pleasure to be with everybody. And maybe that's Fred's genius. Part of his genius . . .

I have to tell you the other thing, too, about *Mister Rogers*. It was totally done on a, I won't say on a small budget, but costuming—in later years it got better. But I know I dressed Betty when she did the rich-lady opera [*All in the Laundry*] with a dress I wore for my daughter's wedding, plus about forty-two pounds of costume jewelry in order to play the rich lady. We sort of dressed ourselves. Carnegie Mellon costume department did a lot of the costumes. And they were wonderful, because that's about as good as you can get when it comes to doing costumes. It wasn't a lavish-budget show.

As far as characters are concerned, or puppets, Lady Elaine was always my favorite. Probably because I envied her ability to just say whatever she wanted to say.

TL: I think a lot of people envy that ability.

AR: It was a wonderful experience. It was thirty-two years! I started in—I can't remember if it was '69 or '70. And then we finished in 200[1], and I missed the last day of taping because I had the flu. Which always made me sad that I missed that.

TL: How would you describe how this show has affected you, and how that has made you the person that you are?

AR: It made me think a lot more about what most of us do naturally. Because Fred was so careful—you've heard [about] the wonderful psychologists that went over every program. Every word. There was no ad-libbing, which wasn't a problem. You learned your script and that was it, and you enjoyed learning the script.

Well, it made me into really a nationally known personality, wherever we went—not today, Tim, because you know the show hasn't been on for so long. But it's nice to have that sort of validation and recognition. It's surprising, the number of people and children who watched.

Bob Dog

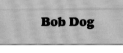

HOME: Neighborhood of Make-Believe

PERFORMED BY: Bob Trow

FIRST APPEARANCE: Episode 1072 (1970)

BOB DOG, PLAYED BY ACTOR BOB TROW dressed in a brown-and-white dog suit, was full of curiosity and excitement, and readily expressed his feelings with his signature dog howl. When he first arrived in Make-Believe, he barked and growled and had a difficult time controlling his urge to bite. King Friday XIII ordered him to go to Some Place Else, where Donkey Hodie helped him to control his growling and barking. Children trying to manage their own urges to bite could see their struggle reflected in Bob Dog's efforts to become tame.

Robert Troll

HOME: Westwood

PERFORMED BY: Bob Trow

FIRST APPEARANCE: Episode 1029 (1969)

ROBERT TROLL CAME TO MAKE-BELIEVE from Westwood in search of his friend Sara Saturday, who was responsible for taming the once-wild troll. He often greeted others with the touch of his extended index finger and the word "Doot!" Robert Troll spoke quickly and in gibberish, which could make him difficult to understand. As Queen Sara said, the best way to understand Robert Troll was to understand his feelings.

OPPOSITE: Neighbor Aber and Lady Aberlin with Robert Troll, who holds King Friday's pet birds, Mimus Polyglottos (a mockingbird) and Troglodytes Aedon (a house wren). The birds are dressed in tutus and attached to balloons after learning to do a balloon dance in Episode 1660.

SNAPPY FACT

Robert Troll's name was a play on the name Robert (Bob) Trow (see page 81), who played the part of Robert Troll. Bob Trow also played the character of Bob Dog, and it did not go unnoticed by those in the Neighborhood of Make-Believe that Robert Troll and Bob Dog had some similar features. In fact, some even found it curious that those two were never seen together in Make-Believe. That changed in Episode 1111, when both Bob Dog and Robert Troll appeared together, though the television viewers saw Bob Dog's costume only from the back.

"In my child development work, I knew that very young children, as they were learning their language, once they mastered their English, they loved playing with words. They loved to do nonsensical stuff. There's something about the tongue that likes playing with syllables. That's how Robert Troll began."

Fred Rogers

I nstead of being ruled by a king and queen, Westwood was governed by Mayor Maggie and her associate mayor, Charles R. "Neighbor" Aber. Of all the neighborhoods that bordered the Neighborhood of Make-Believe, Westwood was the most populated. Residents of Westwood were good and faithful friends to the inhabitants of Make-Believe. They hosted the Bass Violin Festival, helped with the creation of a community swimming pool, and supported the Platypus family after the fire at their Mound.

ABOVE: Mayor Maggie welcomes the Royal Family and Bob Dog to Westwood, where he and Queen Sara each used to live.

RTHWOOD

SOME PLACE ELSE

IGHBORHOOD of MAKE-BELIEVE

SOUTHWOOD

A hand-drawn map of the Neighborhood of Make-Believe and the surrounding communities that was used as a prop in Episode 1618.

Mayor Maggie

HOME: Westwood

PERSONALITY: kind, calm, capable

SPECIAL FRIEND: Neighbor Aber

TALENTS: governing, singing, using American Sign Language

PERFORMED BY: Maggie Stewart

FIRST APPEARANCE: Episode 1402 (1975)

MAYOR MAGGIE WAS THE MAYOR of Westwood. She often had meetings with King Friday to discuss community business. She was fluent in American Sign Language, and she occasionally sang and signed songs with others in Make-Believe. She was a kind and capable leader who assisted citizens all over the Neighborhood of Make-Believe.

Mayor Maggie performed in several Neighborhood operas, and she once served as Queen for a day in the Neighborhood of Make-Believe after switching roles with Queen Sara Saturday.

ORIGIN STORY: Maggie Stewart (see page 85) joined the cast as Mayor Maggie in 1975 because Fred Rogers wanted to feature a strong African American woman in a position of power.

Charles R. "Neighbor" Aber

HOME: Westwood

PERSONALITY: helpful, thoughtful

SPECIAL FRIENDS: Mayor Maggie, Daniel Striped Tiger, Prince Tuesday

TALENTS: singing, dancing, operating large vehicles

PERFORMED BY: Chuck Aber

FIRST APPEARANCE: Episode 1480 (1981)

NEIGHBOR ABER, PLAYED BY CHUCK ABER (see page 86), was a resident of Westwood, where he served as associate mayor beside Mayor Maggie. Throughout Westwood and into the Neighborhood of Make-Believe, Neighbor Aber's compassionate and helpful spirit could be seen in his relationship with all the residents, but especially with the children. He often talked with the young neighbors about their feelings, and he even provided day and night care for Prince Tuesday when King Friday and Queen Sara went away for work.

Neighbor Aber often danced throughout Make-Believe, and he was always willing to lend a helpful hand. Like Mayor Maggie, he was proficient in American Sign Language.

ORIGIN STORY: Neighbor Aber first appeared in the Neighborhood of Make-Believe as a clown delivery person during the Divorce theme week in February 1981. He told Prince Tuesday that he was divorced, and that he missed seeing his children every day.

A Neighborly Chat *with*

CHUCK ABER

Neighbor Aber

CHUCK ABER joined the *Neighborhood* in the mid-1970s by puppeteering and providing the voice for H. J. Elephant III. By the early 1980s, he became more recognizable as "Neighbor Aber," who appeared regularly in both the real Neighborhood and the Neighborhood of Make-Believe.

TIM LYBARGER: How did you find yourself working in the Neighborhood?

CHUCK ABER: During the summer of 1974, Maggie Stewart [Mayor Maggie] suggested to me that I should audition for the Odd Chair Playhouse—a summer stock theater in the Pittsburgh area. I did, and I was cast in a production of *Berlin to Broadway with Kurt Weill.* As fate would have it, Betty Aberlin was also a cast member, and Joe Negri was the music director. As a result of their participation, Fred came to see the show. Fred asked Betty to see if I would be interested in doing something on *Mister Rogers' Neighborhood,* and soon thereafter I became the puppet H. J. Elephant III. It was several years before I first appeared in the "real" Neighborhood, as a uniformed guard to deliver examples of different colors of

gold for Mister Rogers to show his television friends. Through the years, Neighbor Aber eventually became more involved in the show on a regular basis, as the associate mayor to Mayor Maggie.

TL: You mentioned that your first work on the *Neighborhood* was as the puppeteer for H. J. Elephant III. What was it like to be on-screen but not on-screen?

CA: I always tried to emulate Fred's way of bringing the puppets to life—minimal movement and very little emoting.

As far as manipulating the puppet, the only real challenge for me was turning him in the right direction when he was to address someone. Those of us who were working with the puppets had a television monitor below the set so we could see what the camera was showing and, if need be, adjust the position of the puppet. What was on the monitor was reversed from the "live" action, so sometimes those movements and positionings were a little challenging.

Also, whenever there were more than a few puppets in a scene, it got quite crowded down there behind the set, so figuring out just how to get bodies, arms, and puppets all situated and comfortable could be difficult. By the time a scene was rehearsed, however, those challenges were worked out.

TL: Who were some of the more memorable guests you recall visiting the Neighborhood?

CA: An amazing visit to the Neighborhood was by Kent Weber and Shaman—a shy and beautiful wolf. With Shaman was a small and young wolf named Little Dancing Bear who, whenever he wanted, would take Shaman's toy from him. Even though he could have easily insisted on keeping his toy, Shaman never seemed to mind the "theft" by his much smaller friend. It was also interesting to learn that Shaman required his other friend—a large-breed dog, not a wolf—to be within his eyeshot. Kent explained that as long as Shaman could see his buddy, he would be calm and

"Many times I've been told, 'We really need Mister Rogers today!'"

feel safe. Shaman had his own "comfort dog."

And it was always great fun when [children's folk singer] Ella Jenkins dropped by for a visit. She was filled with such joy and music and fun things to do. She always made Fred smile.

TL: Any fun anecdotes you remember from behind the scenes?

CA: In a week of programs titled "You and I Together," I was wearing a gorilla costume in the Neighborhood of Make-Believe. As Neighbor Aber, I wanted to see how I would be treated if I didn't look like myself. At one point, during a break, I heard the piano start the introduction to "Ya Got Trouble," one of Harold Hill's songs [from *The Music Man*]. I began to sing—or speak—the song, and when I turned to see who was playing, I saw that it was Fred! I turned back around and continued to perform. When I was about halfway through, I thought, "Wow! It's amazing that Fred knows this song by heart"—it is not at all an easy song to play. So I turned to look again and saw that Michael Moricz, the music director who

had taken over for Johnny Costa, was sitting at the piano, smiling and playing beautifully, having flawlessly taken over the piano for Fred mid-song. I must admit that all of us in the studio found it more than a little amusing to have this gorilla, Kevin Wendell Gorilla, singing, "Well, ya got trouble, my friend."

TL: Were there any characters or people you especially enjoyed interacting with?

CA: I enjoyed interacting with everyone in the Neighborhood, but I especially liked to be with Mayor Maggie, Lady Aberlin, Daniel Striped Tiger, and Bob Trow (aka Bob Dog and Robert Troll). Mayor Maggie, because we have been together for so many years that there's a comfort and familiarity that makes being with her exceptionally easy and great fun. Lady Aberlin, because her honesty, in life and performance, makes everything real. Daniel, because he represents so much of what we all think, feel, and fear. And Bob Trow, because he was one of the most clever and funny people I have ever known.

TL: What are your thoughts on the recent resurgence of *Mister Rogers' Neighborhood*?

CA: I am thrilled that so many people are celebrating *Mister Rogers' Neighborhood* and Fred's legacy. It is, I believe, a tribute to his message and timelessness that so many people have continued to seek out the *Neighborhood*. I hope that one day the programs will be more easily accessible and available on a daily schedule. I have heard the lament, too often, by parents who wish that *Mister Rogers' Neighborhood* was aired regularly on television. And at least as many times I've been told, "We really need Mister Rogers today!"

TL: Rumors have suggested that you were originally intended to be heir to the *Neighborhood* throne once Fred retired. Any truth to this?

CA: I am always flattered when someone thinks that I was to "inherit" *Mister Rogers' Neighborhood*. To my knowledge, that was never a consideration. It is a daunting and humbling thought, but like those Internet myths about Fred's having been a sniper and having tattoos, there is absolutely no truth to the rumor. Thankfully, because the programs have been preserved, Fred never has to retire.

"I must admit that, the first time I, as Neighbor Aber, was to converse with a puppet, I was somewhat self-conscious and a bit uncomfortable. Before we began rehearsing the scene, I was standing outside the castle, and up popped King Friday. It was incredible! He no sooner said, 'Charles R. Aber, I presume,' than I was entirely at ease. King Friday was so real and alive that I completely forgot that Fred was down there making him move and talk. By the time we were set to record the scene, King Friday was as real to me as Mayor Maggie, Handyman Negri, Mr. McFeely, or Lady Aberlin. Just another part of Fred's genius, I think."

Chuck Aber

H. J. ELEPHANT III (1975) was a resident of Westwood who couldn't read, but he was fluent in understanding sign language. Slightly skilled in boomerang magic, his magic words were "Oh me, oh my." H. J. Elephant III was performed by Chuck Aber and named for the late Senator H. John Heinz III, who was heir to the H. J. Heinz Company and a friend of Fred Rogers.

MR. SKUNK (1975) lived in Westwood and was known to spray when he was nervous or startled. He once sprayed Audrey Duck as she was preparing for her poetry reading at the castle. Mr. Skunk, performed by Chuck Aber, appeared in just six episodes from 1975 to 1987.

NURSE MILLER (1968), a regular character on *Misterogers* on the CBC, provided medical care and encouragement throughout the Neighborhood of Make-Believe. She worked under the direction of Dr. Frogg, and when the Frogg family moved to Westwood, she went with them. Played by actress Maxine Miller, she performed general checkups and assisted with caring for newborns, such as Prince Tuesday. She often followed her medical treatments with a song. Everyone under her care appreciated her kind personality and sincere bedside manner.

THE FROGG FAMILY (1968) included Dr. Frank Lee Frogg, Mrs. Frogg, and their son, Tadpole Frogg. Together, the Frogg family lived in the Neighborhood of Make-Believe fountain, next to the Museum-Go-Round. (In later years, the Platypus family's dirt mound replaced the fountain.) In Make-Believe, Dr. Frogg worked as the resident pediatrician, and Mrs. Frogg served as the curator of the Museum-Go-Round. The family eventually moved to Westwood so that Dr. Frogg could help out at the Westwood Children's Zoo. Mrs. Frogg, who was performed by both Fred Rogers and Hedda Sharapan, was the only member of the Frogg family to appear in episodes after 1979. Dr. Frogg and Tadpole were both voiced by Hilary Bogden.

SOME PLACE ELSE

Some Place Else was home to the Neighborhood School and a potato farm that provided all of Make-Believe with the best potatoes around. Donkey Hodie was the first to settle in this area when he sought a location for his windmill.

DONKEY HODIE (1968), who was voiced by Fred Rogers, was a *"hee-haw"* hardworking potato farmer who initially came to Make-Believe intending to build a windmill behind the castle. (In fact, Donkey's name and love of windmills are a punny nod to the famous literary character Don Quixote.) King Friday objected to the proposed location of the windmill and told Donkey to build it "someplace else." Donkey obliged and moved it to the neighborhood of Some Place Else, where he was the lone resident until the arrival of Harriett Elizabeth Cow.

ABOVE: Lady Aberlin, Lady Elaine, and special guests Bunny Rabbit and Captain Kangaroo, played by Bob Keeshan, visit Donkey Hodie at his potato farm at Some Place Else.

RIGHT: The Washer-Dryer-Sorter-Dumper helped to speed up the preparation of Donkey Hodie's potatoes after harvesting.

HARRIETT ELIZABETH COW (1973), voiced by Bob Trow, was a cow of many talents. In addition to assisting Donkey Hodie on his potato farm, she was deeply involved in the arts. She was a founding member of the Living Prose Society and played both the organ and the clarinet. She also became teacher to Ana Platypus, Daniel Striped Tiger, and Prince Tuesday when the schoolhouse was built at Some Place Else. A kind and caring cow, she often talked with the children about their fears, feelings, and concerns.

SNAPPY FACT

Harriett Elizabeth Cow was named for Fred Rogers' aunt, Harriett Elizabeth Rogers, who was also a teacher.

Southwood was home to the Templeton Jones family and their friend Keith David.

BETTY OKONAK TEMPLETON JONES (1983)

was a talkative resident of Southwood and an old schoolmate of Lady Elaine Fairchilde. She called everyone "hon." She and her husband, James Michael Jones, were married in an episode in 1984. Two years later, they adopted their daughter, Carrie Dell. Betty was voiced by the actor Michael Horton, who described her as a "feisty, babbling Southern matron."

OPPOSITE, BELOW: The Neighborhood School at Some Place Else had three students: Prince Tuesday, Daniel Striped Tiger, and Ana Platypus.

JAMES MICHAEL JONES (1985) arrived in

Southwood from Glassland and married Betty Okonak Templeton. An inventor by trade, he created many interesting gadgets, including a learning machine and a portrait that can look like anyone (also known as a mirror!). Voiced by Michael Horton, James spoke eloquently and was fond of poetry and Latin phrases. While his bride-to-be called the site of their wedding "the wedding place," he referred to it as the *sanctum sanctorum* (meaning "holy space").

KEITH DAVID (1983) was the resident carpenter

of Southwood. He was a friend and neighbor of Betty Okonak Templeton Jones and James Michael Jones, and he acted as best man in their wedding.

NORTHWOOD

Old Goat (along with the less often seen New Goat and Sue Goat) hailed from Northwood—the community responsible for establishing an effective recycling program that resolved the garbage crisis in Make-Believe. Old Goat, who first appeared in Episode 1535, made his presence known when he helped himself to X the Owl's garden vegetables. Eventually, he informed everyone in Make-Believe that Northwood had no food, and they agreed to help. When the surrounding neighborhoods faced a garbage crisis, the goats initiated recycling efforts to reduce waste. He also had an artistic side and recited a poem at the Bass Violin Festival. Michael Horton usually performed Old Goat, but Tom Megalis and Sam Newbury also performed this character on occasion.

VISITORS TO THE NEIGHBORHOOD

Characters from beyond the Neighborhood sometimes visited Make-Believe.

REARDON (1968), played by Metropolitan Opera singer John Reardon, was best known for his baritone vocals and elaborate creativity, which were both major components of the many operas performed in Make-Believe. Frequently commissioned by King Friday XIII, Reardon's operas (written and composed by Fred Rogers) were always entertaining and typically involved many of the neighbors. Reardon's abilities occasionally stretched beyond the stage, and he never hesitated to offer a helping hand. For example, when Handyman Negri attended the Scout Jamboree, Reardon took over the handyman duties at the castle. (For more on the Neighborhood operas, see pages 264–277.)

YOSHI ITO (1971) was a talented opera singer who entertained King Friday XIII and his family. When she delivered his royal plane as a representative of the International Airplane Machine Company (IAMCO, Inc.), he hired her to be his personal pilot. In addition to transporting King Friday to his desired destinations, she helped to locate the Land of Allmine and gave Purple Panda a birthday flight around the moon. She often showed kindness and care to her friends in Make-Believe, encouraging them when they had doubts and fears. She also appeared in various Neighborhood operas.

PURPLE PANDA (1973) was a friendly visitor from Planet Purple, where everything was the same: All girls were named Pauline and all boys were named Paul. Lady Elaine Fairchilde discovered Planet Purple while traveling in her spaceship to Jupiter. For a while, Lady Elaine wanted to adhere to the rules of uniformity that she found on Planet Purple, but her neighbors convinced her that they liked her unique personality. This storyline reflected young children's desire to practice being independent by imposing order on their surroundings, as well as their need to know that they are loved and capable of loving just as they are. Purple Panda was performed by several actors over the years, including David L. Nohling and Matt Meko.

Played by actor Bert Lloyd, **MR. ALLMINE** (1974) was an eccentric visitor to the Neighborhood of Make-Believe. Residing in the Land of Allmine, Mr. Allmine owned an extensive collection of objects. Before learning that you can't take something that doesn't belong to you, Mr. Allmine carried a book in which he wrote the name of any item he wanted to claim as his own. Once he even took Daniel Striped Tiger's clock home with him!

MISS EMILIE, THE POETRY LADY (1968), began visiting the Neighborhood during *The Children's Corner,* when she taught Daniel Striped Tiger his favorite poem: "Be the Best of Whatever You Are" by Douglas Malloch. Later, Miss Emilie, played by Emilie Jacobson, appeared in both the real Neighborhood and Make-Believe. Her poetry was featured in the royal wedding ceremony.

AUDREY DUCK (1971) was an occasional puppet visitor to both the real Neighborhood and Make-Believe. Audrey sometimes traveled with her puppeteer, Susan Linn (see page 98), and at other times with her lion puppet friend, Catalion.

MIME WALKER (1968), played by the actor Jewel Walker, was a visitor to Make-Believe who communicated through the art of mime. After a fire at Corney's factory, Mime Walker was the first person to visit once it had been rebuilt.

A regular character on *Misterogers* on the CBC, **DIGGER DIGORUM** (1968) was an accomplished Latin-speaking archaeologist and King Friday's teacher. For his birthday, she gave the king a magical basket that showed a performance by the Flying Zookeeni Brothers (see page 218) to those who looked inside. Played by actress Anna Haworth, Digger Digorum visited Make-Believe every so often between 1968 and 1975.

MR. ANYBODY (1968), played by actor Don Francks, was a character often seen on *Misterogers* on the CBC. He was known for taking on a variety of roles—such as a stone salesman (0098), a one-man band (1014), or a wedding officiate (1015)—based on his immediate circumstances. He was the veterinarian in the Neighborhood play "Let the Vet Get the Pet" (1110).

PRINCESS ZELDA (1989), played by actress Zelda Pulliam, first visited the Neighborhood of Make-Believe when she and Queen Sara Saturday initiated the creation of a new opera: *Josephine the Short-Neck Giraffe*. Princess Zelda played the role of the young elephant Hazel in the three-part opera (see page 277). When Prince Tuesday struggled with his parents being away from home for work, Princess Zelda comforted and encouraged him through play and song.

In Make-Believe, anything can happen—and anyone can visit!

Van Cliburn (1968)

World-famous pianist Van Cliburn visited Make-Believe several times. He once played piano for Lady Elaine in the "Van Cliburn Room" of the Museum-Go-Round, where she turned him upside down using her magic boomerang.

Tony Bennett (1975)

Lady Elaine had invited singer Tony Bennett to be on MGR-TV, but she was surprised when he showed up to the studio with a sketchpad. She'd been expecting him to sing, not to make art! But Mr. Bennett was a man of many talents. As he drew a picture with pastels, Lady Elaine was disappointed that he wasn't singing. But then she was deeply flattered when he revealed he was drawing a portrait of her. After finishing the drawing, Mr. Bennett sang "It's You I Like" and "Sometimes Isn't Always." Lady Elaine was clearly smitten and liked Mr. Bennett just the way he was, too.

Al Worden (1972)

Astronaut Al Worden, who had been the Command Module Pilot for the Apollo 15 lunar mission in 1971, visited Make-Believe several times. During one visit, he helped Lady Elaine Fairchilde jump to her pretend moon. When he asked to see her boomerang in action, she turned him upside down; he compared his inverted state with the weightlessness of real space flight.

Marcel Marceau (1973)

Marcel Marceau visited fellow-Frenchman Grandpère at the Eiffel Tower before getting into character for his pantomime performance at the castle. Marcel Marceau appeared as a guest in both the Neighborhood of Make-Believe and the real Neighborhood.

Margaret Hamilton (1975)

Actress Margaret Hamilton, known for her role as the Wicked Witch of the West in *The Wizard of Oz*, visited Make-Believe as the character Princess Margaret H. Lizard. She came to see her old college friend, King Friday XIII. She magically changed herself into Margaret Hamilton and then into Princess Margaret H. Lizard.

Classic Moment

**BIG BIRD VISITS
MAKE-BELIEVE**

Episode 1483
Original air date: June 3, 1981

› **IN EPISODE 1483,** which first aired in 1981, *Sesame Street*'s Big Bird visited the Neighborhood of Make-Believe with an entry for the King's "Draw the Neighborhood Contest." X the Owl was so excited to see his feathered friend that he wrote him a welcome poem. Meanwhile, Henrietta fretted that Big Bird was going to take her place as X's best friend. Big Bird reassured her that he was "just flying through" and could never take her place. Henrietta was so relieved that she helped X remember the lines of his poem when he forgot several of them:

OPPOSITE: Sir Thomas T. Tune, played by actor Tommy Tune, meets Lady Aberlin and Daniel in Episode 1594, which first aired in 1988. Daniel is relieved that the very tall Sir Thomas is not a mean giant, while Sir Thomas is relieved to learn that Daniel is not a wild tiger.

"We welcome you on this fine day
And hope that you will stay and stay
Because we call you the Big Bird
We hope that you have also heard
That you are really popular and nice
    and kind and all that.
The end."

"It takes a lot of people to make [our] television program. And all those people care about you. They want to make the best kind of programs they can for families like yours."

Mister Rogers, Episode 1530

In an episode that originally aired in 1972, Bob Brown manipulates a large King Friday marionette from atop the castle while Lady Elaine, Lady Aberlin, and Mr. McFeely look on.

Aerial view of the Neighborhood of Make-Believe, with a puppeteer suspended above the tree so X the Owl can appear to fly. Fred Rogers looks up from below with Henrietta Pussycat on his hand.

With its slow pace, minimalist set design, and low-tech production, *Mister Rogers' Neighborhood* appeared to be a simple television program, but it was built upon an intricate architecture. Each carefully considered component was chosen for specific reasons—all to support the well-being and healthy development of children. "It looks so effortless, and that's the way it should look," Fred once said. "But, there's a lot of effort."

Behind that effort were hundreds of people whose skills, talents, and hard work went into creating nearly nine hundred television episodes over thirty-three years. It takes a lot of people doing a lot of different things to make that much television. Viewers could see Fred, the actors, and occasionally the musicians, but so many others worked behind the scenes to make it all happen. Craftspeople and technical crews worked hands-on in the studio to build sets, create props, and run the lights, cameras, and everything else leading up to "Action!" Producers, directors, associates, assistants, and editors worked tirelessly in pre- and postproduction to prepare and finesse each episode. Employees of Family Communications, Inc., Fred's nonprofit production company, included a small, dedicated staff, each of whom played a vital role in bringing Fred Rogers' vision to life on the screen.

Some members of the staff and crew dedicated their careers to the *Neighborhood* through lengthy tenures with the program. Several of the producers and consultants who worked most closely with Fred at Family Communications, Inc., continue to consult for the organization (now called Fred Rogers Productions).

Central to Fred's life and work was the concept of "deep and simple," which he believed was "far, far more important than shallow and complicated and fancy." This philosophy guided everything about *Mister Rogers' Neighborhood,* both on-screen and off. From the precisely worded scripts and intentional camera angles, to the DIY-feel of paint-and-plywood sets and whimsical, handmade props—all of these pieces came together to create deeply meaningful television.

In many ways, the core messages of *Mister Rogers' Neighborhood* infused the actual *making* of the program. Sets and props didn't need to be fancy or expensive to be interesting or to spark imagination. Directors might have been told to consider elements of childhood development theory when plotting out camera movements. As Mister Rogers sometimes sang, Fred himself liked to take his time "to do it right." This meant he "might do a scene seven times" because he just wanted "it to be comfortable and right." On the other hand, Fred knew how important it is for children to see that everyone makes mistakes, so sometimes the mishaps weren't retaped.

The general vibe on set also aligned with the philosophies of the program. Producer Margy Whitmer remembered that people generally didn't lose their tempers on set. If Fred was frustrated or upset, he didn't yell; instead, he sat down at the piano and played out his feelings. Art crew member Leah Blackwood shared that when there were technical problems and they had to wait for it all to get sorted out, Fred might sit down at the piano and play his song "Let's Think of Something

to Do While We're Waiting," and the crew would sing along.

Fred knew that children sometimes struggle to understand how television works. He thought it was important to pull back the curtain and show them that none of what they saw on TV happened by magic. He often reminded viewers that it's people who make machines and who operate them, just as it's people who make puppets and who make them talk. Likewise, it's people who make television programs. You could also say that it was the people who made *Mister Rogers' Neighborhood* what it was.

At the end of a day of filming, rather than yell, "It's a wrap," Fred would sit at the piano and play out the cast and crew with the song heard at the close of Paramount's "The Eyes and Ears of the World" newsreels.

"The best things of life are way off stage. It's the little epiphanies of life that matter most. It's those moments when somebody will tell you, 'You know you really did help me in a way that you could have never known, just by being there and just by being you.'"

Fred Rogers

The cast and crew in the early 1970s.

People who worked on the program inside WQED's Studio A, where *Mister Rogers' Neighborhood* was filmed for more than thirty years, often noted both how serious and how fun the experience was. Director Paul Lally recalled how he and floor manager Nicky Tallo could be "as serious as heart attacks" on set. "One day we were figuring out something with Lady Elaine at the Museum-Go-Round. I said, 'Nick, look how serious we are.' You would've thought we were doing brain surgery, both of us trying to sort something out. Later on I thought to myself, 'Wait a minute. That's the whole idea!' The trick is, I have to *make* you *believe* it, and that takes work."

Journalists who spent time on the set often reported on the fun and friendly atmosphere. In the 1980s and '90s, when fifteen new episodes of the program were filmed in segments several times a year, the cast and crew would spend months apart. Coming back together on set for the next round of filming could feel like a joyful reunion. In a 1985 interview, Joe "Handyman" Negri described it this way: "I really don't know how it got this way. I guess you could say we're like a family. It's like we've all lived together in another time. We've all known each other in another life."

While not everyone who worked on the *Neighborhood* shared Fred's passion for childhood development topics, there seems to have been a shared appreciation for kindness and whimsy among everyone involved in the program. For

"There were times when my life intersected with a song Fred was singing, and tears would be coming out of my eyes at the light board, no matter how I tried to blink them back. We always believed his message, but once in a while it really 'went in.'"

Frank Warninsky, lighting director

ABOVE: Fred "clowning around" on set with Don Brockett.

OPPOSITE, ABOVE: Fred and Johnny Costa share a laugh on the set in 1992.

OPPOSITE, BELOW: Chuck Aber, Betty Aberlin, and Nick Tallo between takes in the Neighborhood of Make-Believe in 1983.

"When people work very close together to create something that they feel has value that they want to give to their audiences, they become a community. And it's a real blessing to be part of a community of givers. If your main focus happens to be the person who is going to be watching what you're going to be producing, that, to me, is the greatest thing you could ever have."

Fred Rogers

example, production crew member Joe Abeln said that he "got a kick" out of the fantastical elements in the Neighborhood of Make-Believe, and he even played a little game with himself in between scenes sometimes. "I would try to think, 'What would the puppets be thinking?'"

Fred encouraged everyone in the studio to contribute their particular talents to fulfilling his vision, and he acknowledged and appreciated them for the efforts they made. Johnny Costa told an interviewer: "I think that's what makes us almost a family. Fred knows that I have something to give that's important. And he lets me give it and I give it freely and then I'm part of it, a part of his creation. That's what makes us so tight. It's because Fred lets us give."

Hedda Sharapan, who worked closely with Fred for more than thirty-five years, said that he was "very appreciative" of all his coworkers. It was as though he could really *see* them, sometimes in ways they couldn't see themselves. She remembered sitting in a staff meeting where Fred asked for ideas for upcoming theme weeks. "It wasn't one of my strengths to think of the creative ideas he could be doing," she said. "Most of my work was explaining—to try to understand what he was doing and see how he could articulate that to be most helpful for people who might want to use it. I came out of that meeting and I thought, 'Why am I here? I'm not really helpful.'

"I came back to my office, and on my chair was some writing that I had done for him. He had written on top of this, 'Thanks, Hedda. You're a great synthesizer.' And I thought then, 'Okay. It's okay that I'm not the creative idea person here. I'm helpful in a different way. I'm helpful as a synthesizer.' We all had his written notes or comments thanking us for what we were contributing. That's how appreciative he was. He took the time to let us know or to put it in writing."

WHAT WAS IT LIKE TO WORK WITH MISTER ROGERS?

People who worked with Fred Rogers often remarked on the way he took the time to connect with them, and to recognize that they had important lives outside of work. He once sent a cameraman back to the hospital on the day his wife had given birth, even though this meant finding someone else to run the camera that day. He often reached out personally when a coworker experienced a tragedy or death. "When my dad died, Fred was up in Nantucket. He called me at my house," said Nick Tallo. "Anywhere else that you would work, somebody might send you a sympathy card or whatever. But Freddy called me and we talked for forty-five minutes."

"**I never in my life felt like I worked for Fred. I worked *with* Fred, you know, and, to me, that was a big difference.**"

Nick Tallo, floor manager

Mister Rogers spoke to viewers in the warm, conversational style of one friend talking to another. Despite the relaxed, informal tone of the program, most of it was meticulously scripted. The one exception to this was Mister Rogers' conversations with guests. For those segments, he would sometimes give the other person a general idea of the topics they'd discuss, but the interaction itself was a true conversation. But everything else on the program— be it Mister Rogers speaking directly to viewers, or characters conversing in the Neighborhood of Make-Believe—was written to be spoken verbatim. Fred knew that language is a powerful, multifaceted thing, and he conscientiously chose his words to clearly and precisely express his intended meaning.

While Fred wrote most of the scripts, there were several other scriptwriters over the

ABOVE: Producer Sam Newbury (*left*) looks on as Fred and assistant floor manager Jim Seech review changes to the teleprompter script.

OPPOSITE: An excerpt of the original outline of Fred's handwritten script for Episode 1481, which originally aired in 1981.

years, including Guy Urban, Eliot Daley, Betsy Nadas Seamans, and Paul Lally. Daley, who was also executive vice president of Family Communiciations, Inc., explained that each script "was exquisitely crafted so that nothing ever appeared on that screen that wasn't thought through for both intent and probable effect." In order to write for the program, Daley said, he "had to get all the way inside [Fred's] mind, his psyche, his soul. . . . *Mister Rogers' Neighborhood* was a relationship between Fred Rogers and a viewing child, so my challenge and my goal was to understand him with sufficient profundity, complexity, and subtlety that I could prescribe both actions and words for him that were genuine. So that meant we spent a lot of time together, talking about life in general and also collaborating around and fine-tuning what was going to go into a script."

No matter who wrote the scripts, Fred made them his own by tweaking every word and action until he deemed it just right. Fred and the writers also spent a great deal of time consulting with Dr. Margaret McFarland for her expertise on child development topics. For much of the program's run, the closing credits didn't include writers' credits because Fred didn't want children to think that someone else was putting words in his mouth.

Fred wrote his scripts the way he wrote most things: longhand, in his distinctive looping script, on yellow legal pads. He created a lot of material for the *Neighborhood* over the summers at the Crooked House, his family's vacation home on Nantucket. He'd mail the handwritten scripts to his longtime administrative assistant, Elaine Lynch, who would type them up and mail them back to him. Fred loved writing in Nantucket, and he loved the ocean: "I remember writing . . . out in the work house, right there at the lip of the sea. Ah! There's nothing better for me than being right beside the sea!"

A Neighborly Chat *with*

ELIZABETH "BETSY" NADAS SEAMANS

Writer, Actor (Mrs. McFeely)

ELIZABETH "BETSY" NADAS SEAMANS joined the *Neighborhood* in 1972, and she contributed to the series in a variety of ways. Onscreen, she played Mrs. McFeely. Behind the scenes, she was a producer and script writer. She also made short films for the program and created documentary films for Fred's prime-time PBS series *Old Friends . . . New Friends* and *Fred Rogers' Heroes*.

JENNA MCGUIGGAN: How did you become involved in *Mister Rogers' Neighborhood*?

BETSY SEAMANS: I was twenty-three years old. I had a wonderful job at a newspaper, the *Boston Herald Traveler*. And I just suddenly really wanted to write for children's television. I read about Fred, and, through my sister, found somebody who worked for him. It was an associate producer named Diana Dean, and I showed up and asked her for a job. She said, "There are no jobs," and I said, "Well, can I volunteer?" And so I ended up living in the basement of an Orthodox Jewish family's home and helping the children with their homework in the evening for my room and board.

And then during the day I would just go and do whatever I could. They taught me to edit film, and I edited film that was shown on national television within a month of my showing up there. There weren't too many people working there.

They had only been national for about a year and a half when I showed up, and the workload was really beginning to put a strain on everybody. There was lots to do. I remember being assigned to make lunch for Marcel Marceau within, again, that first magical month. Just wonderful assignments. After a while, I got a job helping out with props. I actually helped David Newell— he did props in those days. He did them for a long, long time. And then I got a job as a timer, working with the director in the studio, backpedaling segments to make sure they all fit into the half hour.

Then the really interesting thing that happened was that I heard that they were looking for scriptwriters, because Fred was writing scripts for sixty-five shows a year—thirteen full weeks each year. And he wanted help. I was a writer, even though I was a twenty-three-year-old journalist, but I was a writer and always had been one. I'd probably been in the studio for six months or so before this started bubbling to the surface. So I knew the characters, I knew the puppets, I knew Fred, and I just went home in the evenings and wrote a week of scripts. I was really determined, suddenly, to do this.

I showed them to Fred and he really liked them. He said he had been thinking that it would be good for Mr. McFeely to have a Mrs. McFeely, and he said, "Well, I'll tell you what. How about you write in Mrs. McFeely, and you'll play her?" And I'm like, "No way. I'm not an actress, and I know a lot of actors who are out of work." And he said, "I really think, for a lot of reasons, it would be good for you to do it." For me to play a sixty-five-year-old woman at age twenty-three!

So I said, "Well, I'll tell you what. You have to interview some actresses and then you can choose the one you want." I didn't know Fred well enough

then to know that he would say, "Okay, sure," having absolutely no intention of paying any attention.

By then, finding talent was one of my jobs as an associate producer, so I knew how to find actors and actresses. I rounded up three really great candidates and they went in and talked to Fred and did little bits. And he thanked me and said, "No, I choose you." Which he was going to do all along, anyway.

What I didn't understand in those days was that, the interiors of the program—like what went on in reality in his house and in Bob Trow's Workshop and Betty's Little Theater—turned out to be ad-lib; he really wanted to know the people and to know that they could get into sync with him and that they could think about kids. And I think he had come to trust me, especially after he saw my scripts. He thought I really understood the program. So it wasn't because I was a good actor at all, because I was pretty bad, but because he trusted me to work with him.

So after being there for eighteen months, or a little less than two years, I was writing for the program and I was on the program, and I was twenty-five years old.

JM: You said a lot of what happened between neighbors in Mister Rogers' real Neighborhood, his house and the other neighborhood places, was ad-libbed. In the script, was there something written that you riffed on?

BS: Yes, exactly. Those visits to the neighbors and the Neighborhood were not scripted. Maybe there were two or three lines that you had to remember to say or to point out. They were more conceptual, like, "Remember to talk about this and this and this."

The Neighborhood of Make-Believe is sort of the dream state, but a lot of the things that go on before you get to the Neighborhood of Make-Believe are feeding into that dream. There may be something that has to come up, like about being embarrassed or something, so you might say, "We're going to talk to this musician about whether they ever made a mistake in a performance or with their teacher and how they dealt with it." There were also little factual things, like, "Let's be sure to remember to say that they loved music when they were a very little child, or that they had a special teacher in school."

JM: Often it does feel like people are just talking. I think that's true even of the scripted parts.

BS: The things that were the most scripted are the things that he says to the camera. When he's alone in the house and speaks directly to the camera, that is like a poem. He has really, really worked those over. When I was writing with him, I would probably suggest some of the things he might say, just because I had to write the script from beginning to end. But that was just a sketch for him—he would blow those things out, or completely change them. And of course the Neighborhood of Make-Believe is completely scripted.

JM: What was the process for writing the program?

BS: It followed a very strict outline, which was that I was responsible for three out of the thirteen weeks, and we would do them one week at a time. So when I had a week of scripts that he and I were working on together, I would go to him with three ideas that would be sketched out. There would be a suggestion for the Neighborhood of Make-Believe, because that's the spine, really, of the program. And then suggestions for what kinds of talent might come in

or what kinds of things might happen in the house. Of the three sketches, he would choose one. He might say, "Put this one away and let's work on that next go-round, but this is the one I choose for this go-round."

And then I would really blow them out. I would write a full script for the Neighborhood of Make-Believe. I would really think through, "Okay, where should we go?" We always went somewhere—the little theater, the music shop, whatever. And, generally speaking, what might he do in the interior? And then I would go to him with that outline, and he and I would work that over.

It was very pleasant. It was extremely rigorous, but in a favorite teacher kind of way. If they're challenging you, it's not in any mean way, it's just like, "What about this? And what about that? And why did you say this? And do you think you could try that?" kind of thing. Really, more of a coach.

It was just fun. I don't remember it ever being stressful.

Maybe I was too young to know how stressful it was. I just thought it was super fun, and once we had hammered something out that he thought was pretty close, he would send me over to Margaret McFarland. She would ask me a lot of, "Do you know what young children might think?"

The one I always remember had to do with bees. "Do you know what children feel about bees and the idea of being stung and body integrity and something that enters your body that you don't want?" Of course I had no idea what she was talking about, but it was interesting to learn.

She would go over everything with me in terms of child development, and together we would think about ways to change things. It wasn't always like, "You don't understand this from a young child's point of view." Sometimes she suggested, "Oh, this is an opportunity to explore something. This would be really interesting to preschool children, in this way."

> "People have no idea the care that was lavished on every single word that was written, and on what was offered."

It was this crash course in how little children view the world. They really included me in this whole child-development world in Pittsburgh, which was wonderful. I used to go to the Arsenal Nursery School, where Erik Erikson, [Dr. Benjamin Spock], and different people had been. They had me go to nursery schools and observe young children and really think about young children, not just to be with young children.

Then I would do a big rewrite, I would take it back to Fred, and Fred would smooth it over with me. Then he would write all those intros and stuff—the opening and the close—and then Margaret would come in and work with him. The end of the story was Fred and Margaret, alone, me nowhere to be seen, and then Fred, at the very last, Fred crafting every single thing he said. When he came in the door, and especially when he left, at the end. These were really poems, arias—things that he worked over really, really hard.

JM: So many layers.

BS: People have no idea the care that was lavished on every single word that was written, and on what was offered—not just the care to not do harm, but the opportunity. "We have a chance to share this with children. We have the chance to also share this with parents"—because we knew a lot of parents were watching. It was as much an opportunity as a worry, is basically what I'm saying—to get the chance to talk about the importance of music, or to talk about the importance of feelings, or how the person that you love so much, you can really, really be mad at.

It was great for me. Imagine the chance of a lifetime, being a twenty-five-, twenty-six-, twenty-seven-year-old and getting the permission to have a very complex emotional inner life—and offering that to the world.

JM: **What are some of your favorite memories of working on the show?**

BS: My favorite memories are seeing Fred working with Betty [Aberlin] and Johnny [Costa] and David [Newell]. They are the heart of this matter, in my opinion. And Betty, Johnny, and Fred are the geniuses of the show. They were so creative and so brilliant, and there was something about the combination that was like being in the presence of jazz musicians who were riffing off of each other. Between Betty and Fred, the whole was much greater than the sum of the parts. And the same was true of Fred and Johnny—and then you put the three of them together. The three of them together were really a creative diamond. They were just fabulous. It was exciting to even be on the sideline, to get to see that happen. It was wonderful and unforgettable to anybody that was anywhere near it. It was a privilege.

In the early years, the *Neighborhood* produced sixty-five episodes annually, for thirteen full weeks of programming. Then, when production resumed in 1979 after the multi-year hiatus, the team created fewer episodes, typically making fifteen new episodes per year (for three weeks' worth of programs).

Regardless of the number of episodes being shot, the filming schedule followed the same general pattern. First, they'd film any off-site visits, such as a trip to the zoo or a doctor's office. Next, they'd go to the studio to film all of the scenes in the Neighborhood of Make-Believe. If that group of episodes included any special sets, such as Negri's Music Shop or Brockett's Bakery, those sets would go up next for filming. Then those sets would be put away to make room for the "interiors," which were all the scenes in Mister Rogers' television house. Finally, everything would be edited together to make each episode appear seamless. All in all, in those post-hiatus years, it took about one month on the set to film everything for five episodes.

Fred and the crew watched playback after shooting every scene. If Fred felt that something wasn't quite right, they'd reshoot it—it was always his decision. "I want something to be as clear as possible, and unencumbered," Fred said. "And there are some times I feel that I am clearer than others."

ABOVE: Assistant floor manager Jim Seech holds a cue card for Fred.

LEFT: Fred and staff watch the playback of a scene.

OUTTAKES AND BLOOPERS

ABOVE: Mister Rogers struggles to put up a tent.

BELOW: The cast and crew give Fred a real surprise by including a mannequin among the party guests at Mister Rogers' surprise birthday party in 1988.

Things can go wrong in any neighborhood, even for Mister Rogers. Sometimes, Fred would decide to keep mishaps in the final cut so children could see that mistakes, such as buttoning up your sweater the wrong way, happen to everyone. But sometimes things went a little bit too wrong in the Neighborhood, such as when a chimpanzee pulled apart the scenery and refused to cooperate with Mrs. McFeely, rendering that scene unusable. Or the time Mister Rogers valiantly tried again and again to put up a tent, until he laughingly pitched it across the floor in frustration. David Newell recalled how Fred would always try to make a scene work if he could: "He was such a pro that he could think to himself, 'That could be edited. Let's go on to the next line.' You could see it. I know Fred was thinking, 'Let's try to rescue this.' He was trying to make it work."

Fred was the hands and voice behind most of the puppets in the Neighborhood of Make-Believe. Those who worked with him on set considered him a master puppeteer. Not only could he seamlessly manipulate and voice two puppets at once, he imbued each one with so much personality that viewers might swear they could *see* the characters' emotions—even though most of the puppets' faces were completely static.

Then-assistant producer Hedda Sharapan—who also did the voice of the Mrs. Frogg puppet—said, "If you watch closely to see when Fred made them move, it's not like 'Punch and Judy' where with every syllable the puppet moves its head back and forth. It was just like somehow he understood at what point we needed to see Daniel move his head just slightly, or his hand. He was a genius puppeteer."

Working the puppets was physically and mentally demanding work. Puppeteers often had to kneel behind set pieces with one or both arms raised in the air, all while reading a script taped to the back of the set and looking at a small monitor that showed a reverse image of what was happening on camera. Getting the puppets' movements and positions just right could be challenging, especially if there were a number of puppets in a scene. Puppeteers had to figure out the logistics of all those bodies, arms, and puppets in a small space, as well as compensate for the left-right reversal of what they saw on the monitor.

Some of the puppet characters on *Mister Rogers' Neighborhood* originally appeared on *The Children's Corner,* Fred's earlier children's program with Josie Carey. When NBC decided to air a national version of that program, they commissioned a puppet maker in New York to create larger versions of the puppets. In a letter, Fred recounted meeting those new puppets for the first time: "I remember being 'introduced' to those puppets at a hotel not far from NBC. HRH Friday XIII's crown was much too small to begin with, but they changed that. Lady Elaine was much scarier-looking originally than she was when the NBC people had her remade. I like the NBC one better, now that I think about it."

ABOVE: Producer Sam Newbury and Fred kneel behind the set of the Museum-Go-Round.

OPPOSITE, CLOCKWISE FROM TOP LEFT: Director Paul Lally consults with Fred and Prince Tuesday's puppeteer; Bill Barker with Bill and Elsie Jean Platypus, for whom he provided the voices; Betty Aberlin, Fred, Carol Switala, and Lenny Meledandri under the school set; Michael Horton, Fred, and Lenny Meledandri watch the monitor behind the wall at the Museum-Go-Round.

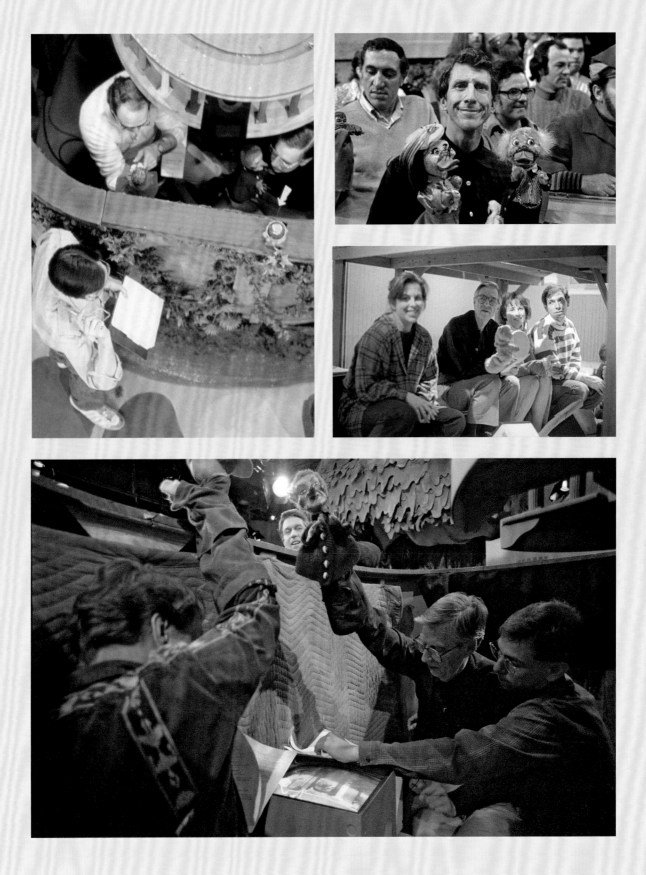

The puppets draped over the tracks in the Neighborhood of Make-Believe as art crew member James Desmone inspects Trolley.

When not on screen, the puppets "rested comfortably in a cozy cabinet in David Newell's office at WQED-TV," recalled actor Chuck Aber. "The fantastic and incredibly talented and conscientious art department for the *Neighborhood* took exceedingly good care of the family of puppets and the wonderful sets. They were always ready to fix or touch up something that needed it."

In fact, the art crew kept special emergency kits on set for quick puppet repairs. They had a kit for touching up Lady Elaine's rosy nose and cheeks, and another for X the Owl's beak. King Friday had a "crown kit" with extra jewels to replace the ones that always seemed to be falling off. And there were "whisker kits" for Daniel and Henrietta. The art crew tried a variety of materials for whiskers over the years. Weed whacker line was too thick. Fishing line could work. But the best whiskers they found were the thin plastic fasteners used to attach tags to clothing, sanded down so they wouldn't be too shiny.

THE ART CREW

The *Neighborhood* art crew was a close-knit, eclectic group of artists, builders, designers, seamstresses, and other creative folk from around Pittsburgh. "It was a wonderful group of people," said Catherine McConnell, who was the art director from 1993 to 2001. "A lot of them were artists who were trying to make a living as artists, and finding work in Pittsburgh was not always easy."

The art department was responsible for designing all of the props and sets for the *Neighborhood*. The handmade aesthetic of the program was deliberate, possibly because Fred didn't want anything to look like it had been purchased from a store. "Fred was about tape and paper," McConnell said. "We would buy things from stores and rip them apart and redo them."

CLOCKWISE FROM TOP LEFT: Art director Jack Guest; painter Leah Blackwood; artists Alexis Samulski and Terrie Godfrey; the art crew in 1995.

OPPOSITE, ABOVE: The puppets snuggled in a case.

OPPOSITE, BELOW: Associate producer Cathy Cohen Droz and prop-master David Morgan prepare Harriett Elizabeth Cow for her first day at the new school in 1979.

Props

Fred's love of whimsy sometimes led him to write story lines with props that would be difficult to make or find in those pre-Internet days—such as a fresh pumpkin in spring or a wading pool in the middle of winter. A script might include something about a "windmill flashlight" without a real explanation of what Fred envisioned. Artists usually had about six weeks to make props. Often, they'd need to make numerous prototypes for Fred, who could better describe what he wanted after seeing what he *didn't* want.

Fred had a particular love for making objects fly in the Neighborhood of Make-Believe. This presented challenges because of course everything had to be created using practical, not computer-generated, effects. There were other art challenges. How do you make cereal drift down from the sky like snow and cover Daniel's clock? How do you create a dinosaur costume for Purple Panda (a costume on a costume!) without making it look like the dinosaur is eating Purple Panda? How do you build a working waterfall and swimming pool for King Friday to swim in?

"There were times where he had no idea how difficult things were going to be when he was writing, but that was part of the challenge," said McConnell. "If he had really known what it was going to take to make them, maybe he wouldn't have put them in the scripts." But, she said, the art crew enjoyed finding ways to make his ideas come to life. "It was nice to be in this creative workshop of interesting people that got together and got to make all this crazy stuff. It was a pretty cool job."

The art department received a list of sweaters and ties Fred was going to wear each day so they could paint the props in colors that wouldn't clash or blend in with his clothing.

ABOVE: An in-progress model of Lady Elaine—a version of the puppet that would have a sturdier body for flying in her helicopter—sits next to the full Lady Elaine puppet.

LEFT: Handyman Negri and Lady Aberlin prepare for splashdown as Lady Elaine returns from her trip to Jupiter in 1972. King Friday, Dr. Bill, Elsie Jean, and Chef Brockett look on.

RIGHT: Jack Guest puts the finishing touches on the new Neighborhood School behind the scenes in Some Place Else in 1979.

ABOVE: Art director Kathryn Borland looks on as her crew installs the upside-down Eiffel Tower in the Neighborhood of Make-Believe.

OPPOSITE, BELOW: Art director Catherine McConnell recalled that one of the biggest challenges her crew faced was during the "Brave and Strong" theme week, when the script called for pieces of cereal to float down from the sky in the Neighborhood of Make-Believe and pile up like snow around the set pieces. They spent several weeks working with actual cereal, but it disintegrated too easily and Fred was unhappy with how quickly it fell. The art crew solved the problem by using foam packing material in the shape of figure eights. Each piece had to be cut in half to make two Os. Next, crew members cut each O into slivers to make many thinner Os, and then dyed them brown to look like cereal.

Sets

Maintaining the sets, especially those in the Neighborhood of Make-Believe, could be challenging. None of them had been built with the idea of lasting for more than thirty years. After decades of use and being shuffled back and forth between warehouses and studios, walls needed to be retaped or nailed back together, and everything needed to be repainted. Sometimes the art department would try to convince Fred to let them update the set pieces, like creating a new Museum-Go-Round, but he liked the old pieces with "lots of layers of paint and glue," said McConnell.

On top of that, or rather, underneath it, the colorful cobblestone walkway that wound through Make-Believe had to be painted fresh each time the set was in production. Kathy Borland, who was an art director and set designer for the last fifteen years of the *Neighborhood*, explained that it took six painters about six hours to paint the floor each time the Make-Believe set was erected in Studio A.

The homespun approach applied to Mister Rogers' house, as well. The closet door in the living room was prone to swinging open on its own. The makeshift solution was a ball of gaffer tape on the floor to keep it shut.

The set for the exterior of the McFeely house and yard, complete with Mrs. McFeely's potting station.

The instruments that filled Negri's Music Shop were on loan from the music departments of Pittsburgh colleges and music stores.

Brockett's Bakery shelves were stocked with goodies from some of Pittsburgh's finest pastry shops. The production crew has fond memories of breaking down the set and feasting on the treats.

LEFT: A view of the set for the television house, with the Neighborhood model in the foreground.

Wardrobe

Mister Rogers almost always wore the same thing: trousers, shirt and tie, and his trusty cardigans and sneakers. In early episodes, he wore sweaters with buttons, but they took too long to fasten, so he eventually switched to zippers. Occasionally he'd change into something other than a cardigan, such as a smock for making art, a tuxedo jacket for the Neighborhood variety show, or a pilot's uniform for a costume party.

The most interesting and ornate costumes usually appeared in the Neighborhood of Make-Believe, especially for the operas. There you might find people in elaborate costumes to transform them into a swan, a kitty, a porpoise, or the personification of the wind, such as when Joe Negri played the part of W. I. Norton Donovan in *Windstorm in Bubbleland*. That costume included Mylar strips attached to his arms and legs that blew wildly while he swung around on a wire. Even the puppets needed special opera costumes, such as when Daniel Striped Tiger played Tiny the Star in *A Star for Kitty* or Lady Elaine played a witch in *Key to Otherland*.

FAR LEFT: Reardon as a swan; Lady Aberlin as Betty; Mayor Maggie and François Clemmons as beavers; Mr. Allmine as Lloyd in the opera *Key to Otherland.*

LEFT: Handyman Negri, Keith David, Miss Paulificate (in bass violin costume), Mayor Maggie, and Lady Aberlin at the Bass Violin Festival that was commissioned by King Friday and held in Westwood.

BELOW: Lady Aberlin and Cousin Stephen Owl skate with Trolley nets in Episode 1682, which first aired in 1995. They needed the nets to catch Trolley, who was speeding too quickly along the tracks in Make-Believe.

The production of the program also depended on the skills and dedication of two sets of union workers employed by WQED: the engineering crew and the production crew, both of which belonged to the International Alliance of Theatrical Stage Employees (IATSE).

Members of the engineering crew were the "eyes and ears" of the program. They included camera operators, audio professionals, and videotape and editing specialists. These were the people who kept the camera steady on Mister Rogers' face and ensured that viewers could hear his quiet voice when he talked. They were the ones who expertly edited together all the segments of an episode (which were filmed out of order) and prepared the final videotapes for broadcast.

Members of the production crew were responsible for readying the studio for filming. They set up the scenery, hung lights, and ran electrical cables. Sometimes they took care of minor repairs or painting the scenery and props. During taping, the production crew became the floor crew. They worked the teleprompter, adjusted the lighting, and operated Trolley. The floor manager and assistant floor manager served as liaisons between the people on set and the director in the control booth.

Nick Tallo worked as a floor manager on the *Neighborhood* for thirty-one years. "My job was to make sure everything was going smoothly, like nobody was taking too much time getting stuff ready for something," he said. "But, basically, everybody was good at what they did, so there was very little of that." Fred, who had worked as a floor manager at NBC at the start of his career, said he considered that position to be exceedingly important. It makes a big difference, he said, "when the people around you are enthusiastic about what you're doing."

> **"Because it was a long-running show, there weren't usually a lot of new problems to solve all at once. Problems came up individually and were solved with all concerned. If costumes could help solve a lighting problem, we worked on it together. It made for quite a relaxed working environment."**
>
> **Frank Warninsky, lighting director**

SNAPPY FACT

When Fred snapped his
fingers during the song at
the end of the program,
everyone in the control
room would snap, too.

CLOCKWISE FROM LEFT: Mister Rogers snaps his fingers
after singing the lyric "snappy new day"; cameraman Bob
Vaughn; production crew in the early 1970s (*standing, from
left*): Frank Warninsky, Nick Tallo, and Joe Abeln, with (*bottom
row*) Paul Pierolo and Jim Seech; Fred and a guest watch
playback.

TELEPROMPTER
NIGHT AND DAY
CARE WEEK -
#1516 - MONDAY
INTERIOR #2
(CONT'D)

WHO MRS. BEASLEY
IS. SHE'S A DAY
CARE GIVER.

(PAUSE.)

OF COURSE, THERE
ARE MANY DIFFERENT
KINDS OF DAY CARE
HOMES OR CENTERS.
BUT ONE THING
THEY'RE ALL SUPPOSED
TO HAVE IS SOMEBODY
WHO REALLY CARES
FOR CHILDREN AND
GIVES THEM GOOD,
SAFE CARE UNTIL
THEIR MOMS OR DADS
COME FOR THEM. IN
MOST DAY CARE PLACES
THE CHILDREN GET TO
LOVE THEIR CARE-
GIVER, BUT THEY
LOVE THEIR MOTHERS
AND DADS EVEN MORE.
THAT'S WHAT MAKES
IT HARD WHEN THE
PARENTS LEAVE.

PAGE 3
#1516-MON
INTERIOR
#2
(CONT'D)

TROLLEY.

MR:
LET'S THINK OF A
TIME IN THE
NEIGHBORHOOD OF
MAKE-BELIEVE WHEN
BOTH A FATHER AND
A MOTHER HAVE TO
GO AWAY FROM HOME
TO WORK.

TROLLEY GOES.

"Fred sounds like he's just talking—but he's reading that verbatim. That stuff is carved in stone on that teleprompter. Jim Seech, the assistant floor director, was a master teleprompter operator. He could move that copy on the mirror so Fred could read it, and it just sounded perfect. Fred's success rate was 98 percent. We rarely did a retake. He really knew what he was doing." —*Paul Lally, director*

Fred's sense of humor sometimes surprised people, even those who knew him well. Writer Betsy Nadas Seamans (who also played Mrs. McFeely) recalls that while Fred himself was always a gentleman, he had a great sense of humor that allowed him to delight in others being a little mischievous.

Members of the *Neighborhood* floor crew were a fun bunch that weren't shy about playing a good prank on the unsuspecting Fred Rogers. People occasionally popped out of the closet to surprise him when he went to hang up his sweater. There was the time they switched out Fred's shoes for similar ones a few sizes too small, leading Fred to crack up laughing in the middle of singing "It's Such a Good Feeling." There was Michael Douglas (later he'd change his name to Michael Keaton), who had the job of catching the film reels that Mister Rogers fed into the wall for Picture-Picture. One time, as Fred slid back the little door in the wall, Michael intoned, "I'm ready to hear your confession, son." Fred burst out laughing. And then there was Nick Tallo, a certified mischief-maker if ever there was one, who took a picture of his bare bottom with one of Fred's cameras. Nick recalls that even after Fred had gotten the film developed, he never said a word about it. But months later, Fred gifted Nick a large framed poster of that exact photo, turning the tables on the roles of prankster and "butt" of the joke.

Lighting director Frank Warninsky rises from behind the Neighborhood model.

THE FLYING ZOOKEENI BROTHERS

On a program brimming with whimsy, one short-lived segment in the Neighborhood of Make-Believe still stands out to fans as especially wonderful and wacky: the Flying Zookeeni Brothers' Daredevil Circus. Originally dreamed up as a joke among members of the floor crew, the Zookeeni Brothers appeared in Episodes 1449 and 1450, which first aired in May 1975. Their performance, a series of spoofs on acrobatic feats using chairs and large wooden blocks, was presented as a special birthday gift to King Friday, which he viewed by looking into Digger Digorum's magic basket.

The troupe, outlandishly outfitted in T-shirts, spandex shorts, and brightly colored tights and capes, consisted of crew members Nick Tallo, Frank Warninsky, Jim Seech, Joe Abeln, and Michael Douglas (Keaton). The group performed alongside the All-American All-Star One-Man-Band, played by crew member David M. Smith, who accompanied the not-so-death-defying acts with his snare drum, cymbal, and kazoo. Peaches and Cream (played by Mary Rawson, who portrayed Cousin Mary

Owl in the Neighborhood of Make-Believe, and Carol Stewart) also helped to highlight the action.

In a 2016 interview, David M. Smith mentioned that the Zookeeni Brothers were not just a one-and-done performance. Their "guerilla circus" performed around Pittsburgh and occasionally included other characters, such as Bronco Cody (played by Smith) as well as the Casserole Sisters: Tuna and Noodle.

Fred and Nick Tallo pose on Mrs. McFeely's motorcycle between takes in 1972.

CLOCKWISE FROM BOTTOM LEFT: Nick Tallo, Mary Rawson, Joe Abeln, David Smith, Michael Douglas (Keaton), and Frank Warninsky.

"I have the most wonderful floor manager in the world: Nicky Tallo. He has an advanced sense of humor. He and Jimmy Seech and [Michael Douglas], those three on the set—we just had a ball. They were just always playing jokes on me."

Fred Rogers

Classic Moment

Episode 1530
Original air date: April 8, 1984

› **MISTER ROGERS WAS** always intentional when it came to answering the many questions that might be running through the minds of his young viewers. In this episode, he offered full transparency as he talked about his job, which was to make television programs. Mister Rogers invited viewers to join him as the camera panned out to reveal that his house was actually a set in a television studio, complete with cameras, crew, and live musicians. He even offered a look at the model neighborhood seen during the program's opening and closing segments.

When asked why he wanted to reveal the behind-the-scenes of the television program to his viewers, Fred said, "People love honesty. They like to be in touch with those who are honest and real."

"The people I work with in this studio are people who know how to make cameras work, and make lights work, and people who know how to play music."

Fred Rogers

A Neighborly Chat *with*

PAUL LALLY

Director

"Fred was not an actor. He was a be-er. He could be who he was. Leave him alone and he would be fine."

An accomplished television producer, director, and writer, PAUL LALLY directed more than one hundred episodes of *Mister Rogers' Neighborhood* from 1982 to 1989. He also earned a writing credit on several episodes.

JENNA MCGUIGGAN: How did you start working on the program?

PAUL LALLY: I answered a tiny ad in *Broadcasting* magazine, about one and a half inches by half an inch. It said: "Wanted. Director for children's television program." That was it. I got the job for two reasons. One, I had about ten years under my belt with television production and children's stuff, and also because I'm a writer, and they were expanding at the time to do some more writing other than just the *Neighborhood*. They hired me as a writer and predominantly as a director.

JM: What was the production schedule like?

PL: Just imagine a ninety-day cycle. In that three-month cycle you would produce five complete television programs from beginning to end, and you just spread that out like butter on toast. You begin with the scripts and then you'd shoot the location pieces, both the ones we filmed with Fred and then the ones we did—like Picture-Picture things—without Fred. (I would write that kind of copy—how people make bicycle helmets or something like that.) Then we'd edit them to time. Constantly we were trying to obey the twenty-six minutes-and-forty-six-seconds runtime, which was pretty sacred back then. You couldn't even be over by a frame. Very tight.

By then you're about six weeks into the sequence, like a month and a half. Then we go into studio production. We'd do the Neighborhood of Make-Believe first. That would be, basically, a week, and then another week with his house—"Fred's interiors" is what we called them.

By now we're two months into it, and we have maybe four weeks left, which is all postproduction. We had an editor who would then start assembling the shows.

"I think the details are why this show worked so well, because they were so well attended to and then hidden."

It's editing and it's taking all the shows, sticking them together. Fred's screening them, making changes, et cetera. Then we do the postproduction with music, with Johnny Costa. We go to a recording studio and Johnny would bring in the trio for the Neighborhood of Make-Believe music—Johnny was there, always, but we didn't have drums or bass while we were filming the Neighborhood of Make-Believe. We figured that all out later.

You have to connect all the dots so that it flows. The whole point is that once Fred walked in the door, he stayed with you for twenty-six minutes and forty-six seconds. That's a big deal for me as a director—a sense of continuity. All the editorial decisions had to match that flow. The overall feel when you stitched it together would be seamless. John Gardner, who was a very famous writer, instructor, and novelist, said your objective in writing is to get somebody to enter a vivid and intense dream, and when it's done, they need to wake up. If they wake up anywhere in the middle, that's because you screwed up.

You used the wrong adjective, a clunky sentence structure. Whatever it is, they woke up, and shame on you. I carried that into the *Neighborhood*.

JM: When I watch these episodes now, as an adult, I'm just so impressed with how seamless it all is. It's really interesting to hear it from your point of view as the director.

PL: I think the details are why this show worked so well, because they were so well attended to and then hidden. When I wrote, it looked on the surface like one thing, but underneath . . . I'll give you a good example. I'd written a script about economics for kids. I would meet with Margaret [McFarland] and talk about the shows I was writing. She'd put her arm behind her, in the small of her back, and sit there, very erect like a ballet dancer sits: "Supply and demand, for a child, is toilet training. They have it and the parent wants it." Can you imagine? She's intuiting what a kid thinks. I, as a writer, and Fred did this, too, had to take that psychological insight and layer it

up artistically and hide it from a child. You and I as adults get it, but for a child, it has to be more symbolic.

So we have Fred playing in the sandbox. He pours water in it and then the water escapes and he stops it from going out. He's demonstrating control as a child might have over his [body functions]. Now, this is serious business here. That's what we did. He's modeling that it's possible to control certain bodily functions, but he's showing you also that it's gonna escape. He's showing you that you can stop it sometimes, but sometimes you can't. And kids are responding to that at a primal level. That makes sense to them.

Fred, obviously, was a master at taking a concept and really making it poetic, and you had to be a safecracker to see what was underneath it. I took pride in that. I would write and go half in a trance to try to find that symbolic thing.

JM: Did you make any special considerations in filming for children?

PL: Fred said, "I have the paint, you have a canvas. Paint." It was very helpful for me to hear that, and it's that simple.

I directed very simply. I believed, and I still do, that I was teaching a five-year-old film grammar. If you and I are watching a show and it's a wide shot, and then we cut to a close-up, as an adult, you'll follow it. But you do this for a kid, and the kid says, "What happened? I was on a street corner, now it's a face. Did we go somewhere?" So I would walk-in my shots. If it was a three-shot, I'd go to a two, then over the shoulder, then a close-up, then back in over the shoulder. I'd walk in and walk out, and it was always only two cameras. I really just enforced that discipline.

The closest I ever would get to Fred was just the bottom of his rib cage and up—it's social distance. He's at the fish tank, that's important talk, so [camera operator] Bobby Vaughn would really creep in, but never any tighter than that. Fred and I talked about this: The only people you see in extreme close-up in your life are your lover or your mother. He said, if it's your mother, it's when she's breastfeeding you. That intense closeness of a face—you associate that closeness with love. I would feed all that into my head as a director and it helped me understand why not to do heedless close-ups.

JM: How did you approach filming the puppets in the Neighborhood of Make-Believe?

PL: Fred told me one time, "With Betty, you're looking at her belief in that puppet—not the puppet." Once I heard that, man, it was like gold. I'd have a big important scene with Betty at the clock, because she was often the pivot in a lot of these emotional moments. I would never take a close-up of Daniel on a key line. Instead, you're watching Betty react to him. You see her belief in the puppet, and it's fabulous. Works every time.

I can remember standing there watching playback of scenes with Betty and Daniel. If we liked it, we'd go on. If not, we'd do it again. We rarely did it again. I would stand there and kind of take a sly look left and right at people gathering around the monitor, and people were just a little hypnotized at the scene. Hypnotized at Betty and Fred's performance with that little puppet—and, I'd like to say, the way I staged it visually. They didn't wake up out of that mini dream for maybe two and a half minutes, and when it would end, there would be that little beat of silence. I'd look at Fred and he'd give me a nod, or a little look, or we'd smile.

JM: What was directing Fred like?

PL: If I told Fred to come in and go to the left—like a director—he would turn into one of those nutcracker soldiers. He'd be useless. He was following somebody else's orders, and he just couldn't. He wanted to be so good at it that he'd just turn into a stick man. I always said to myself, "Why do I tell this guy to do anything?" I would feel terrible.

JM: How did you get around it?

PL: Well, we would do it again, but the next time we did it, I'd keep my mouth shut and he'd find his point. You know, I just said, "You need to slow down." I had to set it up—to direct it in a way that I wasn't directing. Sort of talking to him, saying, "Come on over here," and letting him figure it out. It's just very subtle stuff, to avoid the sense of it feeling forced. Fred was not an actor. He was a be-er. He could be who he was. Leave him alone and he would be fine.

Sometimes Fred needed what I used to call "the bottom of the pool." He needed to push off from something, so he could find out how to work it out. Mostly I'm talking about blocking—moving from A to B. He'd need to see it wrong before he could see the right way.

That said, when Mister Rogers would get ready to leave, he'd have to get his coat on. He'd stand up by the door. We were giving him a countdown—you'd generally count from five minutes, three, two, one, thirty seconds, fifteen . . . By the time he got his coat on, he might have something like forty seconds left, but no one ever worried [about extra time] because Fred would just stand there at the door and go into what I thought of as

his Book of Psalms. He had all these different things he could talk about. "There's no one in the world exactly like you . . ." "All the things that you and I talked about . . ." Those were in his quiver, and he'd just load one awesome arrow after another to fill time. Till he'd finally say, "See you next time." Out the door. Boom. To watch him do it was just genius.

JM: What was it like to work with Johnny Costa, and to see him and Fred working together?

PL: They had kind of a symbiotic relationship. Fred had the composition skill, and Johnny had the arranging skill. He could take Fred's melodic theme and embroider it and make it wonderful—show him sixteen different ways to do one thing.

Fred would bring out the best in Johnny, and Johnny would just deliver. He was remarkable to watch. There's a lot of shorthand going on between them after all that time, where they could solve a musical issue in two seconds. Fred would come bounding out of the set and go over to the piano with Johnny. Everybody would take a little quick breather, they would figure it out, and boom, back he'd go.

There was very much a sense of equality. If you'd have been

there then, Fred would treat you exactly the same way that he treated me, and the way he treated Johnny, and vice versa. I've learned that from him.

JM: What was the general mood on the set like?

PL: I can say this because I couldn't participate, because I was directing. But everybody there (other than me) had a fabulous time, because they were getting together again. It was like a party. That feeling before we would tape would be like people showing up for a surprise party for Fred. It was pure anticipation. And everybody knew everybody. They hadn't been together for three months, or sometimes half a year. There would be just that collegial atmosphere. I was really envious—I was directing, so I had to hit all my marks. But I got to see everybody being happy and it felt terrific just to bear witness. In the ten years that I was there, I got to witness some wonderful human interchanges—honest and happy and loving—and I've been able to carry that forward into my career. I brought all those qualities to other television studios and friends. I carry that little message from the *Neighborhood* to my own neighborhood.

"There's something very mystical and wonderful about how music can touch us. It's elemental."

Fred Rogers

Johnny Costa and Fred Rogers share a moment behind the scenes.

That's What I Sing About

5

**THE MUSIC AND
ITS MESSAGES**

*I*t's a beautiful day in this neighborhood . . ."
From its first tinkling, gliding notes,
the joyful melody of "Won't You Be My
Neighbor?" instantly transports millions
of viewers back to their childhood visits
with Mister Rogers. The song opened almost
nine hundred episodes of *Mister Rogers'*
Neighborhood, and it has become synonymous
with Fred Rogers' inclusive message.

But the music didn't stop at the opening credits. Fred Rogers was a lifelong musician, having learned how to play the piano before he was five years old. Many considered him to be a piano prodigy. In 1951, he received a bachelor's degree in music composition from Rollins College in Winter Park, Florida. Three years later, in 1954, many of the melodies that are now pop culture classics began to take shape on *The Children's Corner*. Over the course of his career, Fred would write the melodies and lyrics for more than two hundred songs.

The significance of music in the *Neighborhood* extended far beyond the songs that Mister Rogers sang. The whole program was steeped in music, thanks in large part to noted jazz pianist Johnny Costa, who served as musical director for more than twenty-five years. The Costa Trio, with Johnny on piano, Bob Rawsthorne on percussion, and Carl McVicker, Jr., on bass, played the music live in the studio during taping, adding a layer of both sophistication and intimacy to the program's musical texture.

The music, often improvised, was like a conversation between Fred and Johnny. Fred said he and Johnny seemed to communicate intuitively through their shared love and understanding of music. Johnny agreed: "I watch Fred, and there must be some kind of telepathy that we're not aware of, because somehow I get the message to play or not to play. I'm sure that some of it has to do with working together all these years, but a lot of it is unexplainable."

Over the decades, Mister Rogers introduced his television friends to a wide variety of musical styles and players. He loved to welcome world-renowned musicians to the *Neighborhood*. "Yo-Yo Ma and Van Cliburn and Itzhak Perlman—all of these people who have come and given their talents so generously on the program," Fred once said. "It delights me to be able to offer that to children. And I hope they delight in receiving it."

Even the *Neighborhood* cast itself was well stocked with incredible musical talent, including jazz guitarist Joe Negri and opera singers François Clemmons, Yoshi Ito, and John Reardon. Cast regulars Betty Aberlin, Maggie Stewart, and Chuck Aber, along with puppeteer Michael Horton, were also trained and accomplished singers. Fred even coaxed David Newell, who played Mr. McFeely and insisted that he "couldn't sing," into singing the "Speedy Delivery" song on occasion. Everyone was encouraged to share their voice.

With its relatable melodies, sophisticated jazz arrangements, honest lyrics, and diversity of voices, *Mister Rogers' Neighborhood* just wouldn't have been the same without the music.

"A SINGING PSYCHIATRIST FOR CHILDREN!"

First and foremost, Fred Rogers considered himself a musician and composer. It makes sense, then, that he used music in so many different ways throughout the *Neighborhood*. Children's programming advocate Peggy Charon called Mister Rogers a "singing psychiatrist for children." Indeed, his songs provided encouragement and life lessons that range from the everyday to the profound. He assured viewers that they could never go down the bathtub drain, and he reassured them that it's okay to wonder and marvel at the world around them. His songs taught children what to do with "the mad" they feel, and encouraged them to be brave and strong. In every episode, he used his songs to solidify the program's core messages in the hearts and minds of all who heard them.

Viewers also saw how people use music to express feelings in healthy ways. Mister Rogers and his musical guests often demonstrated how they used their instruments to convey emotions: to celebrate good feelings, to calm down, or to release anger.

From a young age, music was Fred's way of saying who he was and how he felt. "I was always able to cry or laugh or say I was angry through the tips of my fingers," he said. "I would go to the piano, even when I was five years old, and start to play how I felt."

Fred continued to express his emotions through music as an adult. Fred's coworkers remember how he would retreat to the piano on set to play out his feelings in between filming. David Newell recalled, "When it was a tough day, and the camera went down, or something happened, and we had to wait and wait and wait, Fred would sit down and start playing the piano. You knew Fred was working through his anxiety or his frustrations by sitting down at the piano. He would play 'Misty' a lot. Maybe cuttings from a classical piece or something. Fred loving music so much is what kept him involved. It kept him going on days that he probably was tired. The music meant a lot to him."

OPPOSITE: Mister Rogers observes the musical notations for "Many Ways to Say I Love You."

PREVIOUS PAGES: Mister Rogers watches Johnny Costa play the piano at Negri's Music Shop.

MISTER ROGERS' GREATEST HITS

"Won't You Be My Neighbor?"

"It's You I Like"

"You Are Special"

"What Do You Do with the Mad That You Feel?"

"I Like to Take My Time"

"I'm Proud of You"

"I Like to Be Told"

"Good Feeling"

"Did You Know?"

"You've Got to Do It"

"I'm Taking Care of You"

"You Can Never Go Down the Drain"

"All these songs are really songs about how we feel about ourselves. How children feel about themselves is what I care about most. If we can help our children feel accepted and valued when they are small, they'll have a better chance of growing into adults who can feel good about who they are, too."

Fred Rogers

"It has a musical grid, this neighborhood. It's sort of the heartbeat of it all."

Fred Rogers

Fred Rogers' original composition for "Won't You Be My Neighbor?" (here called "Be My Neighbor?"), which he wrote in July 1963 at his summer home in Nantucket. The song would become the iconic opening theme for the duration of *Mister Rogers' Neighborhood*.

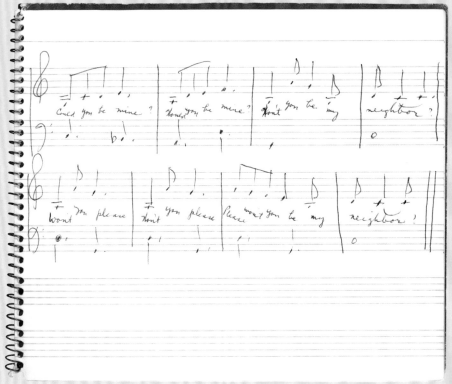

Fred intended for the *Neighborhood* to be watched by children with their parents or caretakers so they could learn and grow together. "Parents don't come full bloom at the birth of their first baby," Fred said. "In fact, parenting is about growing. It's about our own growing as much as it is about our children's growing, and that kind of growing happens little by little."

Every scene, story, and song in the *Neighborhood* was chosen and arranged to support the healthy growth and development of children. Fred built the program around deep and simple messages of love, kindness, peace, and

> ## "Deep and simple are far more important than shallow and complicated."
>
> **Fred Rogers**

respect. These philosophies wove so seamlessly throughout each episode that they were both integral and invisible. They formed the foundation of the program, yet they never came across as intrusive or preachy.

"SOMETIMES I WONDER IF I'M A MISTAKE"

Daniel Tiger's song for "MAKING MISTAKES"   (WEDNESDAY)

~~Sometimes~~ Often I wonder if I'm a mistake
I'm not like anyone else I know
When I'm asleep or even awake
I get to dreaming that I'm just a fake
I'm not like anyone else

Others I know are big and are wild
I'm very small and quite tame
Most of the time I'm weak and I'm mild
Don't you suppose that's a shame?

~~Sometimes~~ Often I wonder if I'm a mistake
I'm not supposed to be scared am I
Sometimes I cry and sometimes I shake
Isn't it true that the strong never break?
I'm not like anyone else I know
I'm not like anyone else

ABOVE: Fred's handwritten lyrics for "Sometimes I Wonder If I'm a Mistake," which Daniel sang to Lady Aberlin in a tender moment during Episode 1578 (originally aired in 1987). Lady Aberlin chimed in with a countermelody, assuring Daniel that he was not a mistake, and the songs combined to become a duet.

Just the Way You Are

IT'S YOU I LIKE

It's you I like,
It's not the things you wear,
It's not the way you do your hair,
But it's you I like.
The way you are right now,
The way down deep inside you.
Not the things that hide you,
Not your toys,
They're just beside you.

But it's you I like.
Every part of you.
Your skin, your eyes, your feelings
Whether old or new.
I hope that you'll remember,
Even when you're feeling blue.
That it's you I like,
It's you yourself
It's you.
It's you I like.

"The greatest thing we can do is to help somebody know that they are loved and capable of loving."

Fred Rogers

OPPOSITE: Handwritten lyrics for "It's You I Like," composed by Fred Rogers in 1971.

MISTER ROGERS OFTEN SAID, "I like you just the way you are." He told children they are loved and capable of loving. In some cases, Mister Rogers may have been the only adult in a child's life offering them this expression of care. For other children, his words were a reaffirmation of their self-worth.

Fred often talked about looking for the "essential invisible" parts of people. Those who knew him commented on his profound ability to discover the thing they were most proud of and shine a light on it. This was another essential part of Mister Rogers' message, which he sometimes expressed in a song: "I'm proud of you / I'm proud of you / I hope that you're as proud as I am." He knew that feelings of pride go much deeper when children own those feelings for themselves.

Mister Rogers helped children to feel good about who they are, but this was a message that went so much deeper than shallow, feel-good sentiment. Mister Rogers communicated to children that each of them was special because there was no one else in the whole world just like them. He wanted children to know that they had value—and so did everyone else.

It's you I like
It's not the things you wear
It's not the way you do your hair
But it's you I like

The way you are right now
The way down deep inside you
Not the things that hide you
Not your toys —
They're just beside you

It's you I like
Every part of you
Your skin, your eyes, your feelings
Whether old or new

I hope that you'll remember
Even when you're blue
That it's you I like
It's you yourself
It's you
It's you I like

EVERYBODY'S FANCY

Some are fancy on the outside.
Some are fancy on the inside.
Everybody's fancy.
Everybody's fine.
Your body's fancy and so is mine.

"You can be an agent of what's good and not have to be terribly direct about it. We have a song on the *Neighborhood* that says, 'There are many ways to say I love you . . .' And there are. And one of the ways is working as well as you can to bring to others what you feel can be nourishing in their lives. It's an offering of love, what we do."

Fred Rogers

Mister Rogers' Neighborhood was an inclusive community where *everyone* was welcomed and appreciated for who they were, regardless of gender, race, nationality, or physical characteristics. Mister Rogers celebrated people's unique skills and personalities, always emphasizing that everyone is valuable, just as they are.

The cast of the program reflected this ethos. Characters such as Officer Clemmons and Mayor Maggie showed viewers African Americans and women in positions of power at a time when societal barriers against women and minorities were pervasive and obvious. In many ways, Mister Rogers was a champion of diversity, and the *Neighborhood* was the first program for children to address these cultural issues through its content.

Mister Rogers also addressed the questions children have about disabilities through matter-of-fact discussions during visits from friends, including series regulars like the McFeelys' television granddaughter Chrissy Thompson, who wore leg braces and used crutches due to spina bifida, and guests like saxophone player Eric Kloss, who is blind. By exemplifying warm relationships with people who look and move in different ways, Mister Rogers showed viewers that *everyone* was included in his Neighborhood and was worthy of love and respect.

ABOVE, CLOCKWISE FROM TOP: Jay Styperk leads Mister Rogers in some exercises; Chrissy Thompson, who played the character of the McFeelys' granddaughter, stops by for a visit in 1985; regular guest Eric Kloss, Betty Aberlin, and Mister Rogers played music together in the Luray Caverns.

"Beside my chair is a saying in French. It inspires me every day. It's a sentence from Saint-Exupéry's *The Little Prince*: 'What is essential is invisible to the eye.' The closer we get to know the truth of that sentence, the closer I feel we get to wisdom. That which has real value in life in any millennium is very simple. Very deep and very simple! It happens inside of us— in the 'essential invisible' part of us, and that is what allows everyone to be a potential neighbor."

Fred Rogers

Mister Rogers and Chrissy Thompson connect on the front porch.

Classic Moment

MEETING JEFF ERLANGER

Episode 1478
Original air date: February 18, 1981

› **IN A LARGELY UNSCRIPTED** segment, a young boy named Jeff Erlanger visited Mister Rogers. Jeff used an electric wheelchair because of a spinal tumor that doctors weren't able to fully remove when he was a baby. After explaining this to Mister Rogers, Jeff joined him in singing "It's You I Like." True to the nature of the *Neighborhood,* Mister Rogers gave all his attention to Jeff as the two of them sang together.

"When we started production that morning, Fred said let's do this one without rehearsal, which was quite uncommon. And when Fred and Jeff sang the song 'It's You I Like' together, and Jeff spontaneously joined Fred—remember, this scene was totally unscripted and unrehearsed or even discussed—it was magical."

Cathy Cohen Droz, director of special projects, Fred Rogers Productions

> ## "Play is often talked about as if it were a relief from serious learning, but for children, play *is* serious learning."
>
> **Fred Rogers**

PRETENDING

**You can try out many things by
  pretending.
Your own makeup play can be
  different every day,
But it's your work, it's important,
  pretend.
You can try out life by pretending.
You can even say you're a baby today
By pretending, pretending.**

Fred considered play to be the "work of childhood" and made it a key component of *Mister Rogers' Neighborhood*. Children are not in charge of much in their lives. The grown-ups are. Play gives children a sense of having some power because they are in control when they play. That helps them let the adults be in charge at other times. When they play and pretend, they are also more open to taking in information for learning.

Besides that, when they play with their friends, they learn how to solve conflicts and get along with others. Playing about scary things even helps children to be braver about those things, because it's like having a rehearsal for their feelings in a safe space.

Mister Rogers' whimsical joy and childlike curiosity guided so much of the play he modeled for viewers, from drawing a picture in the kitchen to building with blocks on the floor. His commitment to playing and learning, even as an adult, kept him open to trying new things, such as break dancing, juggling, and roller-skating. Best of all, play, to Mister Rogers, did not involve the newest and fanciest toys. A block of wood could be a toy truck, a bath towel could become an elephant costume, and a cardboard box could become a television set. All it took was an imagination!

IT'S ALL RIGHT TO WONDER

Did you know when you wonder
   you're learning?
Did you know when you marvel you're
   learning?
About all kinds of wonderful,
All kinds of marvelous,
Marvelously wonderful things?

"The best things in life
are the things that you
can't buy and you can't
even plan for."

———

Fred Rogers

Mister Rogers wanted to help children develop the tools they would need for learning, including permission to wonder, to ask questions, and to try new things. A reporter once asked Fred why he didn't spend more time teaching children "letters and numbers." Fred replied, "I would rather give them the tools for learning. If we give them the tools, they'll want to learn the facts. More importantly, they'll use the facts to build and not to destroy."

Neighborhood viewers also saw that mistakes are a natural part of learning. Mister Rogers let children see him trying new things, even when those things were difficult, such as quick hand motions to a song, juggling, or Chinese calligraphy. Mister Rogers showed children that everyone, adults and children, make mistakes as they learn new things.

I LIKE TO TAKE MY TIME

I like to take my time
I mean that when I want to do a thing
I like to take my time and do it right.
I mean I might just make mistakes
If I should have to hurry up and so
I like to take my time

Unlike most children's programming, the pacing of *Mister Rogers' Neighborhood* was deliberately slow and steady. Each television visit was designed to resemble the flow of real life, with time to think or complete simple tasks. Mister Rogers allowed things to take as long as they needed to take. He also allowed moments of silence to stretch out, with no rush to fill the quiet with unnecessary words or actions. Sometimes he slowed the pace down even further, like when he took a long moment to look at the petals of a flower, or when he set a timer and sat quietly until it went off a whole minute later. There were no quick cuts or jarring transitions. The camera was allowed to linger on a scene, an object, or a person's face. Everything flowed smoothly and seamlessly. Even lively, lighthearted moments felt grounded and mindful. This made the program an oasis of calm for children and their parents.

In Episode 1697, Mister Rogers asks viewers to take a long, careful look at an African violet, and the camera stays fixed on the flower for twenty-five seconds—a far cry from the fast cuts of other children's television programs.

I LIKE TO BE TOLD

I like to be told
If it's going to hurt,
If it's going to be hard,
If it's not going to hurt.
I like to be told.
I like to be told.

Mister Rogers recognized that many things young children do or encounter are new experiences, so he spent time on the program helping to prepare them; a trip to the doctor can be overwhelming, but so can a trip to the grocery store. Facts that are obvious to adults (like knowing you can never be sucked down the bathtub drain) are still mysteries to young minds. Mister Rogers understood that everyday life is full of new and sometimes potentially frightening situations for children. By talking about these things openly and explaining them in a simple, straightforward way, he showed his viewers he respected their feelings. He knew that including children in the discussion of such things helps them to feel safe. Knowing what will happen ahead of time can help to put children at ease, and help them to understand the world around them. By helping children to prepare for new experiences, he also gave them the opportunity to be proud of themselves when they faced new things with knowledge and courage.

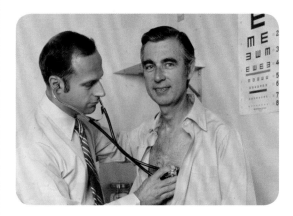

ABOVE: Mister Rogers shows children that haircuts don't hurt.

RIGHT: To help children know what to expect during a doctor's visit, Mister Rogers shows a typical medical exam.

"YOU'VE GOT TO DO IT"

Mister Rogers showed that people learn by doing. Whether it's playing an instrument, painting a picture, or putting on a play, developing a talent requires both imagination and action. "Imagining something may be the first step in making it happen," Fred wrote, "but it takes the real time and real efforts of real people to learn things, make things, turn thoughts into deeds or visions into inventions."

Some things I don't understand.
Some things are scary and sad.
Sometimes I even get bad when
    I'm mad.
Sometimes I even get glad.

Why does a dog have to bark?
Why does an elephant die?
Why can't we play all the time in
    the park?
Why can't my pussycat fly?

Why, why, why, why, why, why
I wonder why.
Why, why, why, why, why, why
I wonder why.

"I do think that the children trust me. If something's going to hurt, I'll tell them. And if it's not going to hurt, I'll tell them."

————

Fred Rogers

Mister Rogers talked honestly about difficult subjects. Just as he helped children to understand new experiences and to deal with their emotions, he helped them think about tough topics such as adoption, death, divorce, moving, and other potentially traumatic events. Even though he simplified things so that young minds could grasp them, he never sugarcoated hard truths or lied. "People long to be in touch with honesty," Fred often said in interviews. Committed to respecting everyone, no matter their age, he was also honest with viewers that some things are hard to understand; not every question has an answer. But talking about hard things can make them more manageable.

MISTER ROGERS TALKS WITH PARENTS

Mister Rogers produced several special programs to help adults talk with children about difficult topics. Some of these specials covered commonplace situations, such as dealing with competition, going to school, or even divorce. In 1968, Mister Rogers presented a very special evening program to help parents talk to and comfort children after the assassination of Robert F. Kennedy. Fred had stayed up all night writing the program, and it aired the day before the funeral. In the Neighborhood of Make-Believe, Daniel Striped Tiger told Lady Aberlin he'd heard the word "assassination" and wondered what it meant. After thinking about it for a moment, she explained that it means "somebody getting killed in a sort of surprise way."

Classic Moment

DEATH OF A GOLDFISH

Episode 1101
Original air date: March 23, 1970

› **IN THIS 1970 EPISODE,** Mister Rogers finds that one of his fish has died. While burying the fish in the yard, he talks with viewers about the feelings that come with such loss, and the importance of talking about those feelings.

"When I was very young, I had a dog that I loved very much. Her name was Mitzi. And she got to be old, and she died. I was very sad when she died, because she and I were good pals. And when she died, I cried. My grandmother heard me crying, I remember, and she came and just put her arms around me, because she knew I was sad. She knew how much I loved that dog."

WHAT DO YOU DO WITH THE MAD THAT YOU FEEL?

What do you do with the mad that you feel
When you feel so mad you could bite?
When the whole wide world seems oh,
   so wrong
And nothing you do seems very right?

What do you do? Do you punch a bag?
Do you pound some clay or some dough?
Do you round up friends for a game of tag?
Or see how fast you go?

It's great to be able to stop
When you've planned a thing that's wrong,
And be able to do something else instead
And think this song.

ABOVE: Fred Rogers in a pensive moment off camera.

ABOVE RIGHT: Mister Rogers showed viewers how he expressed his feelings through music.

Mister Rogers showed that feelings are a natural part of life, and that it's okay to feel angry, sad, or scared. He offered examples of how to deal with emotions, from running fast to pounding clay to expressing oneself with music. He often asked his musical guests to demonstrate how they played their instrument to channel strong emotions, such as happiness, anger, and sadness. These moments showed children that feelings are mentionable and manageable. He helped viewers to know they could stop and think, or they could redirect their energy if they were about to do something they knew was wrong. These were profound and helpful reminders for children and adults alike.

"I have always called talking about feelings 'important talk.' Knowing that our feelings are natural and normal for all of us can make it easier for us to share them with one another. . . . It's only natural that we and our children find many things hard to talk about. But anything human is mentionable, and anything mentionable can be manageable. The mentioning can be difficult, and the managing, too, but both can be done if we're surrounded by love and trust."

Fred Rogers

For more than twenty-five years, noted jazz musician Johnny Costa served as the musical director for *Mister Rogers' Neighborhood*. He and his trio played the music live on set, with Johnny's piano front and center in the soundscape of the program. His signature style accompanied everything from the songs Mister Rogers sang to the improvised "noodling" that underscored Mister Rogers' actions, such as when he fed the fish or made a craft at the kitchen table. Johnny also knew how important silence was to keep children from being distracted when they needed to give their full attention to what Mister Rogers was doing or saying. Indeed, Johnny Costa wove music into the very fabric of the program.

> ## "That cat can play!"
> ___
> **Wynton Marsalis on Johnny Costa**

Fred wrote the melodies and lyrics to the songs he sang on the program, but it was Johnny who arranged those songs into sophisticated jazz pieces. Johnny was known for his jazz chops, but he drew on his training in classical music as well. Beethoven's Piano Sonata No. 3 in C Major inspired the opening riffs of "Won't You Be My Neighbor?"

This freedom to collaborate with Fred and create such high-quality music was integral to Johnny's decision to accept the job of musical director in 1968. He told Fred that he didn't want to play "kiddie" music. That fit perfectly with Fred's approach of introducing children to quality

"Children have ears, and they're people, and they can hear good music as well as anybody else. So I started right from the beginning playing for them as I would for any adults."

Johnny Costa

art and music. "What we do isn't simple," Johnny once said. "Fred doesn't write simple tunes, and the jazz arrangements I do are very sophisticated, too. Fred always says if it's for the children, it has to be the best we can give."

Connecting Through Music

Johnny Costa was born in Arnold, Pennsylvania, about twenty miles northeast of Pittsburgh. He began playing the violin at age five but never really liked it. Two years later, a neighbor who was a professional saxophonist taught Johnny to play the accordion, which he *did* like. In high school he learned piano and began playing professionally around Pittsburgh. After high school graduation in 1940, Johnny started a small band with vocalist Helen Zamperini (whom he would later marry) before moving to New York to work and tour with the Tommy Reynolds band. His musical career was interrupted by military service in the army during World War II, but in 1951 he graduated from Carnegie Institute of Technology (now Carnegie

Mellon University) with dual degrees in music composition and teaching.

Over the next fifteen years, Johnny worked as a studio pianist for Pittsburgh radio and television stations. For a while, he even hosted his own TV show called *The Wonderful World of Johnny Costa,* where he discussed composers and played their music. In 1955 he became a national recording artist and would go on to record fourteen albums over more than forty years.

MICHAEL MORICZ

When Johnny Costa died in 1996, Fred tapped composer and pianist Michael Moricz to be the next musical director. Moricz (*below, second from right*) carried on the tradition of live, in-studio music with Rawsthorne (*right*) and McVicker (*left*) until the final new episode was filmed in 2001. To honor Johnny's legacy, each episode after his death opened with a recording of him playing those shimmering celeste notes at the beginning of "Won't You Be My Neighbor?"

JOHNNY AND VAN CLIBURN

"This is one of my favorite stories about John Costa. I believe it was the twenty-fifth anniversary of Fred Rogers' television show, so they had an affair at Carnegie Music Hall in Pittsburgh. Of course there were a lot of people there, including a lot of people that had been on the show. And one of the people was Van Cliburn, the classical piano player. He was in the audience, and we knew he was going to come up on the stage at some point. But before that happened, John Costa did a bit that he used to do, which is take a tune like 'Won't You Be My Neighbor?' and then take requests from the audience on who their favorite classical composer was, and he would play it in the style of that composer. And if they say Franz Liszt, then he played that. So he does that bit. And then after that here's Van Cliburn. He came up and he gave a nice little talk. But he didn't play—he sat down again. So after the program he came up to talk to John, and John said, 'Van, I was disappointed that you didn't play. I was really looking forward to hearing you play.' And he meant it. Van Cliburn said to him, 'John, after what you did there's no way I could follow that. You think I'm nuts? I'm not going to play.' That was something."

Bob Rawsthorne, drummer, Costa Trio

Fred met Johnny when Josie Carey, who starred on *The Children's Corner*, introduced the two of them. In 1966, Fred and Johnny began a creative collaboration that would flourish until Johnny's death in 1996. People who knew both of them have remarked on their unlikely, but wonderful, friendship. In many ways, the two were like yin and yang; according to Betty Aberlin, Johnny was like "pepper" and Fred was like "salt." Johnny was born to an Italian immigrant family in a working-class neighborhood outside Pittsburgh. Fred, on the other hand, came from a well-off business family in a small town.

Despite their different backgrounds, Fred and Johnny shared a deep connection through music. Fred called Johnny a "sensitive man" and "one of the most gifted musicians" he'd ever met. Johnny was a genius improviser, and he seemed to know intuitively when (and what) to play along to the script, and when to let silence underscore Mister Rogers' words and actions. "Music is rock bottom for Johnny and me, and we communicate on an intuitive substratum that would not be possible if we didn't have a feel for music," Fred said. "It's true that there are no cues. We have a rundown, of course, for the program, and he knows my teleprompter copy. But when I'm working with a craft or something, invariably he'll come in and underline an important issue."

"Road musicians used to watch the Mister Rogers show to hear our jams, especially on Friday. The closing credits were longer on Friday, so we really got to stretch out more with the playing. John would incorporate a little bit of every song that we played during the week into the closing credits. That was a heck of an achievement. John was a genius with that."

Carl McVicker, bass player, Costa Trio

The Costa Trio

The Costa Trio formed in 1969 when Johnny brought on percussionist Bob Rawsthorne and bassist Carl McVicker, Jr. The two Pittsburgh-area musicians had attended college together, and they stayed with the *Neighborhood* until the program ended.

Every so often, the trio members would appear on camera to play with musical guests at Negri's Music Shop. In a 1985 episode, Mister Rogers took viewers behind the scenes to meet the musicians. He asked each of them to play their instruments separately and then together, on a snippet of "Won't You Be My Neighbor?"

ABOVE, LEFT: Johnny Costa and Carl McVicker, Jr., in 1989.

ABOVE: The Costa Trio talk on set. *From left to right:* Bob Rawsthorne, Johnny Costa, Carl McVicker, Jr.

A Neighborly Chat *with*

BOB RAWSTHORNE

BOB RAWSTHORNE played percussion with the Costa trio, working behind the scenes of *Mister Rogers' Neighborhood* for more than thirty years.

TIM LYBARGER: How did you get involved with the *Neighborhood*?

BOB RAWSTHORNE: When the show first started, it was filmed [in] a studio on the University of Pittsburgh campus, and the whole thing was in black and white. It was about [1966]. And it just had the piano on programs, by John Costa. And sometimes they would augment the music, depending on what they had to do. The drummer that John Costa was using at the time was a very good player, but completely nervous when he got on the camera. And they had a script where Mister Rogers was going to talk to somebody about playing on the drum set. He had some [candy] lollipops and stuff— "Could you play it with this . . . ?"

And so the bass player, Carl McVicker, who was a friend of mine from college—we played a lot of gigs together—called me up and said, "You want to do this?" And I said, "Yeah, I'll do it." So I went over there—I'd never met

Mister Rogers before. I put my cases up on his little porch and I went to park. And when I came back I saw Fred Rogers, who picked up a couple cases and took them in. And I thought, "Well, this guy is going to be all right. He's carrying my stuff."

Once in a while, John Costa would call me to do something when they needed a few more musicians. Finally he said to me, "You seem to be the only one interested enough to bring exactly what I want"—because there would be different stuff: temple blocks, bell trees, percussion stuff. So he said, "Do you want this job?" I said yes. So he said, "Okay. I'll give you all the studio work after this." So that's how I got started. And in 1970, we started with a regular trio; before that it was just once in a while.

TL: What was it like playing with Johnny Costa?

BR: Sometimes the word's a little overused when you say "genius," but this guy was truly a genius. You could make a very good case for him being the best piano player in the world. I never heard anybody play it any better than that. Or even as good. I consider myself very fortunate to have wound up with John Costa. I was with him for thirty years.

TL: We've heard over the years that a lot of the music was improvised as you guys went along. How much truth is there to that?

BR: To me, when you watch the programs, the music is like velvet. But some of those days I'd come home and I'd really be stressed out because there was not much room in the production to redo the music when we felt it wasn't right. In other words, the tape could break, an actor wouldn't get a line right, Fred would catch himself looking off of camera— we'd do the scene over. But John Costa was so good, they took for granted that the music was always going to be great. I can remember several times doing something that was sort of hard, and if we needed to do it again, John Costa says, "We're going to keep doing this until we make a mistake." He was a very humorous person.

So throughout the whole time there was always very minimal rehearsal. Fred would come over to the trio before we started to shoot, so we knew what songs were going to be on that day. And he'd go over it, and that was it. And then sometimes he would change things anyway. The way I solved it is I'd turn the sound up pretty good in my headset and keep my eye on the one monitor I had. And then hope for the best, because Fred would pause, say something, and then go on to the song. And the worst thing you could do would be play too early. But we finally got used to doing it.

TL: After thirty years, you start to learn from each other.

BR: Oh yeah. You start to get on to it. If you listen to the closing under the credits at the end of each show, every one of those is completely different. No two are the same. And we did the same song, "It's Such a Good Feeling." The floor manager would stand in front of the band—he knew how much time they had until they got to the very end—he would hold up a sign that would say fifteen seconds. And then he'd say ten seconds, as we're playing. And it's up to John Costa to figure out how he's going to end this. If you listen, it ends like he'd practiced it for a week, but he didn't know how it was going to end until it ended. He went

where his fingers took him. The guy was unbelievable.

TL: On the program, how much instruction was given on what to play and when to play it? It seems like the "We Are Elephants" song is used anytime the word "elephant" is mentioned. Was that kind of thing planned or improvised?

BR: That's improvised by John Costa. They had a script for what we were going to do that day. So let's say we'd have two songs in there. But as far as the incidental music, that was all John Costa making that up. That was all spontaneous. He could include some previous song if there's a reason to do it. Like you say, like an elephant or something, he'd put that in. He'd remember all of that stuff. And then often in the closing he would work those melodies into the closing piece.

He said to me several times, "Bob, you listen to this. This is beautiful." It's like he's hearing it for the first time himself, even though he's playing it. So if you took the music out of it or watched it without that music, it would have a completely different feel to it. The music gives it the continuity.

I would say that after Fred Rogers, the next most important person in the show is John Costa. Fred wrote the songs, but John harmonized them all. That's why you hear those great chord changes. That's all Costa.

TL: How did you feel about appearing on the screen? Was that something that came naturally to you?

BR: That didn't bother me at all. But then a big part of that was Fred Rogers. He had a way of calming down everybody. It was just like he'd ask you the right questions and it just flowed. So he never gave you that chance to get nervous.

One of the most spontaneous things they ever did was after Wynton Marsalis was on. They had a set called Joe Negri's Music [Shop], and they didn't want to just tear it down without filming another segment. The producer asked me, "Can you bring in a couple of different and unusual, goofy-type instruments? We'll make up something."

So we got done with the Marsalis segment and had lunch and went back. They had this little kid's toy piano, and Fred says he's going to play that. Joe Negri played the guitar, and I brought in this thing, it's called a "stump fiddle." It's like a stick with a spring on the bottom and a couple bells and jingles and stuff attached to it. Sort of like a Spike Jones kind of instrument.

So now we start to rehearse for this segment. We end up laughing and the producer said, "Boy, that was great. Would you mind if we kept it?" I said, "No. I don't mind." They decided it's the most spontaneous thing they ever did on the show. And we did it with no rehearsal.

Did you ever see the program with Jeff Erlanger?

TL: That's one of my favorite scenes. You could see it in Fred's face that nobody else on that set mattered at that moment. The set could have been completely empty. It was just him and the kid in the scene.

BR: That's exactly right. And I'll tell you what else, Tim. That scene was not rehearsed. I guess we knew he was going to do that song. But Jeff singing with him, nobody knew what that was going to be. So that whole thing was spontaneous.

TL: That couldn't have been more perfect.

BR: No. And you can see all the emotion and tension; you could cut it with a knife the way it was going on. And that's another thing, when I was playing, I'm thinking, "Oh man. I hope we don't make any mistakes here because we'll never do this again."

TL: It makes the hair on my arms stand up every time I watch it.

BR: That one scene sort of sums up Fred. And he was the same off the camera. If he would be talking to you, he's talking straight to you. He listened to what you say and was genuinely interested in what you do and what you have to say. That's Fred.

TL: Yeah, I've heard that in a conversation he would always turn it back around to you. You would ask him a question, and he would answer it briefly and then ask you about yourself.

BR: That's right. "How do you feel about that?" That was one of his things. We were in Boston one time doing something for the PBS show there. There was a woman who lived in Boston who previously had worked at the WQED studios where we did the show, so she knew Fred well. She invited Fred and the cast to her house for a dinner party. So they send a limo. The limo driver—I still remember his name was Billy—we get in the limo and Billy said, "This is my first day on this job." And Fred says, "Oh Billy, I'm glad to know you. Would you mind if I sat up in the front seat with you?" "Oh no, Mister Rogers. Just get up here."

So we find the house, and Billy's going to stay in the car and wait till we're done. And Fred said, "Oh no, Billy. You're not staying out here. Come up with us." So he comes in and has a great time. To this day I don't know if the woman knows that he wasn't a member of the cast. We get back in the car to go to the hotel and Fred says, "You know what? I've got a cousin that lives right close to here. I'd like to just say hello to him." So Billy finds his house and it turns out the cousin wasn't home. Fred leaves a note under his door, gets back in the car, and Billy said, "I actually live close to here." Fred said, "Do you? I'd really like to see your house." He means this stuff.

TL: Is this with all of you still in the limo?

BR: Yeah, we're still in the limo! So we go to Billy's house. Now Billy is so excited he doesn't even park the car. He just stops it in the middle of the street and gets out. His mother comes to the door and he says, "Mom, I'd like you to meet Mister Rogers." So now Uncle Frank comes down from upstairs in his work clothes. He's on his way to some job, some kind of construction job or something. Billy says, "Mister Rogers, would you mind

In an episode that originally aired in 1973, Bob Rawsthorne shows Mister Rogers and Joe Negri a collection of gongs.

if I took a picture of you with my mother and my uncle?" "Oh no, that's fine." Well, that's done. And then Fred says, "Now you go line up over there with your family. I'm going to take your picture." And there's Fred, he's taking this guy's picture. I've seen him do this other times. That's the way he was.

TL: What are your thoughts on the legacy and the resurgence of the *Neighborhood* that's come about in the last few years? How has this message and neighborhood survived fifty-plus years?

BR: Oh, I think it's the message that Fred brought to children. His message overall was, "You're special. There's nobody else like you. And I like you just the

way you are." That's the overall message of the whole thing.

I'd have to say I feel I've really been fortunate to have ever been a part of that. And I'm proud of what we did, what we accomplished. Fred Rogers always said, "You never know who's listening." Which turned out to be true. There's a drummer in Pittsburgh now that's like the main jazz guy. I talked to him and he said, "I used to lay in bed and listen to you, how you played those brushes. You're the main reason I took this up." Well, Fred's right— you never know who's listening.

📺

Over the years, Mister Rogers introduced his television friends to a host of accomplished musical guests who played songs from a variety of genres, including jazz, classical, rhythmic percussion, and African folk music. Cellist Yo-Yo Ma, who became good friends with Fred, once noted, "In this neighborhood, all types of music are included, so it's every child's music." Whenever Mister Rogers asked his guests how they used music to express their emotions, they responded thoughtfully, demonstrating with their instruments how they might play when they were feeling angry, sad, or happy. These moments, which were often unscripted, gave the musicians a chance to love their art in front of others, a teaching technique that Fred had learned from his mentor, Dr. Margaret McFarland. "The best teacher in the world," Fred said, "is somebody who loves what he or she does, and just loves it in front of you." He knew that this kind of enthusiasm could inspire children to want to try new things.

With his musical guests by his side, Fred also emphasized the role that practice and persistence play in learning to make music. He knew it was helpful for children and adults alike to hear that adults have had to persevere in order to overcome challenges and deal with making mistakes. Again and again, Mister Rogers reminded viewers that

ABOVE, LEFT: Yo-Yo Ma and his son, Nicholas, with Mister Rogers.

ABOVE, RIGHT: Fred Rogers with the Uptown String Quartet.

ABOVE: Wynton Marsalis on an episode that originally aired in 1986.

OPPOSITE: Mister Rogers looks on as Delfeayo Marsalis, Joe Negri, and Branford Marsalis play "Won't You Be My Neighbor?" (1990).

it's okay to try new things, to do something poorly until you can do it well, and that it's through *doing* that people bring ideas and creativity to life. In fact, it's not just okay to do these things, it's wonderful!

Wynton Marsalis (1986)

Mister Rogers met acclaimed jazz trumpeter Wynton Marsalis at Negri's Music Shop. Marsalis told Mister Rogers that he got his first trumpet at age six, but it wasn't until he was twelve that he started practicing seriously. Joe Negri and the Costa Trio soon joined them in the back room, and the musicians played "It's You I Like" before launching into a blues jam session.

Joe Negri recalled how Marsalis "wanted to test the water a little bit and test us," suggesting that they play before the rehearsal. "We jammed on some blues, and after about five or seven minutes, he said, 'Terrific, okay. Let's go.' And then we did a couple of Rogers songs, and we all got along."

ABOVE, LEFT: Yo-Yo Ma and his son, Nicholas, with Mister Rogers.

ABOVE, RIGHT: Fred Rogers with the Uptown String Quartet.

ABOVE: Wynton Marsalis on an episode that originally aired in 1986.

OPPOSITE: Mister Rogers looks on as Delfeayo Marsalis, Joe Negri, and Branford Marsalis play "Won't You Be My Neighbor?" (1990).

it's okay to try new things, to do something poorly until you can do it well, and that it's through *doing* that people bring ideas and creativity to life. In fact, it's not just okay to do these things, it's wonderful!

Wynton Marsalis (1986)

Mister Rogers met acclaimed jazz trumpeter Wynton Marsalis at Negri's Music Shop. Marsalis told Mister Rogers that he got his first trumpet at age six, but it wasn't until he was twelve that he started practicing seriously. Joe Negri and the Costa Trio soon joined them in the back room, and the musicians played "It's You I Like" before launching into a blues jam session.

Joe Negri recalled how Marsalis "wanted to test the water a little bit and test us," suggesting that they play before the rehearsal. "We jammed on some blues, and after about five or seven minutes, he said, 'Terrific, okay. Let's go.' And then we did a couple of Rogers songs, and we all got along."

CLOCKWISE, FROM TOP LEFT:
Virtuoso violinist Itzhak Perlman (1993), who trained at the Academy of Music in Tel Aviv and the Julliard School, talked about needing to use crutches as a result of having polio, and how he uses his strong arms to play the violin.

Rita Moreno (1975), Broadway singer and actress, sang "It's You I Like," accompanied on piano by musical director Johnny Costa.

The Harlem Boys Choir, directed by Dr. Walter Turnbull (1991), sang several songs for Mister Rogers.

A Neighborly Chat *with*

YO-YO MA

Cellist **YO-YO MA** visited the *Neighborhood* three times, and he and Fred formed a special friendship that would last for the rest of Fred's life. In 2014, Yo-Yo Ma received the inaugural Fred Rogers Legacy Award to commemorate the ten-year anniversary of the Fred Rogers Center at Saint Vincent's College.

TIM LYBARGER: How did your friendship with Fred begin?

YO-YO MA: It was around 1985, because that's when Nicholas, my son, was probably around two years old. Nicholas, as a toddler, was fascinated with Mister Rogers. One day a friend, Jill Philipson, who worked at WGBH, passed along the message to say, "Would you like to appear on *Mister Rogers' Neighborhood*?" What father would not say yes to appear on a show that his son is really interested in? So I jumped at the chance to appear on the show.

All I knew about Mister Rogers was that he was the host of a show that my son really loved. And we had watched him and thought he was a very, very gentle person. I think anybody who meets him realizes what an extraordinarily sincere person he is, and one of the ways it appeared to me was that when he talked to me on the set he put his face incredibly close to mine and said, "Yo-Yo. It is so nice to see you."

It wasn't until afterward that I realized, "That's the way *Nicholas* would talk to me." Because children get really close to you, and they're examining your face. They're usually fascinated with noses, with people's glasses, with the movement of someone's mouth. So they haven't developed that social space, and Mister Rogers knew that and, I think, deliberately did that so that he is putting himself in the child's shoes. Which was amazing.

Much later on, I realized that the space between his presence on the screen and the child watching was, to him, a sacred space. So he projects that incredible sincerity that one feels when you see him get into the mind of the child. It's a very deliberate way to communicate, and that's something that was really extraordinary.

"He was an incredibly creative person who was able, with the help of a devoted team of people, to create a whole world that was just devoted to addressing children's inner lives."

We had this first meeting, and I learned that he was, in fact, a music major in college and that he played the piano really well, and that Joanne also was a pianist and had a piano duo. I realized that they had deep relations with music. We shared a common bond.

A little while later, I think he was doing a fathers and sons episode, and he invited Nicholas to be on the show. We all met the Rogers family—and my wife, Jill, and my daughter, Emily, came along—and so I think we became enveloped in the *Mister Rogers' Neighborhood* family. Fred was incredibly nice—just someone we adored. And, of course, it was the same with members of the cast. Later on, Nicholas was on the show again as an adolescent teenager, and he played the piano with me. Over the years, I stayed in touch with Fred. Again, the relationship was such that whenever I showed up in Pittsburgh we would see one another. Usually in the morning

because Mister Rogers goes to bed fairly early. Fred and Joanne might show up at a concert once in a while and we'd see each other then.

TL: Are there particular things you learned from Fred Rogers?

YM: I have to tell you a couple things. One thing is an extraordinary part of knowing Mister Rogers and having been on the show: he got a lot of letters. I know that because whenever anybody wrote to him about the music segments that we did, he would actually send me a photocopy of the letter and his response. And it wasn't like, "Oh, thank you for your lovely note. I hope everything's well." No, they were detailed letters and answers, thoughtfully written.

TL: Why do you think he sent those letters to you?

YM: Because that's part of the relationship, you know? I was on

the show, and he was sharing the response of someone who kind of got interested in music because of it. He wanted me to know about it. It was a result of extending his friendship.

And it was so incredibly astounding to me that he would do that. When I first met him, I was starting a career playing cello and responding to some people writing letters. And so, somewhere, subliminally, I thought, "You know, that's the way to do things." So it was a kind of modeling, of saying, "You treat others with the respect that they give you." If you are in some way in the public eye and someone responds to that, you owe them a reply, a human response, not just "Thank you for your inquiry, here's a photo." That was a tough model to follow, because who has the time, right? And who cares enough to do that? But he set the bar, and whether I succeeded or not—and very often I didn't—I knew that it was the thing to do.

Occasionally we'd have breakfast, and every person—from the waitstaff or the kitchen staff, the fellow diners—would just come by and say, "This is what your show has meant to us." Unfailingly, he was present and gave people time—I don't know how he did it, but he did it. So that was also a lesson in how to be.

He's a person who keeps on giving past his lifetime, as evidenced by the growing interest. He was not just someone doing a children's show, but rather someone who has become, because of the first principles of his values, a powerful spokesperson for a way of being in today's world, for children and adults.

With the documentary [*Won't You Be My Neighbor?*] and the Tom Hanks film [*A Beautiful Day in the Neighborhood*], it's almost like, here's this man who's been doing these things, never broadcasting "This is who I am. This is why I'm doing this." Instead, focused on the relationship and the child's needs.

And that's another lesson, I think, which is so important. If you're going to be someone's advocate, you do it 100 percent. His testimony, that moment when he testified in front of Senator Pastore—the passion with which he recited: "What do you do with the mad that you feel?" It's one of those moments where his absolute sincerity and vulnerability became the greatest strengths, that actually spoke to someone who was not initially given to funding the nation's public television. But boy, he cut right through the defenses. He spoke to something very, very deep inside the senator that made

him say, "Yes. I see the value in what you're doing."

TL: You mentioned Fred and Joanne's deep relationship with music. Will you tell us a bit about that?

YM: Music, I think, for both of them, is a form of spiritual communication. It's revealing one's inner core in life, and I think Mister Rogers and Joanne, each in their own way, are incredible. They are people who really speak from their inner core in life, and therefore also in music, and I think that they have a deep appreciation of different types of music.

I think Fred was a very good jazz pianist and also, from a track I heard, a wonderful composer. He wrote contemporary music. He was very multifaceted, and the fact that he wrote all the music, he acted in all the parts, and all the voices are his, so he's what one might call a performance artist. He was an incredibly creative person who was able, with the help of a devoted team of people, to create a whole world that was just devoted to addressing children's inner lives. That includes real life and make-believe life, and really trying to separate between the two. He understood how important it was to have a strong inner life,

because that inner life is what can sustain people through tough times.

What I realize in hindsight—as I discover so much more about the man, about Fred and Joanne and their wonderful children—is how intricate and deep and complex their lives must have been in order to create this real simplicity. The simplicity is the result of a tremendous amount of pruning to get to the essential.

TL: After appearing on the *Neighborhood* program a few times, then all these years later with Morgan Neville essentially saying you were the inspiration for his interest in creating a documentary about Mister Rogers—what are your thoughts on being part of such an influential and long-lasting legacy?

YM: What an extraordinary privilege to have known him and in some way participated in some episodes. It was for me an incredible blessing, and it happened so organically. It was a purposeful life that he wanted to lead. The *Neighborhood* program was Fred's mission, and I feel that I'm still learning from him.

STOMP (1995)

Mister Rogers visited a rehearsal for the percussion group STOMP. Some of the group members talked about how they'd been tapping and pounding out songs since they were children. They demonstrated how they used buckets, pipes, and their own bodies to create rhythms. Mister Rogers got in on the action, pounding on blue barrel drums and wielding a push broom.

"We did a week about being angry, and one of the things important to Fred and important for kids to learn is that it's okay to be mad, but it's not okay to hurt anybody. A lot of times he'll say, 'Pound some clay or go outside and run around. Get that angry feeling out and then you can deal with whatever's wrong.' So I happened to see STOMP, the performance group. I was just blown away and thought, 'We've got to figure a way for Fred to have them on the program.' That was a big deal, to convince him to do that; it's just not who he is. But there's one piece that they play with these tubes that's very soft. So I put together this clip of some of their performances, and I made sure that was part of it. I think that helped a lot. And then he met them and we couldn't get him to stop talking with them and hanging out with them. I was like, 'We have a plane to catch!'"

Margy Whitmer, producer

"I LOVE OPERA DAYS!"

While music often filled the Neighborhood of Make-Believe, opera days were truly special. With their whimsical plotlines, elaborate costumes and sets, and winsome songs, the operas charmed viewers and cast members alike.

The idea to include operas in Make-Believe came from Fred's time as a music composition major at Rollins College. That's also where he met John Reardon, who would go on to be a well-known baritone with the Metropolitan Opera in New York—and also to appear in all of the Neighborhood operas. Several other cast members were also accomplished opera singers, including François Clemmons and Yoshi Ito. Nearly everyone in Make-Believe—people and puppets alike—participated in the operas in some way.

At the start of a typical opera week, Reardon would arrive in Make-Believe and King Friday would commission an opera to be performed by week's end. The puppets had different ideas about what role they wanted to play—parts that wouldn't ordinarily go together, but Reardon helped them (through Fred's genius, of course) make a story and create songs to sing. After Reardon created a story, he rehearsed some of the songs with the puppets and neighbors through the week. By Friday's program, when nearly the whole episode was given over to the opera, the viewers were familiar with some of the songs and the story, but it was also a wonderful surprise to see it all come together with sets and costumes.

By being able to see the artistic process unfold, children learned about creativity and collaboration. Just as Mister Rogers wanted children to understand that people *make* things in factories (such as crayons and graham crackers), he wanted them to understand that they can *create* things using their imaginations, be it a television program, a painting, or a song. In one episode, Mister Rogers told the children, "An opera is just a story for which you sing the words instead of say them."

The *Neighborhood* presented fourteen operas, all written by Fred. Over the years, the story lines, sets, and costumes grew increasingly complex, though almost all of them included a love story, as is typical of classical operas. The first, called *The Babysitter Opera,* featured four characters and one set, and lasted just ten minutes. The final opera, *Josephine the Short-Neck Giraffe,* featured fifteen characters and spanned three whole episodes. Perhaps more than any other element of the program, the operas allowed Fred and the cast to embrace the fanciful fun of the Neighborhood of Make-Believe, where anything can happen. In a 1999 interview, Fred reminisced enthusiastically about the operas, saying, "Oh, what a good time we've had with them!"

Fred with members of the cast of 1982's *Spoon Mountain* opera. *From left to right:* Joe Negri, Chuck Aber, Audrey Roth, Fred Rogers, Don Brockett, and Betty Aberlin.

"It helps children to see people dressed up in costumes, pretending, and singing their thoughts instead of saying them, knowing it's all right to sing sad and angry songs, as well as happy, carefree ones. I hope these operas can encourage children to express who they really are, and in doing so, help them to feel better about themselves."

Fred Rogers

The Babysitter Opera

(APRIL 1968, EPISODE 0045)

This short opera tells the story of a son who is upset when his mother must leave him with his grandfather and a babysitter while she goes out. They comfort him, and he eventually settles down to sleep. When his mother returns, she breaks the fourth wall and addresses the audience: "And so you see, ladies and gentlemen, by this opera, that mothers can go out, but they come back."

OPERA CAST & CREW

LADY ABERLIN AS MOTHER

DONKEY HODIE AS SON

HENRIETTA PUSSYCAT AS BABYSITTER

JOHN REARDON AS GRANDFATHER

X THE OWL—STAGE MANAGER (CREW)

Campsite Opera

(JUNE 1968, EPISODE 0084)

In this whimsical love story, the Hobby Horse Express man arrives with a letter for campsite owner Lady Elaine, informing her that Benjamin Franklin will be coming to stay. Meanwhile, a photographer also arrives, looking for a place to spend the night. The Hobby Horse Express man and the photographer fall in love, and the happy couple ride off on their matching hobbyhorses.

OPERA CAST

JOHN REARDON AS HOBBY HORSE EXPRESS MAN

LADY ELAINE FAIRCHILDE AS CAMPSITE OWNER

X THE OWL AS BENJAMIN FRANKLIN

LADY ABERLIN AS PHOTOGRAPHER

CHEF BROCKETT AS COVERED WAGON

Lost and Found Teddy Bear

(APRIL 1969, EPISODE 1055)

In this opera, the first to be shown in color, a teddy bear goes missing while dancing and singing with the young lady who owns him. Together with a policeman, the young lady searches for her lost teddy bear and determines that he has gone out to sea. She travels the world with a whaling captain, but no one they meet has seen the missing bear. Finally, the policeman brings news that the teddy bear had been napping under his couch all along!

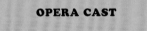

OPERA CAST

DANIEL STRIPED TIGER AS TEDDY BEAR

LADY ABERLIN AS YOUNG LADY

OFFICER CLEMMONS AS POLICEMAN

TROLLEY AS OCEAN WAVES

JOHN REARDON AS WHALING CAPTAIN

KING FRIDAY XIII AS KING

QUEEN SARA AS QUEEN

ROBERT TROLL AS WHALE

X THE OWL AS BENJAMIN FRANKLIN

HENRIETTA PUSSYCAT AS FRANKLIN'S MOTHER

ELSIE JEAN PLATYPUS AS LOCH NESS MONSTER

DR. BILL PLATYPUS AS BAGPIPE PLAYER

Pineapples and Tomatoes

(APRIL 1970, EPISODE 1125)

While Benjamin Franklin meets with the operator and the vice president of the Pineapple Can Telephone Company, a call comes in from an angry housewife who likes tomatoes, expressing her distaste for pineapples. The vice president visits her at her house, hoping to change her mind about his favorite fruit. After some prodding, he learns that she loves tomatoes because she loves the color red. Benjamin Franklin invents pineapple cans in new colors, including red, and all is resolved when the housewife gets a new red telephone can. The opera ends with a love song sung by the vice president and the operator, who admit to having feelings for each other.

OPERA CAST & CREW

LADY ABERLIN AS OPERATOR

LADY ELAINE FAIRCHILDE AS HOUSEWIFE WHO LIKES TOMATOES

X THE OWL AS BENJAMIN FRANKLIN

JOHN REARDON AS VICE PRESIDENT OF THE PINEAPPLE CAN TELEPHONE COMPANY

CORNFLAKE S. PECIALLY—TELEPHONE EQUIPMENT (CREW)

DANIEL STRIPED TIGER—COSTUMES (CREW)

HENRIETTA PUSSYCAT—COSTUMES (CREW)

The Uncle of the Monkey

(APRIL 1971, EPISODE 1169)

The scene opens on the zookeeper caring for a talking parrot, a duck, and a horse. Over at the monkey house, the organ grinder is upset that no one wants to pay for his music. Defeated, he gives his monkey and his organ to the monkey's uncle, who converts the organ into a popcorn maker. This gives the organ grinder a renewed sense of purpose and confidence, and he decides he will continue his work at the zoo.

OPERA CAST

LADY ABERLIN AS ZOOKEEPER

BOB TROW AS PARROT

DANIEL STRIPED TIGER AS DANIEL DUCK

INO A. HORSE AS HORSE

JOHN REARDON AS ORGAN GRINDER

ROBERT TROLL AS MONKEY

CHEF BROCKETT AS MONKEY'S UNCLE

MISS PAULIFICATE AS MONKEY'S AUNT

The Snow People

(APRIL 1972, EPISODE 1245)

Henrietta Pussycat is practicing the skill of concentration with her teacher. They imagine François Clemmons and Yoshi Ito are playing badminton. Lady Aberlin ruins the game by trying to steal the shuttlecock. When they ask her to leave, she and the witch at the Place of Mischief make it snow, turning the others into frozen snow people. Now concerned for her friends, Lady Aberlin recalls that it takes "a very special teacher and a warm pussycat" to melt the snow. When Henrietta arrives, everyone concentrates and the snow melts.

OPERA CAST

HENRIETTA PUSSYCAT AS STUDENT

JOHN REARDON AS TEACHER

FRANÇOIS CLEMMONS AS BADMINTON PLAYER

YOSHI ITO AS BADMINTON PLAYER

LADY ABERLIN AS SELF

LADY ELAINE FAIRCHILDE AS WITCH

CHEF BROCKETT AS CHEF

MISS PAULIFICATE AS CLEAN-UP FRIEND

ABOVE: François Clemmons and Yoshi Ito sing a duet after being turned into snow people.

BELOW: Henrietta and the others concentrate on melting the snow.

Potato Bugs and Cows

(APRIL 1973, EPISODE 1300)

Priscilla Cow is lonely. She befriends a potato bug, and then she wants to *be* a potato bug, because they're so groovy! Horatio Potato Bug agrees to teach her how to be one. When Priscilla's mother learns of her plan, she calls on the farmer for help. He enlists the aid of King Clemmons, who enlists the help of Joe Bull. Back at the barn, Priscilla is about to leave the farm with the potato bugs when the King and Joe Bull convince her that cows can be groovy, too.

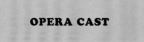

OPERA CAST

LADY ABERLIN AS PRISCILLA COW

CHEF BROCKETT AS HORATIO POTATO BUG

HARRIETT ELIZABETH COW AS MRS. COW

JOHN REARDON AS FARMER

FRANÇOIS CLEMMONS AS KING CLEMMONS

LADY ELAINE FAIRCHILDE AS FARMER'S WIFE

YOSHI ITO AS PILOT

JOE NEGRI AS JOE BULL

MISS PAULIFICATE AS IDAHO POTATO BUG

ABOVE: Priscilla's quiet and lonely barnyard.

BELOW: Horatio Potato Bug teaches Priscilla Cow the groovy potato bug song and moves.

All in the Laundry

(APRIL 1974, EPISODE 1370)

In this opera, a photographer snaps a photo of overworked Gillespie, an employee of the Latrobe Laundry and Dry Cleaning Company (LLDCC). Outside the store, the photographer greets Miss Morgan, who sees the photo of Gillespie and decides he's the man of her dreams. Gillespie then sees a picture of Miss Morgan and falls in love with her. A wacky series of missed connections ensues until the two meet and truly fall in love. The wealthy Miss Morgan buys the LLDCC so she and Gillespie can work side-by-side.

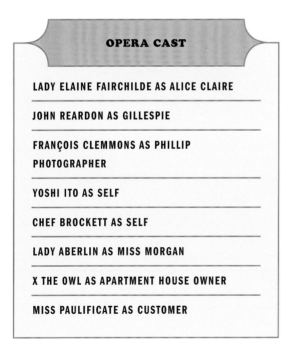

OPERA CAST

LADY ELAINE FAIRCHILDE AS ALICE CLAIRE

JOHN REARDON AS GILLESPIE

FRANÇOIS CLEMMONS AS PHILLIP PHOTOGRAPHER

YOSHI ITO AS SELF

CHEF BROCKETT AS SELF

LADY ABERLIN AS MISS MORGAN

X THE OWL AS APARTMENT HOUSE OWNER

MISS PAULIFICATE AS CUSTOMER

ABOVE, FROM TOP TO BOTTOM: Chef Brockett, Yoshi Ito, Miss Morgan, and Gillespie look at a photograph; Miss Morgan and Gillespie fall in love; a quadrillion-dollar-bill prop used by Miss Morgan to buy the LLDCC.

Key to Otherland

(APRIL 1975, EPISODE 1425)

Betty falls asleep on the beach and dreams that an old key she's found unlocks the door to Otherland. There she and her brother Lloyd are confronted by a wicked witch and her elephant sidekick. The witch captures Lloyd, imprisons him in a glass box, and forces him to exercise. Betty rescues Lloyd with help from a swan, two beavers, and the elephant. The swan falls in love with Betty and decides he wants to leave with her. Betty awakens on the beach and realizes it was all a dream. She buries the key back in the sand for someone else to find, so they can have dreams of their own.

OPERA CAST

LADY ABERLIN AS BETTY

MR. ALLMINE AS LLOYD

LADY ELAINE FAIRCHILDE AS WICKED WITCH

H. J. ELEPHANT AS ELEPHANT

JOHN REARDON AS SWAN

FRANÇOIS CLEMMONS AS BEAVER

MAYOR MAGGIE AS BEAVER

MISS PAULIFICATE AS MOTHER SWAN

CHEF BROCKETT AS FATHER SWAN

"Where is the door that this key was made for?"

Lady Aberlin as Betty

Concept drawing of the set for the witch's taffy factory.

Windstorm in Bubbleland

(MAY 1980, EPISODE 1475)

This opera is set in a place called Bubbleland, where everyone loves their bubbles, and no one ever wants to hear bad news. Television news anchor Robert Redgate reports on a new product from the National Bubble Chemical Company called "Spray Sweater," which comes in an aerosol can and is billed as "the ultimate protection for your precious bubbles." The manager of Betty's Better Sweater Company crashes the broadcast and blows the whistle on Spray Sweater: There's nothing inside the can but plain old air!

As Friendly Frank the Porpoise reports on the perfect weather in Bubbleland, Hildegarde Hummingbird swoops in to warn of an upcoming windstorm. No one wants to acknowledge such bad news, so she leaves Bubbleland.

Robert Redgate and the Betty's Better Sweater Company manager visit the National Bubble Chemical Company to confront its president, W. I. Norton Donovan, about the fraudulent Spray Sweater, which is causing too much wind in Bubbleland. Mr. Donovan reveals his true identity: the Wind.

The citizens work together to build a wind-blocking wall at the docks, but the Wind is a fierce and mighty foe. Finally Hildegarde returns and uses her strong hummingbird wings to overpower the Wind, who is forced to retreat. Bubbleland is saved, and everyone learns that people are more important than bubbles.

OPERA CAST

JOHN REARDON AS ROBERT REDGATE

LADY ABERLIN AS BETTY'S BETTER SWEATER COMPANY MANAGER

FRANÇOIS CLEMMONS AS FRIENDLY FRANK THE PORPOISE

LADY ELAINE FAIRCHILDE AS HILDEGARDE HUMMINGBIRD

CHEF BROCKETT AS BANANA BOAT CAPTAIN

MISS PAULIFICATE AS BUBBLE VENDOR

HANDYMAN NEGRI AS W. I. NORTON DONOVAN AND THE WIND

"There's never any trouble here in Bubbleland . . ."

Spoon Mountain

(JULY 1982, EPISODE 1505)

Prince Extraordinary and Betty Green of the park service climb Spoon Mountain to rescue Purple Twirling Kitty from Wicked Knife and Fork. Wicked Knife and Fork reveals that all he ever really wanted was a spoon, and the prince tells him he can make himself some spoons at the castle. The group returns to the castle, Betty and the prince announce they are in love, and Wicked Knife and Fork declares that he will choose a new name for himself.

OPERA CAST
JOE NEGRI AS STORYTELLER
CHEF BROCKETT AS KING KITTYPUSS
MISS PAULIFICATE AS QUEEN MUMSIEBELLE
CHUCK ABER AS PRINCE EXTRAORDINARY
LADY ABERLIN AS BETTY GREEN
OFFICER CLEMMONS AS COMMODORE
JEFF SHADE AS PURPLE TWIRLING KITTY
BOB TROW AS WICKED KNIFE AND FORK

A Granddad for Daniel

(MAY 1984, EPISODE 1535)

It's Grandparents' Day, and Daniel Mefford is wishing he could see his granddad, who left long ago. Daniel joins his mother, a trolley conductor, on her way to the jungle. They are joined by several passengers, including a drinking-straw salesman who has traveled the world. When the trolley arrives at the jungle, the passengers realize that the drinking-straw salesman is actually Daniel's granddad! Together in celebration, the Meffords take a trolley ride around the world.

OPERA CAST

DANIEL STRIPED TIGER AS DANIEL MEFFORD

NEIGHBOR ABER AS CHARLES MEFFORD

OLD GOAT AS GOAT

LADY ABERLIN AS MRS. MEFFORD

JOHN REARDON AS SALESMAN

BOB DOG, CHEF BROCKETT, AND
MISS PAULIFICATE AS FISH

BETTY OKONAK TEMPLETON JONES AS STARFISH

OFFICER CLEMMONS AS OFFICER ON DUTY

A Star for Kitty

(MAY 1986, EPISODE 1565)

Kitty asks for a small star named Tiny for her birthday, but Tiny doesn't want to be found, so he hides inside a tube of Superbright toothpaste. When Kitty learns that Tiny doesn't want to leave the sky, she agrees to leave him in his night-sky home. This act of kindness helps her to twinkle and shine.

Half-Moon and Other Half-Moon at Twinkling Class.

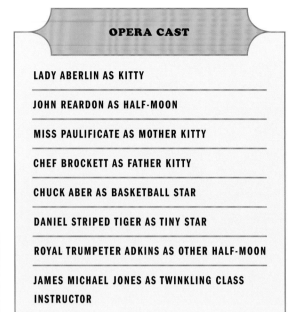

OPERA CAST

LADY ABERLIN AS KITTY

JOHN REARDON AS HALF-MOON

MISS PAULIFICATE AS MOTHER KITTY

CHEF BROCKETT AS FATHER KITTY

CHUCK ABER AS BASKETBALL STAR

DANIEL STRIPED TIGER AS TINY STAR

ROYAL TRUMPETER ADKINS AS OTHER HALF-MOON

JAMES MICHAEL JONES AS TWINKLING CLASS INSTRUCTOR

Josephine the Short-Neck Giraffe

(MAY 1989, EPISODES 1608, 1609, 1610)

The final Neighborhood opera, *Josephine the Short-Neck Giraffe,* spanned three episodes.

Although her friends like her just fine, Josephine the giraffe is upset because her neck is too short and it makes her feel different from all the other giraffes. Josephine's friend Hazel the elephant tells her she's going to school to learn to read and play the trombone. Hazel says Josephine should come to school and learn to grow.

The next day, Josephine's mother encourages her to try going to school. Hazel and Josephine set out together, but Josephine worries. At the school, the principal directs Hazel to the music room and takes Josephine to the A.A.A. room—the Attractive Active Animals room! There, Josephine meets her teachers and classmates, including Samuel S. Snake, who doesn't know how to hiss, and J.R., an extremely shy, tall giraffe.

J.R. tries to talk to a sullen Josephine, but he stumbles over some of his words. Josephine says that he can grow out of his shyness, but she'll always look the way she does. J.R. tells Josephine that he thinks she looks nice. He wins her over. Josephine feels more comfortable with how she looks and who she is.

Josephine and Hazel stop to talk to Frog, Tree, and Sunflower.

OPERA CAST

BETTY ABERLIN AS JOSEPHINE GIRAFFE

DANIEL STRIPED TIGER AS SUNFLOWER

CHUCK ABER AS THE VOICE OF FROG

BOB DOG AS TREE

MICHAEL HORTON AS THE VOICES OF BUTTERFLY, BIRD, AND BEE

HANDYMAN NEGRI AS FATHER ELEPHANT

PRINCESS ZELDA AS HAZEL

MISS PAULIFICATE AS MOTHER ELEPHANT

MAYOR MAGGIE AS MRS. GIRAFFE

CHEF BROCKETT AS MR. BULLDOG

BARBARA RUSSELL AS POSY

MARY RAWSON AS ROSY

BOB TROW AS THE VOICE OF SAMUEL S. SNAKE

NEIGHBOR ABER AS J.R. GIRAFFE

WINNIE FLYNN AS MRS. MONGREL

CLOCKWISE FROM TOP: Set for Josephine's outdoor scenes; candid cast photo; Betty Aberlin and Maggie Stewart consult with Fred.

OPPOSITE: Fred's first sketch of the story for *Josephine the Short-Neck Giraffe*, written in 1950 while he was at Rollins College.

Once upon a time there lived a very unhappy giraffe whose name was Josephine. All day long Josephine would set in the forest and watch her friends eat the tender leaves from the highest parts of the trees, and she would simply sigh and cry. She was ~~unhappy~~ SAD because she had a very short neck - in fact ~~her neck~~ it was so short, it looked more like a cow neck: than a giraffe's. ~~and~~ Ever since she could remember, all she ever wanted was a long neck. ~~(one a) longer a long neck~~ She was sure that when she was seven her neck would stretch and look like the number of her years ~~but~~ yet her seventh birthday had come and gone and still her neck stayed short.

One day shortly after her seventh birthday Josephine decided ~~to~~ find help from the famous psychiatrist Artur, the lion. Because of her constant worry concerning her short neck, she had developed a "cow complex" and could no longer tend to

Classic Moment

SHARING A WADING POOL

Episode 1065
Original air date: May 9, 1969

> **ON A WARM DAY IN THE NEIGHBORHOOD,** Mister Rogers invited Officer Clemmons—an African-American police officer—to join him as he soaks his feet in some cool water. It was a subtle yet powerful response to the racial boundaries and tensions of the 1960s, specifically around sharing public swimming pools. After Office Clemmons and Mister Rogers cooled their feet in the wading pool, they used the same towel to dry off. This seemingly simple interaction conveyed a deep message of friendship and acceptance. More than twenty years later, in 1993, the two re-created this scene during Clemmons's final appearance on the program.

Mister Rogers' Neighborhood A VISUAL HISTORY

A Neighborly Chat *with*

FRANÇOIS CLEMMONS

Officer Clemmons

"It's a whole lot more than playing and splashing around in a pool."

François Clemmons

FRANÇOIS CLEMMONS joined the cast of *Mister Rogers' Neighborhood* in 1968 in the role of Officer Clemmons, a member of Neighborhood law enforcement. By the mid-1970s, his role transitioned to that of a music teacher whose studio was located next door to Mister Rogers' house.

TIM LYBARGER: How did you become involved with the show?

FRANÇOIS CLEMMONS: My relationship started with Fred at Third Presbyterian Church in Pittsburgh. I was working on my master's at Carnegie Mellon and I auditioned for John Lively, who was the organist there at Third Presbyterian Church, and he hired me. He introduced me to Fred Rogers. As a matter of fact, Joanne Rogers sang in the choir. Much to my surprise and joy, she sat right next to me. So sure enough, he introduced me and said, "Joanne, this is François. He's never met Fred Rogers, and we would like to have those two get together," because Fred was a composer and he was doing this new television program. John was the one who said, "I think he would be wonderful on that show," and Joanne agreed.

TL: Do you remember what year this was?

FC: Fall of '67. I guess he was still getting his act together, no pun intended. Setting it up and putting out feelers and testing stuff. I sang a program of American Negro spirituals on Good Friday before Easter. When it was over, I swear, everybody came up and shook hands and said, "My goodness. What a wonderful, wonderful, deeply touching, meaningful event. Thank you." Well, at the end of this line of people was this humble, understated, sincere-looking person: Fred Rogers. He came over, and the thing I remember is he was very, very nondescript. He wasn't someone that made an impression. Joanne and John Lively were making a fuss, in a good sense of the word. I was thinking, "She married him?" Because she was lively . . . a pepper woman. She was so jovial; she could tell a joke and have you laughing. When she kept saying, "Meet my husband," I kept thinking to myself, "I don't need to meet anybody else. You are wonderful." Well, when I finally met him, I thought, *"Him?"* I sincerely did. But the occasion went very well. We were all civilized people. He was incredibly gracious and humble, so there was no other way to treat him.

We decided to all get together and have lunch soon. They arranged a date for us to meet at Stouffer's in Pittsburgh. When I walked in, we sat and we had light conversation about music. I soon discovered he was quite knowledgeable and that he loved opera. I love opera, too, and I of course had studied at Oberlin, so we had something to talk about. Music really was a common bond. I was surprised at how eclectic his taste was, because mine is very eclectic. A lot of times you have classically trained musicians and they only want Mozart or Bach or Schubert. And then you find the other side, the jazz musicians, and they only want Miles Davis and people like that. It's one or the other. Here was someone like me, who just liked some of everything.

Lunch lasted for at least two hours. He was a great, great listener. I never had such a warm, affectionate introduction to a stranger than I did in that lunch with him. I was just amazed, as I thought about it later on. What a nice man. And it was genuine! He wasn't one of those insincere nice men. It really was a dynamic energy between us. He said, "Come on over to the station. Let me show you around." So I went with him. When I went inside, he continued his explanation of what he was doing on *Mister Rogers' Neighborhood*. I met the producer and the people involved in the office, the coordinators. People were helping in all different levels. They were so nice. But there was one thing that puzzled me and stayed with me quite a long time. When he put his hand inside the puppet and started talking to me, I had a strange reaction to the puppet.

TL: In what way?

FC: I was uncomfortable because I didn't feel a man, a mature heterosexual man, would play with puppets like he was playing, and change his voice. I'm a ghetto man from Youngstown, Ohio. My father worked in a sawmill. My stepfather worked in the steel mills. They were not educated people, so I grew up in a household where men were kind of rough. I never saw a black man playing with puppets. So when I saw Fred and heard the voice that he took on, I thought

François and Fred in 1972.

"There were racial problems. I said to him, 'This is horrible, what those people are doing.' He and I were there talking. We were looking at each other. I know that he was feeling my pain because, for me, it wasn't just about water and a swimming pool, it was racism that I was feeling, pain. He sat and prayed, 'What can we do, God?' The universe gave him such a powerful answer, the simplest thing in the world. 'Sit there with that boy and put your feet in the water, and let them see.'"

François Clemmons

---

it was childish. I was dismissive because it was—it seemed to be something a young child would do, but not a forty-year-old man.

TL: How did you adapt your thinking after you joined the cast?

FC: First of all, I related to the puppets as a facet of his personality. King Friday's one side, Queen Sara's another side, Lady Elaine's another side, X the Owl is another side. When I talked to the puppets, I was really talking to him. I never got over that. I never saw Queen Sara as a separate entity. I never saw King Friday as a separate entity. I think that was my cultural limitation.

I know this sounds crazy, but Fred helped me to understand I needed to learn to play. I had lived such a deprived childhood; I had not properly played. I began to get to know more about what had been missing from this wounded soul that had been brought to him. There had been so much lacking and so much neglect that I had put a shell around myself. Fred said, "Go out and have a good time, but you have to have it a certain way. There are certain things that you can do and certain things you cannot do. But you must find hobbies, things that you like to do, things that you can do that are safe, that are healthy—that will help you to be stronger, that help your mind. There's some healing that has to go on here, François. And the only way you can heal is play."

When I met Fred and we started talking, he said, "What was it like to go to bed hungry? What was it like to live in a shelter a couple nights, François?" That's something he didn't know. He became my mentor, my teacher, my guru. But I became his teacher of what it was like to only have one pair of pants, one pair of shoes. He didn't know anything about that. Fundamental things that he took for granted, I did not.

Those were the kinds of things we talked about. I was the wounded singer who harbored a lot of anger. The more I was able to talk about it and deal with it, the healthier I got, and my singing got better. That was the most remarkable thing. I had a great teacher. His name was Lee Cass, at Carnegie Mellon. But it wasn't just his technique teaching me, it was Fred's emotional release that was also teaching me. I was fascinated by the fact that I could have a session with Fred and come away singing better. There was a freedom that came into my voice and to my singing because it also had to do with self-worth. Once I got under Fred's wing and [started working with] Lee Cass, they made me feel that I could go anywhere and sing, and sing well, and be acknowledged as a worthwhile, strong, serious artist.

TL: Talk a little bit about how music in the *Neighborhood* was used to communicate Fred's message.

FC: Well, children love music, and they learn, I think, very quickly from music. Fred had ideas that he wanted to communicate. I think [music] was a quicker way to communicate some of those

"[Johnny] made me feel like I was the best singer in the world."

ideas so that people could think about them later on. Sometimes just a word or two, a turn of a phrase, sticks with us longer if you can remember the sound or remember the unique words or the way he put it together. So I think that he had a very, very valuable talent because his music was perfect for the children. In some cases, it stayed with us as adults.

TL: How about the operas? What stands out to you?

FC: First of all, they were highlights for me because they really gave me a lot of singing to do. In the operas, a lot of times Fred would write something special for me. I liked that, and I liked working with the cast together with John Reardon, who was our king—he really was the one that we all looked up to. He had been in school at Rollins with Fred. To see those two together was so nice. They were very dear friends. He was so knowledgeable and sang very beautifully all the time. He helped to set a high

standard of professionalism and preparedness and friendliness at the same time.

TL: What kind of memories do you have of the musicians on the program?

FC: The first one right off the bat is Johnny Costa, of course. He and I had a very special symbiotic relationship. I made some of the best music in the world when I worked with Johnny, because he understood that I'm a tenor. He made a real effort to have stuff in the right key for me. He babied my voice, and that's what a singer needs—an accompanist. He was a great soloist, but he understood that when he was an accompanist, it wasn't about Johnny, it was about me. He made me feel like I was the best singer in the world.

He's really a beacon. He's a light. People who are into music listen for him. They want to hear the opening and anything he does in between. But they really love that dazzling ending that he does. No matter where I go, people say, "Who was that pianist? He's just got silver fingers." It's wonderful, the way he does that. He's made it into something very, very special. In fact, sometimes when they were writing the music and putting out that first songbook, it was too damn hard. They actually had to put out another one to make the music easier, because those first- and second-grade teachers couldn't play it.

Another standout was Mary Lou Williams, the pianist. She lived in Pittsburgh. I went over to her house and she taught me how to scat.

TL: There's an episode where you're with her at the studio.

FC: She taught me how to do it. It's on the soundtrack of *Won't You Be My Neighbor?* She took a liking to me. That's the only way you could say it, to tell the truth. She cooked dinner for me and said, "You can come over here and see me anytime you want to." I was thinking to myself, this busy, wonderful, world artist who traveled everywhere, she was Duke Ellington's pet. She was his protégée. When she was thirteen, fourteen, fifteen, he took her everywhere and showed her off. She was a magnificent artist and improviser. He said she was the greatest genius he had ever met. He had her up there on that level.

Then of course, Reardon, he became my friend. He was also like a big brother. He really talked to me about what the life was like in New York. The first trip I ever really made to New York, he took care of me. Fred said, "This is my best friend. Here's his number. Give him a call. He knows you're

coming and he will take care of you." He was a wonderful guy.

TL: Tell me more about your memories of others in the cast.

FC: Betty Aberlin was very, very funny. She had a great sense of humor. I loved working with her, absolutely loved it. She always thought she was like my big sister. She was two years, I think, older than me. Right from the very beginning when I joined the company, Betty decided to show me around and take care of me and make sure I didn't blunder something horribly or whatever. I had been on the show twenty, twenty-five years and she was still doing that. She really did have a tremendous warmth toward me.

Audrey [Roth] was also like that. She was always bringing food. If I got hungry, Audrey had something in that damn purse. She and Brockett were kind of a duo together.

And Joe Negri, who's just easygoing. He was so freaking laid-back. It was a pleasure when Joe was there. He was not competitive or inappropriate in any way. He was always supportive.

Joe and Johnny—both of those guys were dynamic musicians. Johnny also used to tease me a lot because I was doing opera and

he was doing jazz. We used to say we got exchanged at birth.

I used to love it when we got together, *all* together. I loved the camaraderie.

After a couple years on the show, because I won the Metropolitan Opera's auditions in Pittsburgh, I went on to Cleveland and New York. I was in New York City at some point, '72, '73. I thought, "My family is in Pittsburgh. I wish I were in Pittsburgh with my family." That was when I realized how important the program was for me.

I have gotten the blessing of the friendship of being one of Fred's children or disciples, whatever you want to call me— his neighbor. People everywhere I have gone love Fred Rogers. I've been given the benefit of the doubt and name recognition everywhere. I wouldn't have had this kind of a career that I do have, had it not been for him.

I had to be careful sometimes talking to guys at the Metropolitan Opera, because I said to them, "I've already started at the top. I started with the best." You don't get any better than Fred. You get something different, but you don't get anything better.

📺

"Television has the chance of building a real community out of an entire country. . . . One of the dividends about being on so long is that children who grew up with the *Neighborhood* can be having children and also grandchildren. . . . It's like an old classic book. If your parents read a certain book to you that their parents read to them, and they have that warm feeling about being read to, they pass that on to their children. There isn't anything like that as far as comfortable roots are concerned. It's fun to be part of that kind of tradition."

Fred Rogers

Fred Rogers introduces children to Daniel Striped Tiger in 1970.

It's Such a Good Feeling

6

F red Rogers' timeless messages of self-worth, peace, and love have left an indelible impression on multiple generations of television viewers. For five decades, Fred brought his deep knowledge of child development to television, and children all across the country benefitted.

From the earliest days of his career, Fred secured his place as an educational and cultural luminary who worked for the good of all. In 1969, his testimony before the United States Senate helped to unlock funding for the Public Broadcasting System, saving it from near-certain demise. Throughout his lifetime he received innumerable honors and awards, many of them in recognition of his contributions to the healthy development of children. Decades later, in the age of social media, Fred's words of comfort and advice are regularly shared online.

There are countless stories of how Fred and the *Neighborhood* touched people's lives. Children with critical illnesses often requested to meet Mister Rogers, and many did through the work of the Make-A-Wish Foundation or through Fred's personal efforts. And then there are the private stories of how Fred helped people he never even met—stories of children who relied on Mister Rogers to be the one caring adult voice in their world; stories of mothers and fathers who found guidance for dealing with the roughest parts of parenting young children; and stories of adults who found comfort, hope, and even the will to live through Mister Rogers' messages. In these and so many other ways, Fred's words and actions have rippled far beyond their original moments.

Fred passed away in 2003 from stomach cancer, but his memory and spirit live on. Memorials and tributes to Fred continue to flourish through books, artwork, and films. His influence endures

Mister Rogers reveals to viewers how he made Daniel talk and move in a 1995 episode.

through the work of Fred Rogers Productions, the organization Fred started in 1971 under the name Family Communications, Inc. Today, Fred Rogers Productions produces popular children's programs, including *Daniel Tiger's Neighborhood,* the first program to be spun off from the original *Neighborhood.*

Furthermore, the Fred Rogers Center for Early Learning and Children's Media at Saint Vincent College—located in Fred's hometown of Latrobe, Pennsylvania—carries on the *Neighborhood* legacy through professional development and educational opportunities for today's leaders in child development. The Fred Rogers Center also hosts the official Fred Rogers Archive, which houses thousands of items spanning his life and career, providing scholars the opportunity to delve into Fred's work.

Fred Rogers has had an immeasurable impact on multiple generations of television neighbors. Through his *Neighborhood* he has provided countless individuals with a priceless sense of belonging, value, and importance—a timeless message in our ever-changing world.

ABOVE: Mister Rogers talks to elementary school students in Chicago.

OPPOSITE: Members of the cast, staff, and crew wearing sweaters and ties as a tribute to Fred on the last day of filming in December 2000.

Despite his usual promise at the end of each program that he would be back, there was, sadly, a final episode of *Mister Rogers' Neighborhood,* filmed in December 2000. The production's final week—a five-episode series about art appreciation—capped off 895 *Neighborhood* visits across four decades.

Even so, Mister Rogers never implied in that final episode that the program was ending. Just as he always did, he promised to return before walking out the door with a wave and a smile.

Fred had specifically scripted this action so that any series of episodes could be viewed in any sequence without losing continuity. Always calculating every episode down to its finest detail, Fred planned his final episode doing what he had done for his entire career—providing thoughtful comfort and stability to his young television neighbors. So even though production ceased, episodes continued to air on PBS stations around the country.

Fred Rogers took seriously his many roles in life—father, husband, minister, teacher, musician, writer—and scores of people have found inspiration in his insight, wisdom, and message. But what inspired Mister Rogers?

During Fred's time on the Rollins College campus, he regularly observed the words etched in marble on a wall near Strong Quad: *"Life is for service."* He took these words to heart and even carried them on a piece of paper in his wallet for many years.

> ## "We deal with such things as the inner drama of childhood. We don't have to bop somebody over the head to . . . make drama on the screen. We deal with such things as getting a haircut, or the feelings about brothers and sisters, and the kind of anger that arises in simple family situations. And we speak to it constructively."

Testimony by Fred Rogers to the U.S. Senate, May 1, 1969

THE PASTORE HEARINGS

In 1969, Fred Rogers testified before the U.S. Senate Subcommittee on Communications in support of maintaining government funding for public television. Up against a proposal to cut the budget by half, Fred wowed the tenacious subcommittee chairman, Senator John Pastore, and helped to secure approximately $20 million in funding. Without that appropriation, the fledgling public television network may never have been able to establish a foothold. Fred's steady, heartfelt testimony continues to resonate today and is often referenced any time the government considers cutting funding for education or arts programs.

Fred dedicated his life to serving children and families, through his work in his secular television ministry and beyond. He wrote dozens of books for children and parents. He inspired thousands of graduates through his dozens of commencement addresses. His production company, Family Communications, Inc., developed an array of resources to benefit young children and families, including training programs for police on the impact of violence on young children; workshops for educators on strategies for helping young children understand their feelings; as well as pamphlets to advise families on childcare, school, moving, death, divorce, and other issues.

JOHN O. PASTORE
UNITED STATES SENATOR

May 8, 1969

Dear Mr. Rogers:

Your gracious and thoughtful letter thrilled me as much as the sincerity of your presentation before the Committee the other day.

As honestly as I can say it, I believe that the parents of America owe you a debt of gratitude for your splendid program and the fine effect that it has on children.

Now, to give you a chuckle: The day you appeared before my Committee, without even knowing that you had testified, my son, Dr. Pastore, who is located at the Yale-New Haven Hospital, called me on the telephone to tell me how impressed he has been with your program and how nice I should be to you. He told me that my grandson, Gregory, who is four years old, has three great idols--Mr. Rogers, his daddy, and his grandpa--and, remarkably enough, in that order, which places me at the bottom of the totem pole.

You say that you would like to meet me personally sometime. This would, indeed, delight me very much and I suggest that whenever you are in Washington, you telephone me so that we can have lunch together at the Capitol.

Looking forward to seeing you, and with warmest personal regards, I am,

Sincerely yours,

John X Pastore

Mr. Fred Rogers
Station WQED
4337 Fifth Avenue
Pittsburgh, Pennsylvania 15213.

Fred Rogers received a wide range of awards and recognitions for his contribution to children's television and his dedication to the lives of children and families. The archive at the Fred Rogers Center contains box upon box of awards and plaques, but Fred repeatedly emphasized that it's not "the honors and the prizes and the fancy outsides of life which ultimately nourish our souls."

Fred endeavored to be a gracious receiver in everything he did. "I want to learn how to be the best receiver that I can ever be because I think graceful receiving is one of the most wonderful gifts we can give anybody," he said. "If we receive what somebody gives us in a graceful way, we've given that person, I think, a wonderful gift."

ABOVE: Fred Rogers was inducted into the Television Hall of Fame in 1999. Twenty-nine-year-old Jeff Erlanger presented Fred with the award, leading to a touching surprise reunion. Fred often cited Erlanger's visit to *Mister Rogers' Neighborhood* in 1980 as one of his favorite moments on the program. In his acceptance speech, Fred gave his audience the gift of a few moments of silence in which to think about the people who had loved and encouraged them throughout life.

RIGHT: A ten-foot-tall, seven-thousand-pound bronze sculpture of Mister Rogers, seated and in mid–shoe change, was unveiled on Pittsburgh's North Shore in 2009. Created by sculptor Robert Berks, the memorial is called *Tribute to Children*.

PREVIOUS PAGES: An overhead view of Fred in his television living room between takes.

In 2002, Fred received the Presidential Medal of Freedom, the highest civilian honor bestowed by the U.S. government. It was presented by President George W. Bush, who stated, "Fred Rogers has proven that television can soothe the soul and nurture the spirit and teach the very young."

As the 1970s drew to a close, the VCR began making its way into households across the country. When the legal question of recording copyrighted broadcasts surfaced, Fred Rogers testified in 1979 on behalf of VCR manufacturers. He favored the position that, by recording his program, families could enjoy it together at a later time: "I just feel that anything that allows a person to be more active in the control of his or her life, in a healthy way, is important."

ABOVE: Fred greets an excited Chatham University graduate after his commencement speech in 2002.

BELOW, LEFT AND RIGHT: Fred received numerous honorary degrees from colleges and universities from coast to coast, including one from Dartmouth College, where he began his college career in 1946, and where he delivered his final commencement address in 2002.

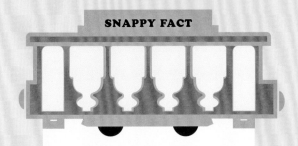
Fred received a total of forty-three honorary degrees from 1973 to 2002. Each one came with an academic hood—those colorful collars worn atop commencement gowns. The sashes of velvet and satin were transformed into two colorful quilts, made by Mrs. L. R. Lefever, a friend of Fred's, and Catherine McConnell, a fiber artist and the art director for the *Neighborhood* in the 1990s.

RIGHT: Detail of one honorary doctorate hood quilt, housed at the Fred Rogers Archive in Latrobe, Pennsylvania. The quilts serve as beautiful reminders of the way Fred had an impact on thousands of graduates through the dozens of commencement addresses he delivered.

"Those of us in television are chosen to be servants. It doesn't matter what our particular job; we are chosen to help meet the deeper needs of those who listen, day and night."

Fred Rogers

A Neighborly Chat *with*

BILL ISLER

Former President and CEO of the
Fred Rogers Company

BILL ISLER joined Family Communications, Inc. (later renamed Fred Rogers Productions) in 1984 and served as president and CEO of the company from 1987 to 2016. He is also the former executive director of the Fred Rogers Center for Early Learning and Children's Media at Saint Vincent College.

TIM LYBARGER: How did you initially become involved with Family Communications?

BILL ISLER: I was in graduate school at the University of Pittsburgh and one of my major professors was Margaret McFarland. I got to know Margaret, and she asked me if I would like to go to the premiere of a new series on hospitalization and children by a friend of hers, Fred Rogers. This would have been about 1973, '74. I went, I met Fred, and we stayed in contact.

I was in state government at the time. I was in charge of early childhood education and was an executive assistant to the secretary of education. Fred would come to Harrisburg for various reasons. One was the Pennsylvania Public Television Network; the other was to speak with people in the legislature and

the governor. And when Governor Thornburgh was governor of Pennsylvania, and his term began in '79, Fred was a close personal friend of his and his wife, Ginny. We had [Fred] come up for the International Year of the Child to talk about children and television, and to do some advocacy on the part of the state library system, to really promote work in libraries for young children and families.

It was at that time that Fred asked me if I would consider coming back to Pittsburgh—I was born and raised in Pittsburgh—and working with him and Family Communications. And I initially was not interested—I really loved what I was doing in Harrisburg, and I was working for a great secretary and great governor. I then was asked to reconsider, and I did. I came in late '83 to be part of Family Communications.

TL: You started at Family Communications in the mid '80s, and you were there through your retirement just a few years ago. You formed a very close friendship with Fred over the years. What was it like to work so closely with him?

BI: It was a delight to be able to work with this man. He was incredibly creative. I saw the creativity just grow every time he did something, every *Neighborhood* that he wrote, the new neighborhood that he wrote when he wrote *Old Friends . . . New Friends.* When he was working on speeches, when he was involved in either local or national organizations or events, as a member of an advisory committee or board—I really got to see a lot of aspects of Fred's creativity and genius. And I don't use that word, "genius," lightly.

As good as he was as somebody who could speak to and write for children and young children, he had a tremendous business sense, too. And there was nothing, from a business point of view or a personal point of view, that we didn't talk about. It was always fascinating to me when opportunities would come about, and we would talk through them.

Fred was not interested in licensing, and he was not in it for the sale of products. Fred was in it to really commit, as he would say, his life to the ministry of talking with children and families via the media. But knowing that we had to raise money to keep the program on, and knowing that there were some good opportunities to get his message out through music, for instance, or home video—Fred was very realistic about that. I got to see a lot of facets of Fred that really made me respect him more with each passing year.

TL: As the head of the company, what kind of challenges did you face?

BI: Fred was asked to do a lot. He did a series on hospitalization. He did a series called *I Am, I Can, I Will,* which was for children with disabilities. He did a series for migrant children, he did a series on childcare. He did a series of programs and then print materials to go with them, on divorce and death. Take a look at that body of work. It's far more extensive than just the *Neighborhood,* but it's based on his uncanny ability to be able to write for children, and for parents to use it as a parenting tool. The challenge was to pick the projects that Fred felt could do the most good for children and families. Because the opportunities were there all the time.

TL: What was the process for narrowing down those topics?

BI: There were a lot of discussions in the office. Fred had really good advisers. It was in many ways a group process, but Fred would always be the one to make the final decision. And that was understood and accepted as part of the process. It was, in a sense, Mister Rogers' neighborhood, and Fred was the leader.

TL: Did it happen often that the group felt one way and Fred in the end said, "No, I think I'm going to go this way"?

BI: It didn't happen often, but it happened. And Fred would give explanations about why. It would happen in the process of producing a *Neighborhood.* He would say, "I don't think I wrote that right." Even when we were writing the series of ten First Experiences books, Fred would make changes up until the time his manuscripts were submitted to the publisher. And he always made them better. He was always thinking and rethinking. And sometimes that would be problematic—not for Fred, but for those of us who were working with him, saying, "We know the manuscript's due. We know this is due. But . . ." He was not impossible. He was open to question, he was open to comment, and he was open to suggestion.

TL: Is there an instance that stands out to you that embodies the kind of person that Fred was to work with?

BI: One of the examples is the way he and Margy [Whitmer] worked on putting the First Experiences book series together. I remember that Jane Breck, who was a local pediatrician, was one of the pediatricians in the book. And at the time, the publisher was not real fond of having a woman on the cover. But Fred was adamant about diversity. We did a book on going on an airplane, and it was an African American male flight attendant. Fred was insistent, and on things like that, he would not give in. We wanted to do *Going to the Potty,* and we were concerned about how that was going to look, but Fred was adamant that we could do a good book with good photos. I was always impressed with how Fred, in a very, very calm way, could explain why he wanted to do something or why something was important.

TL: You had a big hand in the establishment of *Daniel Tiger's Neighborhood,* which came after Fred passed away. What would Fred think of *Daniel Tiger*?

BI: I think what most people don't know is that Fred always felt that the *Neighborhood* could go into animation. That the Neighborhood of Make-Believe could live on. I mean, again, this was not an ego thing for him, but he did all the music, he did all the puppeteering, he was the adult facilitator for children. There were a lot of roles he played, but he felt that the Neighborhood of Make-Believe, with the puppets and the characters and who they were and the way they were known, that it's something that could continue.

We were in California on a couple of occasions and talked to animators. What Fred found out is that animation is much faster than live action. But Angela Santomero and the folks that work with her—Kevin Morrison, 9 Story—were all able to slow down and do what Fred did. To have Daniel ask you to reflect— "Have you ever thought . . ." —much like what Fred did.

Angela was a student of Fred Rogers and a student of the *Neighborhood,* and used it in her work. And she had met Fred on a number of occasions. They had corresponded. It was natural, in my mind, to work with Angela (as well as other people). But obviously *Daniel* was really the strength, it was what's propelled the company into where it is now. I mean, it's continuing in Fred's work and legacy and reputation.

TL: As you look back over your time with Family Communications and then into the Fred Rogers Company as it evolved, what do you see as some of the most impactful work that you were involved with?

BI: The continuation of the *Neighborhood.* In my mind, it continued to speak to children and families and the issues that children and families face. It

> "Every time there is a crisis, 'look for the helpers' comes up. That's pretty powerful, for him to reach back into his childhood and to share that with all the generations that have come after him."

continued to be developmentally appropriate. To me, we're a hallmark of children's television. When you watch children's television today, you see a lot of elements that were integral to the *Neighborhood,* like how people make things. You now see that incorporated into a lot of other children's programming.

The *Neighborhood* now speaks to four generations. I mean, that's something else that is really important to stress. We're going into the fourth generation. There are just so many things that were gratifying to see come to fruition in being every bit as accepted today as they were when Fred first produced the program. Like any great work that anybody does, it continues for generations. I think what may surprise some people is how long and how strong Fred's legacy has continued to be part of American life. Every time there is a crisis, "look for the helpers" comes up. That's pretty powerful, for him to reach back into his childhood and to share that with all the generations that have come after him.

TL: When you joined Family Communications, did you ever think that we would be where we are today, with the legacy and the message still carrying on strong?

BI: I don't think any of us expected it, but I think that one of the things that it speaks to is the power of video. Because we still have video of him. I mean, the company still uses what I would call his PSAs [public service announcements], and they're as fresh today as they were when they were written. Many were written for specific incidents but are used today in a more generic way or for another community issue. I think the power of video is something that has really continued to promote Fred's work.

Morgan Neville's documentary [*Won't You Be My Neighbor?*]— the success of it, in terms of the number of people who have seen it—speaks again to what Fred's life and message mean to people. And what's interesting to me is having people who are seeing it and are seeing Fred for the first time, and getting how important that message is, and knowing that it has value and importance in our lives.

Fifteen years after his death, I think he is as important and as prominent in American life as he was in the later years of his life.

"LOOK FOR THE HELPERS": FRED IN THE AGE OF SOCIAL MEDIA

The Internet has created new ways for people to connect as neighbors across any distance. In the sharing culture of social media, people often turn to the comforting words of Mister Rogers in times of disaster, tragedy, or crisis:

> My mother would say to me, "Look for the helpers. You will always find people who are helping." To this day, especially in times of disaster, I remember my mother's words, and I am always comforted by realizing that there are still so many helpers—so many caring people in this world.

Mister Rogers' message was steadfast over his fifty years in television, but the way society views him has changed over the years. No longer is he simply the sweater-wearing, soft-spoken man who talked to children about feelings. Mister Rogers has become a source of inspirational wisdom for children and adults alike. In many ways he is a cultural icon, and some talk about him almost as a saint. But Fred himself would have pushed back against this, gently reminding us that each and every one of us is important and special, just the way we are.

Mister Rogers talks with students at Mesa Elementary School on the Navajo reservation in Shiprock, New Mexico.

FRED ROGERS PRODUCTIONS

Fred Rogers' nonprofit company, Family Communications, Inc., continued to work on a host of children's media resources after his death in 2003. Now known as Fred Rogers Productions, in 2012 the company debuted *Daniel Tiger's Neighborhood,* an animated series that is built on the foundation of Fred's Neighborhood of Make-Believe. The program follows the children of the puppets from the original series, and stars Daniel Tiger, the sneaker-clad, red-cardigan-wearing four-year-old son of the beloved puppet Daniel Striped Tiger. Fred Rogers Productions, which is based in Pittsburgh, is also responsible for other popular children's programs, including *Odd Squad* and *Peg + Cat.*

ABOVE: Daniel Tiger (*center*) with his friends (*left to right*): Katerina Kittycat (Henrietta Pussycat's daughter), Prince Wednesday (Prince Tuesday's younger brother, son of King Friday and Queen Sara); Miss Elaina (daughter of Lady Elaine and Music Man Stan), and O the Owl (nephew of X the Owl).

LEFT: Daniel Tiger's home contains many iconic reminders of Mister Rogers' television house, including a stoplight, Trolley bench, and a fish tank.

Planned under Fred Rogers' guidance and established in 2003 at Saint Vincent College in his hometown of Latrobe, Pennsylvania, the Fred Rogers Center for Early Learning and Childhood Media supports and enriches the important work of those who help children learn and grow across multiple disciplines, including early learning, education, communication, health, media, and more. By focusing on strengthening human relationships and promoting meaningful uses of digital media and technology, the Fred Rogers Center supports the current practice and ongoing development of child-serving professionals; expands educational opportunities for undergraduate students; and collaborates in public service and applied research with educational and research institutions and community organizations.

Fred Rogers offered a distinctly deep, simple, and compassionate voice for the healthy social-emotional development of children and the adults who care for them. As the official home of the Fred Rogers Archive, the Center also makes available unique resources that help to deepen the collective understanding of the rich legacy of Fred Rogers and illuminate his continued relevance and applications of his messages today.

> "I'd like to be remembered for being a compassionate human being who happened to be fortunate enough to be born at a time when there was a fabulous thing called television that could allow me to use all the talents that I had been given."

Fred Rogers

OPPOSITE, ABOVE: The Fred M. Rogers Center building on the campus of Saint Vincent College in Latrobe, Pennsylvania, is home to the Fred Rogers Archive.

OPPOSITE, BELOW: The multimedia Fred Rogers' exhibit, located on the upper level of the Fred M. Rogers Center building, is open to the public.

F red Rogers' lasting impact and appeal are evident across a wide swathe of popular culture, from the delightful to the ridiculous to the sublime. He has been mentioned in television shows and movies, parodied by the likes of Eddie Murphy on *Saturday Night Live,* and animated for the cartoon *Arthur.* In 2018, Google even created a stop-motion animation Google Doodle to commemorate the fifty-one-year anniversary of the show's first taping.

Fred has inspired theme park attractions, been honored in restaurants with sandwiches bearing his name, and been the foundation for so many performers and educators who respect his timeless message. Fred Rogers is commemorated in museums such as the Senator John Heinz History Center in Pittsburgh, the Pittsburgh Children's Museum, and Smithsonian's National Museum of American History.

ABOVE: A collection of memorabilia at the Fred Rogers Archive.

Won't You Be My Neighbor?

In the summer of 2018, the documentary film *Won't You Be My Neighbor?* debuted in theaters across the country and helped to bring Mister Rogers back to the forefront of American culture. Directed by Academy Award–winner Morgan Neville, the movie examined the life and legacy of Fred Rogers, illuminating the care and deep intentions behind the program. Neville revealed a side of Fred Rogers and the *Neighborhood* that many people had never considered: one of courage, innovation, and radical thinking about television's potential—and the importance of nurturing children by focusing on the essential core of what makes us human. "I felt that this was a voice I don't hear any more in our culture," Neville said. "That kind of grown-up, caring, empathetic kind of voice that's looking out for the best of all of us."

For perhaps the first time, millions of people began to understand the rigor and scope of Fred's work. The response to the film was overwhelmingly positive and emotional. David Newell visited one theater that placed packages of tissues near the entrances, with a note encouraging people to take some. Hedda Sharapan noticed that audiences often stayed in their seats through the film's end credits, "as though they needed to stay in that presence" a little longer.

Neville wanted the film to go beyond evoking nostalgia, and Sharapan notes that people aren't just *watching* it; they're *using* it. She's heard many stories of people striving to be kinder, and in her work with educators, she's seen the film used as a training tool to highlight the messages of the *Neighborhood*.

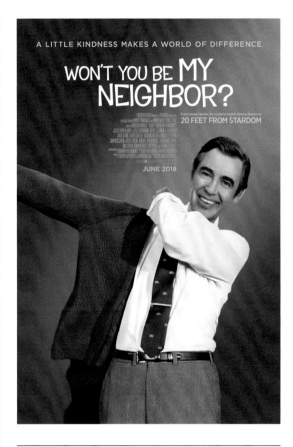

The poster for the 2018 documentary film *Won't You Be My Neighbor?*

It's tempting to wonder what Fred would think of the film. "All I can say is what Joanne told me," Neville told *Pittsburgh Magazine* shortly before the film premiered. "When we finished the film, I screened it for her; I don't think I've ever been so nervous screening a film. The first thing she said was, 'Fred would've loved it.' That's the best review you're going to get."

A Beautiful Day in the Neighborhood

Eighteen years after the crew of *Mister Rogers' Neighborhood* broke down the sets for the last time, many of them came together again to help bring it all back to life—this time for the big screen. In November 2019, TriStar Pictures released *A Beautiful Day in the Neighborhood*. Directed by Marielle Heller

ABOVE: Tom Hanks stars as Mister Rogers in TriStar Pictures' *A Beautiful Day in the Neighborhood.*

RIGHT: A 3-D sketch of Mister Rogers' television house set created by the film's art director, Greg Weimerskirch.

OPPOSITE: Mister Rogers (Tom Hanks) meets journalist Lloyd Vogel (Matthew Rhys).

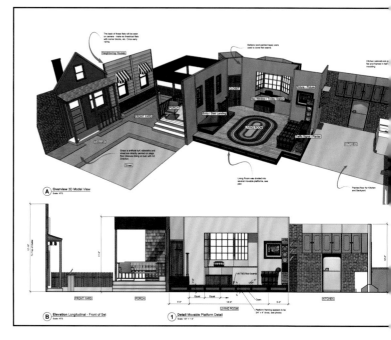

(screenplay written by Micah Fitzerman-Blue and Noah Harpster), the film is based on the true-life friendship between Fred Rogers and journalist Tom Junod, which developed in 1998 when Junod profiled Mister Rogers in an *Esquire* magazine article titled "Can You Say . . . Hero?" In the film, two-time Oscar-winner Tom Hanks plays Fred Rogers, and Matthew Rhys plays the part of Lloyd Vogel, a character based on Junod.

To capture the essence of the people and places of *Mister Rogers' Neighborhood*, Hollywood

> ## "I've never, in my entire life, gone into a place where a place from my past has been meticulously reconstructed. And I'm telling you, it's a jolt. It really is. It's kind of a beautiful thing."
>
> Tom Junod

paid Fred Rogers' real neighborhood a visit. The movie was shot on location in Pittsburgh and in Studio A at WQED, where every episode of *Mister Rogers' Neighborhood* had been filmed. Members of the film crew consulted with people who had worked on the program, and some of them still live and work in the Pittsburgh area.

"As a Pittsburgher, I'm totally proud of that fact," said Greg Weimerskirch, the film's art director. "We have a great film community here, I mean it's really tops. I've worked in Los Angeles for a number of years and our construction people and our scenics are on par with them, so we're all very proud."

Re-creating the Neighborhoods

Fred Rogers deliberately planned every element of *Mister Rogers' Neighborhood*; he had a specific vision or purpose for every scene, character, line of dialogue, set piece, and prop. It only made sense for the filmmakers to follow his lead: Those charged with re-creating Fred's world for *A Beautiful Day in the Neighborhood* were determined to replicate each detail as faithfully as possible.

Knowing that generations of *Neighborhood* fans would scrutinize every detail of the sets, the crew worked to "get as many details as accurately done as possible," said set decorator Merissa Lombardo. The work started nine to ten weeks before they even began filming the movie, with Lombardo and her team researching and sourcing all of the materials, fabrics, and patterns. "Everything in there, we made. It wasn't borrowed," she said. Even the sweaters that Tom Hanks wears as Mister Rogers were made by hand, a tribute to the ones knitted by Fred's mother.

David Newell, who played Mr. McFeely and also handled many of the program's props over the years, picked out the original kitchen curtains. He'd chosen their blue seascape design because it reminded him of Nantucket, where Fred and Joanne Rogers had a summer home.

The Model Neighborhoods

Re-creating one beloved element in the kitchen required especially intense work. The models of the Neighborhood of Make-Believe that sat on the blue corner shelves had been handmade by Bob Trow, who passed away in 1998. The film's art department scanned the original models and used a 3-D printer to create duplicates. Once printed, the replicas were then sculpted and completed by hand in order to impart a homespun feel.

The film crew paid equal attention to creating the miniature neighborhood that was shown in the program's opening and closing credits. "That was one of the more complicated things, because we had to re-create something that was there in every episode, and we were starting from scratch to re-create that," explained production designer Jade Healy. "Two model makers who worked on the original model came in [to work on it]. That's been one of the greatest pleasures of this movie: the amount of people in this town who have come to work on this project, who worked on the original show, who knew Mister Rogers."

The Neighborhood of Make-Believe

Art director Greg Weimerskirch recalled that many of the set pieces in the Neighborhood of Make-Believe presented specific challenges. To get everything just right, crews studied photographs and, when possible, measured the original set pieces, including King Friday's castle and X the Owl's oak tree, which are both housed at the Senator John Heinz History Center in Pittsburgh. According to Weimerskirch, "The castle was incredibly hard to duplicate because it's a very organic shape; there's nothing coplanar. It's all molded. The other thing we noticed, watching the show over the years, is the more it was used, the more it kind of collapsed on itself. So this is the 1998 to 2000 version, where if you look closely, the towers are kind of leaning in on each other."

For the sake of authenticity, the Make-Believe set pieces were built just like the originals—with lightweight wood held together with nails, not screws. Production crews took care to re-create

OPPOSITE, ABOVE: The front porch set as seen in *A Beautiful Day in the Neighborhood*.

OPPOSITE, BELOW: The kitchen set re-created for the film.

the backs of the set pieces in Make-Believe as meticulously as the fronts. This included adding the bits of writing that were found on the backs of the originals and sanding everything down so it looked aged. Healy said they paid special attention to the tiny details and markings that reflected how those original set pieces may have been "beaten up" from decades of use.

She noted that creating the oak tree was "really exciting because it is so textural. It was like we were trying to understand how they built it or what they did. We got to talk to people who actually worked on it, and they gave us the information and we built it exactly that way." Weimerskirch added that they had to "figure

out how the puppeteers actually work within these things. Like the tree: In order to access [Henrietta's] little house, the puppeteer from the inside has to get their hand all the way through that limb and up into the house. So it's very difficult to do."

The Trolley

Crews also had access to the original Trolley and worked with a Pittsburgh design and fabrication shop to "replicate almost every part exactly as it was," Weimerskirch said. "We also duplicated the mechanisms that drive it almost to a T. Except for the motor, everything else was milled to be as close to the original as possible."

SNAPPY FACT

The film crew worked to make the sets as authentic as possible in every way, even down to the felt-tip pens and yellow legal pads Fred used in his office. "Every detail, maybe we don't see it, but we want to try to have it on the set," said set decorator Merissa Lombardo.

Behind the Scenes of Studio A

To re-create the behind-the-scenes sections of Studio A, where the television program was made, the film crew committed to using as much of the older technology—cameras and monitors—as possible. "Whenever you're dealing with the older technology on film, there's so many ways to do it, and it's nice if you can do it as realistically as possible," said Lombardo. To that end, they tracked down three of the big Ikegami film cameras like the ones used to record the television program and had them shipped from London. They even considered how those old cameras would have affected the colors of the sets and worked to match everything in the movie to what viewers had seen on television.

The film crew considered even the smallest details of the re-created iconic Neighborhood set pieces (*left to right*): Daniel's clock; King Friday's castle; and the model Neighborhood.

"The thing about the color is that you are looking at footage that was shot on the Ikegami, which gives you a very different color than what you actually [see]," said Healy. "If you look at that color and you try to match it to a swatch, you're going to be off. So it's like this backwards way of trying to figure out what was the actual color that they shot. The [television program's] art director [Kathy Borland] had some photos she shared

with us. So we would sit down with all these swatches and be like, I think it's that gray, and hope for the best."

Pittsburgh Embraced *A Beautiful Day in the Neighborhood*

Fred Rogers lived most of his life in the Pittsburgh area, and he is still one of the city's best-loved neighbors. People working on the film noticed that nearly everyone they talked to in Pittsburgh had fond memories of the *Neighborhood* or a Mister Rogers story of their own.

"There is so much love for him here," said actress Susan Kelechi Watson, who plays the character of Andrea Vogel. "[In Pittsburgh] you get a feeling of what [may have] inspired him."

ABOVE: The cameras, monitors, and other studio equipment used in re-creating the sets were true to the time period of the original filming.

OPPOSITE: Two-time Oscar-winner Tom Hanks portrays one of America's most cherished icons, Mister Rogers, on the set of TriStar Pictures' *A Beautiful Day in the Neighborhood*.

Actress Maryann Plunkett, who plays Joanne Rogers in the film, recalled several interactions she witnessed between Joanne and local onlookers during filming: "When we were shooting, there were some people who'd come up and say, 'As a kid I grew up watching [*Mister Rogers' Neighborhood*] and it affected me. It meant the world to me.'"

Production designer Jade Healy noted, "One of the greatest pleasures of this movie is the amount of people in this town who have come to work on this project who worked on the original show." Even regular community members were happy to help with anything related to the *Neighborhood*. "I went to a woman's house to buy her couch [for the movie]," Healy said, "and she was like, 'Just take it for free. This is for Fred.'"

Casting Fred Rogers

It seems that Tom Hanks was destined for this role. Who better to portray the nicest man to ever be on television than the actor often referred to as "the nicest man in Hollywood"? Maryann Plunkett put it this way: "He seems like the perfect man to play Fred Rogers because there is a decency to him. A genuineness." She noted that the actors didn't try to imitate their real-life counterparts, but rather, to "get to the essence of who these people are."

Arjun Bhasin, the film's costume designer, said that transforming Tom Hanks into Fred Rogers came organically: "I feel like Tom has a Rogers-esque vibe anyway; that's very much his character, and it seemed like a natural fit. And everyone in the world expects them [Hanks and Rogers] to be the same kind of person, so I didn't have a lot of hard work to transform him. It seemed like a very natural transformation."

Even the *real* Joanne Rogers felt that Tom Hanks resembled her husband—especially when he was wearing the "wig and eyebrows," she said.

Carrying Forward Fred's Kindness

The cast and crew of *A Beautiful Day in the Neighborhood* hope that the film inspires audiences to live out Mister Rogers' message of compassion. Director Marielle Heller said: "At a time when the world feels divided, Fred's message of kindness is even more important. His radical kindness, one which does not discriminate, resonated with all of us, and we hope it resonates with audiences. We all feel like we've been forever changed by working on this movie, and we thank Fred for that gift."

A Neighborly Chat *with*

TOM JUNOD

In 1998, **TOM JUNOD** was assigned to write a feature story about Fred Rogers for *Esquire* magazine. The two men became friends. The story of that friendship is the basis for the feature film *A Beautiful Day in the Neighborhood*.

Q: Tell us about where you were in your career at the time when you got this assignment.

TOM JUNOD: I had just come to *Esquire* from *GQ* and at *GQ*, I had experienced more professional success than I had ever experienced in my life. I had done story after story that were boundary breaking in a lot of ways. I was definitely of the opinion that I had to top myself at all times, that I had to top other writers.

Q: When you got the assignment to profile Fred, take us into getting that assignment, your reaction to that assignment, and what your preconceptions were going into it.

TJ: Well, we were doing this hero story, this heroes issue, and somebody at the magazine thought it would be really kind of funny having me, this kinda hotshot sort of badass guy doing a story on Fred Rogers. And so, it was intended as like this juxtaposition of good, Fred, and bad, me—a role that I was definitely willing to step into and willing to play at the time. I was fairly pleased because I thought that this was my chance to not just explore goodness, but to see all of that which lurks behind it.

Q: Did you believe the story of Fred Rogers or did you think, I'm gonna find the seamy underbelly?

TJ: You always think that you're gonna find the seamy underbelly—at least I certainly did. And the amazing thing about it was Fred wasn't having any of that. Fred saw me, sized me up and went to work. He had that amazing gift of looking at a person and seeing what that person needed, and that he was gonna minister to that person. That person, in this particular case, was me. I look back on it now and realize how purposeful Fred was and how kind of relentless he was in doing that.

But the really interesting thing, at the time, was that it was just like incoming. It was like, I'm gonna take a picture of you, Tom. Oh, I'm gonna have Joanne call you. I'm going to write you a note and this and that. What? What? What? Maybe from the beginning to the end in this particular story, I was off balance, and he kept me off balance.

Q: What is the side of him that people don't know? The side that is off-screen? Or is there a different side?

TJ: Behind the soft-spokeness, behind the sort of extroverted kindness, behind all that, he was made of iron. He would not do what he did not want to do and he was gonna do what he did want to do. And that was the person I saw from the beginning to the end.

Q: What did that say about your relationship with respect to trust and things like that?

TJ: I think that's what he just kept on sort of pounding to me, that I was a good person. I think that he was an extremely complicated man. I think that, at the same time, his theology, his worldview, was exceedingly simple. He kept things extraordinarily simple: You are special. The universe/God loves you. You are worthy of my trust. You are a good person. Those are the things that he told me. They're not particularly complicated notions. But the difference with Fred is that he enacted them. He lived them. There was not a moment with Fred that you were with him that those very, very simple notions weren't part of the conversation and what was happening. That's an incredible experience, to experience goodness, to experience his goodness, to experience your own goodness.

Q: What was it like for you coming on set for this film and seeing the *Neighborhood* set and seeing Tom [Hanks] as Fred?

TJ: I've never, in my entire life, gone into a place where a place from my past has been meticulously reconstructed. And I'm telling you, it's a jolt. It really is. It's kind of a beautiful thing.

And then seeing Tom as Fred—I saw him first on one of the monitors. I was not in the studio when they were taping him originally. I was in the side room and looking at him on the monitors. And . . . it kinda rounded off my relationship with Fred and my memories of Fred in a way.

Q: Talk about Joanne and your relationship to her—what you saw between her and Fred.

TJ: I never met anybody like Fred. I've never met anybody like Joanne. I think that Joanne knew how special Fred was and that he was a really different sort of person. I do believe that she allowed him to be that person—encouraged him to be that person. And I think that he absolutely realized how special Joanne is.

This is not news to anybody who knows Joanne, but she has the world's greatest laugh and the world's most infectious laugh. But also, she's as tough as nails.

Q: What's your hope when people see this film, the message that it gives, the takeaway from it, the experience of it?

TJ: His spoken message is simple, but the message of his life is not simple, because the message of his life is goodness in action. If the movie captures that . . . maybe we should all aspire to be a little better.

"I'm just so proud of all of you who have grown up with us. And I know how tough it is some days to look with hope and confidence on the months and years ahead. But I would like to tell you what I often told you when you were much younger: I like you just the way you are. And what's more, I'm so grateful to you for helping the children in your life to know that you'll do everything you can to keep them safe and to help them express their feelings in ways that will bring healing in many different neighborhoods. It's such a good feeling to know that we're lifelong friends."

Fred Rogers

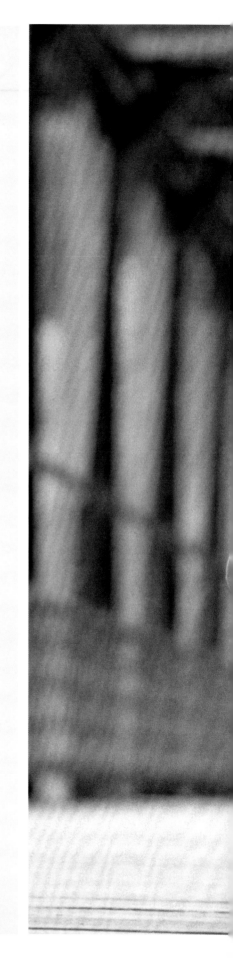

RESOURCES

THEME WEEK TOPICS (1979-2001)

Alike and Different (1987)	Episodes 1581–1585
Art (1991)	Episodes 1641–1645
Be Yourself: That's the Best (1997)	Episodes 1716–1720
Brave and Strong (1996)	Episodes 1706–1710
Bubbleland (1980)	Episodes 1471–1475
Celebrate the Arts (2001)	Episodes 1761–1765
Celebrations (1986)	Episodes 1561–1565
Competition (1981)	Episodes 1481–1485
Conflict (1983)	Episodes 1521–1525
Creativity (1982)	Episodes 1501–1505
Curiosity (2000)	Episodes 1751–1755
Dance (1987)	Episodes 1571–1575
Day Care and Night Care (1983)	Episodes 1516–1520
Discipline (1982)	Episodes 1491–1495
Divorce (1982)	Episodes 1476–1480
Dress-Up (1991)	Episodes 1636–1640
Environment, The (1990)	Episodes 1616–1620
Everybody's Special (1995)	Episodes 1686–1690
Families (1985)	Episodes 1551–1555
Fast and Slow (1995)	Episodes 1681–1685
Fathers and Music (1990)	Episodes 1621–1625
Food (1984)	Episodes 1536–1540
Friends (1982)	Episodes 1506–1510
Fun and Games (1989)	Episodes 1601–1605
Games (1983)	Episodes 1511–1515
Giving and Receiving (1998)	Episodes 1721–1725
Goes to School (1979)	Episodes 1461–1465

Going Away and Coming Back (1994)	Episodes 1676–1680
Go Stop Go (1999)	Episodes 1741–1745
Grandparents (1984)	Episodes 1531–1535
Growing (1991)	Episodes 1631–1635
Helping (1996)	Episodes 1701–1705
Imaginary Friends (1992)	Episodes 1646–1650
Josephine the Short-Neck Giraffe (1989)	Episodes 1606–1610
Kindness and Unkindness (1988)	Episodes 1591–1595
Learning (1992)	Episodes 1651–1655
Little and Big (1998)	Episodes 1731–1735
Love (1993)	Episodes 1661–1665
Mad Feelings (1995)	Episodes 1691–1695
Make–Believe (1982)	Episodes 1501–1505
Makes an Opera (1980)	Episodes 1471–1475
Making and Creating (1986)	Episodes 1556–1560
Making Mistakes (1987)	Episodes 1576–1580
Mouths and Feelings (1990)	Episodes 1626–1630
Music (1985)	Episodes 1546–1550
Nighttime (1988)	Episodes 1586–1590
No and Yes (1985)	Episodes 1541–1545
Noisy and Quiet (1999)	Episodes 1736–1740
Pets (1982)	Episodes 1496–1500
Play (1981)	Episodes 1486–1490
Playthings (1986)	Episodes 1566–1570
Ready to Read? (2000)	Episodes 1756–1760
Secrets (1988)	Episodes 1596–1600

Sharing (1997)	Episodes 1711–1715
Superheroes (1980)	Episodes 1466–1470
Then and Now (1993)	Episodes 1666–1670
Things to Wear (1994)	Episodes 1671–1675
Transformations (1996)	Episodes 1696–1700
Up and Down (1992)	Episodes 1656–1660
What Do You Do with the Mad That You Feel? (1995)	
	Episodes 1691–1695
When Parents Go to Work (1989)	Episodes 1611–1615
When Things Get Broken (1999)	Episodes 1746–1750
Windstorm in Bubbleland (1980)	Episodes 1471–1475
Work (1984)	Episodes 1526–1530
You and I Together (1998)	Episodes 1726–1730

CLASSIC EPISODES

Episode 0001 (1968) Misterogers' Neighborhood Goes National

Episode 1001 (1969) The First Episode in Color

Episode 1015 (1969) The Royal Wedding

Episode 1101 (1970) Death of a Goldfish

Episode 1478 (1981) Meeting Jeff Erlanger

Episode 1481 (1981) Visiting the Crayon Factory

Episode 1530 (1984) Behind the Scenes

Episode 1587 (1988) Mister Rogers Goes to Russia

SELECTED TITLES

A Beautiful Day in the Neighborhood by Fred Rogers and Luke Flowers (Quirk, 2019)

Dear Mister Rogers: Does It Ever Rain in Your Neighborhood? by Fred Rogers (Penguin Books, 1996)

Everything I Need to Know I Learned from Mister Rogers' Neighborhood by Melissa Wagner and Fred Rogers Productions (Potter, 2019)

First Experiences: Going to the Potty by Fred Rogers, photographs by Jim Judkis (G.P. Putnam's Sons, 1986)

First Experiences: Making Friends by Fred Rogers, photographs by Jim Judkis (G.P. Putnam's Sons, 1987)

First Experiences: The New Baby by Fred Rogers, photographs by Jim Judkis (G.P. Putnam's Sons, 1985)

First Experiences: When a Pet Dies by Fred Rogers, photographs by Jim Judkis (G.P. Putnam's Sons, 1988)

The Good Neighbor by Maxwell King (Abrams Press, 2018)

Let's Talk About It: Divorce by Fred Rogers, photographs by Jim Judkis (PaperStar, 1998)

Let's Talk About It: Extraordinary Friends by Fred Rogers, photographs by Jim Judkis (Puffin, 2000)

Life's Journeys According to Mister Rogers, Revised, by Fred Rogers (Hachette, 2019)

Many Ways to Say I Love You: Wisdom for Parents and Children from Mister Rogers (Hachette, 2006)

Mister Rogers' Neighborhood: Children, Television, and Fred Rogers by Mark Collins and Margaret Mary Kimmel (University of Pittsburgh Press, 1996)

The World According to Mister Rogers, Revised, by Fred Rogers (Hachette, 2019)

You Are Special: Words of Wisdom from America's Most Beloved Neighbor by Fred Rogers (Viking Penguin, 1994)

WORKS CONSULTED

Fred Rogers Archive. Fred Rogers Center for Early Learning and Children's Media at Saint Vincent College. Latrobe, Pennsylvania.

Fred Rogers Exhibit. Fred Rogers Center for Early Learning and Children's Media at Saint Vincent College. Latrobe, Pennsylvania.

BOOKS

Collins, Mark, and Margaret Mary Kimmel (eds.). *Mister Rogers' Neighborhood: Children, Television, and Fred Rogers.* University of Pittsburgh Press, 1996.

King, Maxwell. *The Good Neighbor: The Life and Work of Fred Rogers.* New York: Abrams Press, 2018.

Rogers, Fred. *Dear Mister Rogers, Does It Ever Rain in Your Neighborhood?* New York: Penguin Books, 1996.

ARTICLES

"Before *Mr. Rogers' Neighborhood* came *Misterogers* on CBC." CBC Archive. June 20, 2018.

Briggs, Kenneth A. "Mr. Rogers Decides It's Time to Head for New Neighborhoods." *New York Times.* May 8, 1975.

Chau, Elaine (producer). "The Canadian Story Behind *Mister Rogers' Neighborhood.*" CBC Radio. June 6, 2018.

DeFrancesco, Joyce. "A Life Well-Lived: A Look Back at Fred Rogers' Life." *Pittsburgh Magazine.* April 2003.

Fletcher, Christopher. "One Last Time." *Pittsburgh Magazine.* March 2001.

Hart, Ron. "The Music of Fred Rogers' Neighborhood." *JazzTimes.* July 19, 2018.

Hartlaub, Peter. "'Dead' and Fred: George A. Romero's connection to Mr. Rogers." *SFGate* blog. May 13, 2010.

"A Hero's Heroes: Fred Rogers' response to our September 2002 question: Who is your hero?" *Pittsburgh Magazine.* April 2003.

"Johnny Costa: Pianist for *Mr. Rogers' Neighborhood.*" Pittsburgh Music History. https://sites.google.com/site/pittsburghmusichistory/pittsburgh-music-story/jazz/modern-era/johnny-costa.

Junod, Tom. "Can You Say . . . Hero?" *Esquire.* November 1998.

Kimmel, Margaret Mary, and Mark Collins. *The Wonder of It All: Fred Rogers and the Story of an Icon.* Latrobe, Pennsylvania: Fred Rogers Center for Early Learning and Children's Media at Saint Vincent College. September 2008.

Kris, Deborah Farmer. "The Timeless Teachings of *Mister Rogers' Neighborhood.*" PBS for Parents. http://www.pbs.org/parents/rogers/the-timeless-teachings-of-mister-rogers-neighborhood.

Laskas, Jeanne Marie. "Zen and the Art of Make Believe." *Pittsburgh Magazine.* October 1985.

Laurich, Alice. "Meet Mister Rogers." *Focus Magazine, Tribune Review.* June 23, 1974.

Llana, Sara Miller. "How Canada Helped Make 'Mister Rogers' Neighborhood.'" *The Christian Science Monitor.* July 20, 2018.

"The Method Behind the Magic." PBS for Parents. https://www.pbs.org/parents/rogers/the-method-behind-the-magic.

Nedeff, Adam. "Violent Images: The Assassination Special." The Neighborhood Archive. http://neighborhoodarchive.com/articles/20131122_violentimages/index.html.

Pesci, Jennifer. "Family Values." *Pittsburgh Magazine.* January 1998.

Rogers, Fred, with Kathryn Brinckerhoff. "I Like You Just the Way You Are." *Guideposts.* September 1980.

Sciullo, Maria. "Live and Lively, Early Days of *Mister Rogers' Neighborhood* Began with a *Corner.*" *Pittsburgh Post-Gazette.* February 19, 2018.

Sedgwick, John. "Who the Devil Is Fred Rogers?" *Wigwag*. November 1989.

Shanley, Mike. "Joe Negri: *Mister Rogers' Neighborhood* Guitarist." *Jazz Times*. July 1, 2004.

WEBSITES

Fred Rogers Productions: www.fredrogers.org and www.misterrogers.org

Fred Rogers Center for Early Learning and Children's Media at Saint Vincent College: www.fredrogerscenter.org

Joe Negri "About" page: www.joenegri.com

PBS for Parents: *Mister Rogers' Neighborhood*. www.pbs.org/parents/rogers

The Neighborhood Archive, curated by Tim Lybarger. www.neighborhoodarchive.com

VIDEO AND FILM

Fred Rogers: America's Favorite Neighbor. Hosted by Michael Keaton. WQED, 2004.

Mister Rogers and Me. Directed by Benjamin Wagner and Christofer Wagner. PBS, 2012.

Mister Rogers: It's You I Like. PBS, March 2018.

"Neighborhood Colleagues Remember Fred Rogers." *OnQ*. Hosted by Chris Moore. WQED-TV, 2003.

"Remembering Mister Rogers." *OffQ*. Hosted by Chris Moore. WQED-TV, 2003.

Rogers, Fred. Acceptance Speech: Lifetime Achievement Award, Emmy Awards, 1997. Video.

———. Induction Speech: Television Academy Hall of Fame, March 11, 1999. Video.

———. Commencement Address. Dartmouth College, 2002. Video.

Speedy Delivery: Serving Mister Rogers' Neighborhood Since 1967. Directed by Paul B. Germain. SpeedyFan Entertainment, 2008.

Won't You Be My Neighbor? Directed by Morgan Neville. Focus Features, 2018.

INTERVIEWS

Clemmons, François. "Walking the Beat in *Mister Rogers' Neighborhood*, Where a New Day Began Together." StoryCorps, interview by Karl Lindholm. Aired on *Morning Edition*, *NPR*, March 11, 2016. Audio.

Daley, Eliot. Interview by Tim Lybarger, *Neighborhood Archive Podcast*, episode 0014, September 15, 2012. Audio.

Rogers, Fred. Interview by Karen Herman. Archive of American Television, July 22, 1999. Video.

———. Interview by Joan Rivers. *The Tonight Show*, 1986. Video.

———. Interview by John Donvan. *Nightline*, July 13, 2001. Video.

———. Interview by Charlie Rose. *Charlie Rose*, September 20, 1994. Video.

———. Interview by Charlie Rose. *Charlie Rose*, May 13, 1997. Video.

Seamans, Elizabeth Nadas. Interview by Richard Paradise. Martha's Vineyard Film Center, Martha's Vineyard, Massachusetts. Video.

ACKNOWLEDGMENTS

This book would not have been possible without the staff of Fred Rogers Productions, including Paul Siefken, Kevin Morrison, Matt Shiels, Brittany Smith, Jack Rowley, and Micah Southwood.

Special thanks to Cathy Cohen Droz, Hedda Sharapan, and Margy Whitmer for their generous gift of time and invaluable insights into the mind and heart of their colleague Fred and the work of the *Neighborhood*.

To David Newell for always being ready with a Speedy Delivery of stories, history, and lore of the *Neighborhood*, and for carrying forward its timeless legacy every time he speaks, whether in costume or not.

And to Emily Uhrin for accommodating our many requests and sharing the treasure trove of the Fred Rogers Archive with us. Thanks also to the staff of the Fred Rogers Center, especially Karen Struble Myers.

Big thanks to the team at Clarkson Potter for bringing this book to life, especially Angelin Borsics for her encouragement, patience, and outstanding editorial guidance; Danielle Deschenes for her magical design skills; production editor Patricia Shaw, copy editor Lawrence Krauser, and proofreader Edith Baltazar for their expert eyes on the text of this book; and Kim Tyner, Jessica Heim, and Philip Leung for bringing the photographs to life through the proofing process.

Deep appreciation to everyone—cast, crew, coworkers, friends, guests, musicians, and neighbors—who shared their experiences of being part of the *Neighborhood*: Chuck Aber, Betty Aberlin, Joe Abeln, Leah Blackwood, Kathy Borland, Jim Bruwelheide, François Clemmons, Andrew Gordon, Bill Isler, Tom Junod, Paul Lally, Susan Linn, Yo-Yo Ma, Catherine McConnell, Carl McVicker Jr., Joe Negri, Barbie Pastorik, Bob Rawsthorne, Adair Roth, Betsy Nadas Seamans, Nick Tallo, and Frank Warninsky.

Neighborly thanks to Tom Hanks for his eloquent foreword to the book. And many thanks to the following people at Sony Pictures and in the crew of *A Beautiful Day in the Neighborhood*: Marielle Heller, Kristie Alarcon, Greg Weimerskirch, Jade Healy, Arjun Bhasin, Marissa Lombardo, Susan Kelechi Watson, and Maryann Plunkett.

Thanks to our intern, Marisa M. Andrews, for all of her work behind the scenes. To photographer Lynn Johnson and Miriam Intrator at the Lynn Johnson Collection: Ohio University Libraries for opening their archives to us. Thanks also to the following photographers for their contributions to the book: Matt Bulvony, Terry Clark, Kira Corser, Dave DiCello, Susan Gray, Lilo Guest, Jordan Hainsey, Richard Kelly, Jim Manzella, Mark Murphy, Walt Seng, Sandy Speiser, William Wade, and Jack Weinhold.

Thank you to Courtney Keel Becraft at the Senator John Heinz History Center for generously sharing your resources and photographs; to James Okonale at the McFeely-Rogers Foundation; to

Wenxian Zhang and Darla Moore at the Rollins College Archive; and to Brooke Thompson-Mills for her assistance.

Thanks to Katie Funaki and Megan Hedges at Rewind Memories in Squirrel Hill for your quick work.

Personal thanks from Melissa: Thank you to my neighborhood helpers and personal connectors: Isaac Bower, Ellen McGrath Smith, Lauren Stern, and Lisa and Ben Collier. Loving thanks to my family, especially my brother, for handling so much so I could focus on work, and to Chris and Helena for your patience, support, and hugs.

Personal thanks from Tim: Thank you to all of those at Fred Rogers Productions—especially Kevin Morrison—for continued support of the Neighborhood Archive, and to Melissa Wagner for inviting me to be a part of this wonderful book project. To the Neighborhood Archive audience, I am grateful for each and every one of you as that labor of love has grown far beyond anything I ever could have imagined.

Personal thanks from Jenna: I'm grateful to the spirit of Fred Rogers for showing up in unexpected ways throughout the writing of this book. Deep love and thanks to my husband, James, who loves me just the way I am, and who has taught me to be proud of myself. In the words of Donkey Hodie, "I want you, *hee-haw!* Just you."

PHOTO CREDITS

Personal photographs and ephemera reproduced courtesy of the McFeely-Rogers Foundation, with the help of the Fred Rogers Archive and the Fred Rogers Center at Saint Vincent College. Unless noted below, all other photographs and ephemera reproduced courtesy of Fred Rogers Productions. Numbers in parentheses indicate clockwise placement (from the top left) on the indicated page.

Courtesy of **Joe Abeln:** pages 121, 185, 215 (2), 218 (2); courtesy of **Leah Blackwood:** 203 (2); **Matt Bulvony:** pages 37, 92 (1), 131 (2), 169 (2), 172 (2), 175 (3), 246 (2), 257 (1); © **Terry Clark:** pages 77 (1), 140, 153 (2); © **2019 CTMG, Inc.** All rights reserved. Photos by **Lacey Terrell:** pages 6–7, 312 (1, 2), 313, 314 (1, 2), 316 (1, 2), 317, 318, 319; **Department of College Archives and Special Collections, Olin Library, Rollins College, Winter Park, Florida:** pages 16 (1, 2), 17 (2); © **Kira D. Corser:** page 93; courtesy of **Dartmouth College Library:** page 298 (2, 3); © **Dave DiCello:** page 297; courtesy of **Focus Features LLC:** page 311; courtesy of **The Fred Rogers Center at Saint Vincent College:** pages 299, 309 (1, 2); **Lilo Guest:** pages 277, 278 (1, 3); **Jordan Hainsey:** pages 22–23, 23 (2), 139 (2), 143 (3), 160–61, 271 (3), 272 (2), 310; **The Lynn Johnson Collection, Mahn Center for Archives and Special Collections, Ohio University Libraries:** pages 51, 52–53, 122–23, 159, 182, 186 (1), 199 (4), 200–201, 210–11, 225, 228, 290, 298 (1), 304–5, 322–23; courtesy of **Tom Junod:** page 320; © **Richard Kelly:** pages 54 (1), 56, 57, 58, 59, 62 (1), 67, 85, 88 (1), 102 (1, 2), 103, 118, 120, 127 (1), 132, 137 (2), 150, 203 (4), 206 (2), 208–209, 237 (1), 242, 249, 288, 291; **James Manzella:** pages 47, 66 (1), 69, 98 (2), 106, 125, 184, 203 (3), 211 (1), 215 (3, 4), 217, 226, 240 (1), 241 (2), 246 (1), 248 (1), 256; **Catherine McConnell:** pages 88 (2), 202 (1), 205; **Mark Murphy:** pages 186 (2), 198, 203 (1), 220, 232; courtesy of the **National Archives:** page 296 (2); **Leonard Schugar:** pages 114–15; courtesy of the **Senator John Heinz History Center:** pages 63 (1, 2, 3), 72–73, 116–17; **Walt Seng:** pages 78, 260; **Sandy Speiser:** pages 68, 129 (2), 222, 251 (1), 278 (2), 281; © **susangrayart.com:** pages 99 (2), 257 (2), 258 (3), 259 (1), 263 (1, 2); © **Television Academy, Hall of Fame 1999:** page 296 (1); **William Wade:** 84; photography by **Jack Weinhold:** pages 30, 32 (2); courtesy of **WTAE:** page 25

INDEX

INDEX

BOOK AND COVER DESIGN BY Danielle Deschenes
ILLUSTRATIONS BY Max Dalton
JACKET PHOTOGRAPHY BY The Fred Rogers Company
SEE PAGE 329 FOR PHOTO CREDITS

10 9 8 7 6 5 4 3 2 1

First Edition